MARILYN
AND ME

Susan Strasberg

MARILYN AND ME

Sisters, Rivals, Friends

WARNER BOOKS

A Time Warner Company

Grateful acknowledgment is given to quote from the following:

"The Falling Star" by Sara Teasdale. Reprinted with permission of Macmillan Publishing Company from *Collected Poems of Sara Teasdale*. Copyright 1930 by Sara Teasdale Filsinger, renewed 1958 by Guaranty Trust Co. of N.Y.

"Mr. Sandman" by Pat Ballard, Edwin H. Morris & Co., copyright © 1954.

"Whatever Lola Wants" by Richard Adler and Jerry Ross, Frank Music Corp., copyright © 1955.

"Hey There" by Richard Adler and Jerry Ross, Frank Music Corp., copyright © 1954.

"Heat Wave" by Irving Berlin, Irving Berlin Music, 1933, copyright renewed. All rights reserved.

Included in this book are excerpts from "Father of the Star" by Lewis Funke, which appeared in *Pageant* magazine in 1956, and an excerpt from "She Did It All by Herself" by Marcia Benton, which appeared in *Movie Magazine* in 1956. Regrettably, these publications are no longer in existence, so formal reprint permission could not be requested.

Warner Books, Inc., 1271 Avenue of the Americas, New York, NY 10020

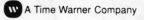 A Time Warner Company

Printed in the United States of America

LIBRARY OF CONGRESS CATALOGING-IN-PUBLICATION DATA

Strasberg, Susan.
　　Marilyn and me : sisters/rivals/friends / Susan Strasberg.
　　　　p.　cm.
　　ISBN 0-446-51592-2
　　1. Monroe, Marilyn, 1926–1962.　2. Strasberg, Susan.　3. Motion picture actors and actresses—United States—Biography.　I. Title.
PN2287.M69S75　1992
791.43′028′092—dc20
　　[B]　　　　　　　　　　　　　　　　　　　　91-50609
　　　　　　　　　　　　　　　　　　　　　　　　　CIP

Book design by Giorgetta Bell McRee

With respect, love and gratitude to all the great teachers in my life—
past, present, future, known and unknown.

She was so lovely and too young to die. God bless her. . . . I never met Marilyn Monroe, but if I had, I would have tried very hard to help her. . . . A sex symbol is a heavy load to carry when one is tired, hurt, and bewildered.

CLARA BOW,
The "It girl" of the silver screen
1905–1965

All so-called "primitive" societies have at their head important people with special powers. These people have the ability to transform themselves in public performance from their normal personality into somebody or something else: a god or animal, ancient ancestor, or representation of a spirit. Their crucial role in society is to transcend the boundaries of their own identity, follow a path to personal knowledge, and, in dramatic performance, to lead their audiences into ritual journeys into their own psyches. They are mystics, magical seers, and creators of visions. These people, commonly called shamans, sorcerers, or medicine men, were the first actors.

BRIAN BATES,
The Way of the Actor

Intense emotion is stressful, and we look to artists to feel for us, to suffer and rejoice, to describe the heights of their passionate response to life so that we can enjoy them from a safe distance, and get to know better what the full range of human experience really is. We may not choose to live out the extremes of consciousness we find . . . but it's wonderful to peer into them. We look to artists to stop time for us, to break the cycle of birth and death and temporarily put an end to life's processes. It is too much of a whelm for any one person to face up to without going into sensory overload. Artists, on the other hand, court that intensity. We ask artists to fill our lives with a cavalcade of fresh sights and insights, the way life was for us when we were children and everything was new.

DIANE ACKERMAN,
A Natural History of the Senses

PROLOGUE

Hollywood, California, 1991

IN THE SPRING OF 1954 I WAS SO YOUNG I still thought I knew everything. I was fifteen years old and in Hollywood. One halcyon May day, long before smog, Vietnam, the Kennedy assassinations, women's lib, AIDS, and global warming, I briefly met Marilyn Monroe on the set of *There's No Business Like Show Business*. When she said good-bye to me that afternoon, she said she would see me in New York. But I knew I would probably never see her again.

Marilyn was the quintessential child of Hollywood. Born and bred there, she'd overcome her horrendous early years of family insanity and abandonment to become the newest sex goddess of the silver screen. She was a star, but she wasn't considered an actress. Although none of us knew it then, she was to be the last of the victim sex symbols created by the studio system, a dying dinosaur that she helped to destroy. My father stood for truth, reality, art—to me Marilyn seemed the opposite. She represented glamour, sexuality, and fantasy, the "anything goes" girl.

By contrast, I was a young actress from a New York theatrical family. I'd been raised surrounded by books, classical music, writers, actors, and directors. My father, Lee, had cofounded the acclaimed Group Theatre in the thirties. Then he became artistic director of the Actors Studio, whose members included Jimmy Dean, Marlon Brando, Paul Newman, Steve McQueen, and Geraldine Page. Pop was known as an intellectual, a great teacher, and the father of "the Method." My mother, Paula, a beautiful, warm, vibrant young actress in the Group Theatre, had continued to perform while coaching and teaching others. Her acting career ended when she was blacklisted by the infamous McCarthy committee, which destroyed the lives of so many talented artists.

I was sure Marilyn and I had absolutely nothing in common. The distance between our worlds was so much greater than the three thousand miles between New York and Hollywood, I knew it could never be crossed.

Now, thirty-eight years later, I am—oh, God!—fifty-two, old enough to finally realize that *never* is one of those words that, after I say it, I eat it for lunch the next day. I did see Marilyn again. Like Goldilocks with the Three Bears, she would eat from my plate, drink from my cup, and sleep in my bed. In less than a year from our brief encounter, this blond bombshell fell into the midst of my emotionally land-mined family. Both our lives had changed drastically. My burgeoning career propelled me into the limelight. Her nine-month marriage to baseball great Joe DiMaggio ended in divorce. She fled Hollywood to make a new life in the East. There she chose my father to be the keeper of the flame, the caretaker of her luminous, underrated talent. Over the next eight years she became a private acting student of my dad: his favorite protégée, a second daughter to my mother, who coached her in all her films, a benefactor to my younger brother, Johnny, and an older sister to me. She was the adopted third child in our family.

Our door was open to many artists, but Marilyn was special. She was welcomed in our home even at five in the morning and there was a bed for her and arms to hold her. She permitted us to see her angels and her demons without fear of rejection. She was accepted unconditionally.

Growing up during that decade of dreams, I had one constant, insatiable, unfulfilled, secret longing. I wanted to be like Marilyn because I thought that was the only way to win my father's love and approval—as she had.

In those tumultuous, lightning-struck years, I became a star on stage and screen, fell in love, and had my heart broken. My father's prestige soared with the reputation of the Actors Studio and the actors he had trained and influenced. Marilyn fought to claim her "grail," the respect and acknowledgment she so desperately sought through her work. In her personal life the ticking time bomb of her unconscious emotions gathered momentum. The sex goddess became the outlaw goddess: marriages, divorces, pills, politics, alcohol, awards, illnesses, men, and scandal. My mother nudged, nursed, nurtured, and dedicated her prodigious energies to all of us.

For eight years Mother, Marilyn, and I, three women of different generations, tap-danced for the love of one remarkable man, "Pop."

We all traveled first class on the great American *Twentieth Century* express train with an open ticket to wherever we wanted to go. The only limits were in our minds. Our baggage held talent, fame, success, fortune, youth, beauty . . . Only one thing eluded us: happiness. In those days I was so young, I still believed in happy endings.

I wish this story came out like a popular novel: all villains punished, all heroines rewarded, a "happily ever after" finale. But it's real life—there are no villains or heroes, just us, human beings, with our egos, insecurities, jealousies, hopes, dreams, and desires. There can't be an ending, happy or otherwise, because even death doesn't end love.

In the software of my brain, on some level of reality in my

memory between time and space, life and death, then and now, my family, Marilyn and I are all eternally entwined like the strands of the double helix of the DNA. Marilyn and I made the journey, crossing that enormous sea of differences that had seemed to separate us. And it turned out that the longest distance we had to travel was from the head to the heart. During that journey we made together, she became my sister, my rival, and my friend.

Marilyn changed my family's life and we changed hers. And nothing was ever the same again.

Two self-portraits painted and titled by Marilyn
and given to me on Fire Island in the summer of 1955.

" lonely "

" life is wonderful
so what the hell "

They thought, How can a girl with success, fame, youth, money, beauty . . . how could she kill herself? Nobody understood it because those are the things that everyone wants; they can't believe that life wasn't important to Marilyn Monroe, or that her life was elsewhere.

MARLON BRANDO

1

IN 1953 ELIZABETH II BECAME QUEEN OF ENGLAND as Marilyn Monroe became the new queen of Hollywood. Eisenhower was president. McCarthy was in power in his Senate committee, destroying lives while claiming he was saving the country from communism. Playwright Eugene O'Neill died, and Arthur Miller wrote *The Crucible* about the Salem witch hunts. Jonas Salk developed the polio vaccine. The Rosenbergs were executed. Norman Vincent Peale's *The Power of Positive Thinking* was a hit. Alfred C. Kinsey's *Sexual Behavior in the Human Female* was published. The contraceptive pill was available. Edmund Hillary and Tenzing Norgay reached the top of Mt. Everest as the first atomic shells were being fired in the United States. Burt Lancaster and Deborah Kerr shocked the nation and thrilled me at fourteen, making love on the beach in *From Here to Eternity*. Radio stations blared

"How Much Is That Doggie in the Window?" and "Stranger in Paradise." While the New York Yankees defeated the Brooklyn Dodgers in the World Series, Dark Star won the Kentucky Derby, a 25–1 long shot. We didn't have to lock our doors in New York City, and my friends and I were wearing full skirts with appliquéd poodles and crinolines and ballet slippers or white buck shoes. Jolting Joe DiMaggio, the king of baseball, was courting his queen of hearts, Marilyn Monroe, an affair I followed faithfully in the fan magazines. At fourteen I was becoming an actress. I'd already made my theater debut and played Juliet in *Romeo and Juliet* on live television. My parents said nothing but let me do more TV, so I figured they hadn't been horrified by my acting. But I had my heart set on doing movies. This was a dream I kept to myself because I was worried it would be considered a betrayal of my father's commitment to the theater. Mom and I must have shared this illicit desire because at the end of 1953 she promised to take me to Hollywood when she went the following spring. I was thrilled; I knew wonderful things were just around the next corner. My life was changing as rapidly as the world's was.

In the new year Senator McCarthy was formally censured and condemned by the Senate. Aldous Huxley wrote *The Doors of Perception*. Vietnam was divided into north and south. Nasser seized power in Egypt. Toscanini retired. *On the Waterfront* won the Academy Award, bringing the Actors Studio and my father as its artistic director to greater worldwide prominence; the Method was becoming a household word. We worried about fallout and radioactive strontium 90 in our food. The first woman ran the mile in under five minutes and as the Hit Parade played "Young at Heart," I was getting ready to turn sweet sixteen.

Nineteen fifty-four was the year Anne Frank and Marilyn Monroe entered my life and changed it forever.

* * *

A friend had invited me to visit 20th Century-Fox studios to meet the newest star in the Fox firmament, Marilyn Monroe. Her life was familiar to me from the gospel of the movie magazines I read avidly each month. She was the most human of the stars I read about because there was so much about her early life: the little girl rejected by an insane mother, father unknown; her adoption by foster families who abused her; her molestation by an older man; a meteoric rise to stardom after a litany of abandonments and near disasters. After innumerable disappointments, she'd overcome all adversity. She was Horatio Alger and Helen of Troy. She'd found the love and approval she'd been deprived of in her childhood. Her public adored her, approved of her, protected her. Her life was dramatic enough to be a movie. It had a better plot than most of the ones she'd starred in so far.

Photoplay, Silver Screen, Modern Screen, Natalie Wood, Marilyn Monroe, Clark Gable, Doris Day, Montgomery Clift, Elizabeth Taylor, Rock Hudson . . . names like poetry. Loves, divorces, successes, sorrows. They were living, I wasn't. Natalie Wood was my age, Marilyn was only twelve years older. I'd have to hurry to catch up.

I was also going to watch the filming of *Desiree*, with Marlon Brando as Napoleon. This really excited me because I'd already met him in New York and had gotten a wild crush on him. Unfortunately he hadn't crushed back. Yet!

The sky was clear blue, the color of Paul Newman's eyes. "Just another lousy day in paradise," griped the native Angelenos. In the still heat, not a palm frond stirred. Nothing moved fast but the sports cars and my racing pulse because I was going to see Marlon again. The last time, I'd been at a party in New York, safety-pinned into one of my mother's dresses. Marlon arrived in a jacket, jeans, and silk ascot, bare-chested, no shirt in the middle of winter. Mother tried to burst my romantic bubble: "He'll probably get pneumonia." It didn't work.

My mother assured me that I was going to be a big star just like Marilyn, soon.

I knew that I was on the yellow brick road to Oz, that I would find fame, fortune, and, most important, love. When I found and kissed the right frog, I'd be happy and live a perfect life, forever. But impatiently I wanted more, faster, now, yesterday!

Steffi Skolsky had invited me to the Fox lot. Her father was columnist/producer Sidney "But don't get me wrong, I love Hollywood" Skolsky. My mother wasn't coming because she was involved with family business. I was relieved, as we had been together constantly this trip. She managed to embarrass me to tears ("Oh, pleeaasse, Mother!) with her unrelenting bragging about my career. She introduced me to all her Hollywood friends from the war years, when she and my father had lived in Los Angeles and my dad had been under contract to Fox as a director. She hoped they'd cast me in their movies. Ever since her own career had been so unceremoniously ended by the blacklist, all her considerable energies not devoted to my father and his career went into my burgeoning one. My younger brother, Johnny, was lost in this rush; he was going to be the family doctor, which meant he didn't need as much attention as I did. Mother told anyone who asked, "Johnny is the only member of the family who has no theatrical ambitions, thank God he's a born scientist. Though," she added, "Hippocrates called medicine an art, not a science." I loved Mother but she gave new meaning to the word *chutzpah*.

Tights, Napoleon/Marlon was wearing tights, chewing gum, and playing baseball between scenes; he was almost naked. I didn't know where to look, so I whipped off my horn-rims. I hadn't read Dorothy Parker for nothing. With 20/400 vision, my eyesight made everything look like a Renoir painting. I flirted with Marlon, who seemed to flirt back, but I couldn't tell. It was awful being fifteen and jailbait.

Movies were magical. The camera on a huge crane moved like a high-powered, streamlined, prehistoric monster. Orson Welles had described film as "a ribbon of dreams" and I knew I was destined to be in those dreams. I imagined what it would be like seeing myself up there on celluloid, dancing magnetic molecules, larger than life.

Sidney went ahead to visit Marilyn. I wanted to meet her. Who in America didn't? I just hated leaving Marlon. While Steffi dragged me away, I daydreamed that I was his Desiree, feeling the cool Mediterranean breezes of France waft across my bared bosom.

First I heard her voice, half-playful child's, half-sensual, seductive woman's, crooning, "We're having a heat wave . . ." Then I saw her shimmering under the Technicolor lights. I'd met and known lots of stars. Marilyn was different. She seemed to flicker like a flame giving off a nimbus of light. I thought it was trick lighting until I stood next to her. She still glowed, managing to radiate sex and innocence together. I wondered how she did it.

They were shooting the "Heat Wave" number for the film *There's No Business Like Show Business*. She was working hard, but botching take after take. I felt a little superior because I was a "serious" actress. The musicals I loved were Fred and Ginger swirling chiffon, virtuoso feet tapping to "Heaven, I'm in heaven . . ."

Tension on that set grew so visceral that I felt it gathering in the muscles in the back of my neck and shoulders. The atmosphere on the cavernous sound stage was like the moment before a big storm breaks.

Marilyn's outfit was high plumed headgear, flowers stuck in it, giant hoop earrings, three-inch heels, red toenail polish, a two-piece costume so tight that her body was like a sausage squeezed into a skin, and an overskirt with ruffles, print pattern, and a polka dot petticoat. She was larger than life, an all-American blond Chiquita banana commercial, only beautiful.

She was lip-synching, which is singing to a prerecorded song to match the lip movements. She had to dance without running out of breath, hit her camera marks, the musical notes, and her key light all at the same time. She was obviously having problems. Who wouldn't, with this series of tasks? There was a lot of low cursing going on when she flubbed a take, as if she were doing it on purpose. I knew she wasn't. As my father said, "No actor *wants* to be bad." She was obviously trying desperately to do it right, pouring sweat under the hot klieg lights. Her thick pancake had tear runs of perspiration. She kept looking anxiously over to a corner, where a tall man in a dark business suit was half-hidden in the shadows, watching her every move.

"That's DiMaggio," Steffi whispered. I turned to stare at him.

"He doesn't like anyone to look at him," she hissed, too late. "He doesn't like it when she does sexy things like this." I thought, What did he expect her to do instead? That's what she did. If she had been a bird, would he have asked her not to fly?

"I know," I whispered back, feeling very in. I'd read all about how DiMaggio wanted to change her. He wanted her to wear high-necked dresses, be more demure. Marilyn wanted to please him and do anything he wanted to make him happy.

The makeup man, body makeup people, and a hairdresser hovered just out of camera range like the pit crew at a car race. Between takes they rushed in to patch Marilyn up.

"Lights, camera, action!" They really said that.

"Quiet . . . roll." *Cahck!* The clapboard held up in front of her face, with the number of the take, name of the picture, director, and cameraman, banged shut. "Take twenty." The camera whirred, the music began.

She started singing and dancing as if it were the thing she

wanted to do more than anything else in the world; as if one hundred people weren't waiting for her to make a mistake, as if the man she loved weren't watching and judging, as if it weren't a hundred degrees under the lights, and as if a million dollars weren't riding on her performance. She flashed a two-hundred-watt smile as she swayed, sashayed, and swung those hips. "We're having a heat wave, a tropical heat wave, it isn't surprising the temperature's rising, you certainly can, can can. . . ." And with one emphatic bump and grind of her behind, she tripped and fell smack on her ass.

Empathizing with her completely, I gasped out loud. Then I felt sorry for her. She looked so embarrassed and dazed as people rushed to lift her up and make sure she wasn't hurt. I heard lots of "Shit!" and then "Cut!" and "Five-minute break!" were called. Marilyn made a beeline, half limping, for the man in the shadows.

"Joe." She rushed at him with the enthusiasm of a football tackle, arms open to embrace him, her face lit up with welcome. As she neared him, he seemed to withdraw behind some invisible shield, tightening his body against her. He became more taciturn than before, if that were possible. He resembled an Italian marble sphinx.

She froze for a moment, like a pointer. A fleeting expression of rejection flitted across her heavily made up face. I felt with her again. Joe reacted to her the way my father did to me when I ran to hug him.

"Gosh," Marilyn said, grimacing, "I almost got makeup on you." Then, like a good little girl who's been chastised, she circumspectly kissed him on the cheek.

Sidney had waved us over, and I stared up at Marilyn. She was so big. Of course I was only five feet one inch, and I was wearing flats. I swore my mother was going to have to buy me high heels. Marilyn was five nine in her heels, and that giant headdress gave her another foot at least. She was a Carmen Miranda goddess who towered over me and just about everyone else near her. Sidney, Steffi, and I, all under five three, looked like midgets standing next to her.

When I shook hands with her, she said, "Hi, I'm Marilyn," as if I didn't already know. Her voice was whispery and breathy. She seemed nice but preoccupied. I took the opportunity to give her the once-over, makeup, hair, body, so I could tell my mother every detail. There was a lull in the conversation. Marilyn fidgeted nervously. Steffi, like a party hostess, turned to her and asked, "What kind of character were you doing in that song? You were marvelous." Marilyn looked surprised and started to stutter and stammer some reply, "Sh-she's a . . ." Sidney glared at his daughter.

At that moment a body makeup woman came over, and Marilyn, with visible relief, said, "Gee, I've got to fix my makeup, excuse me, but will you all come to my dressing room in five minutes?" She was addressing the three midgets, who all nodded assent simultaneously. She gave a quick kiss to "Slugger" and left. DiMaggio in his business suit was sweating profusely. He wiped his brow and faded back into the shadow with his silent companion, a man who looked like someone out of an old George Raft movie. He'd been so inconspicuous, I hadn't even noticed him. Mr. DiMaggio, from the glimpse I'd had of him, was good-looking, but kind of stolid and low-key, old, compared with her, although he seemed nice. Nice in my vocabulary was the kiss of death. Exciting, sexy, wild, crazy, gorgeous, were more to my taste. He was definitely not my type, though actually I wasn't sure what my type was yet. But I knew for sure that Marlon was closer to it than Joe. Marilyn had seemed intimidated by her Yankee baseball legend, but I wasn't. After all, my father, brother, and I were Giants fans.

As soon as the three of us were alone, Sidney turned to Steffi furiously. "What's the matter with you?" he seethed. "You know better than that!" He sounded like my father when he got mad. I started to shake.

Steffi seemed genuinely bewildered. "What did I do?"

"It's what you said. You know she's playing a whore. You know Joe is sensitive about what she does, why did you have to say anything?"

It seemed crazy to me that Marilyn, the most desirable woman in America, would be worrying about playing a part her boyfriend didn't like. My first part had been a young French streetwalker. I'd gotten good reviews, and I was still a virgin. It was acting, that's what actresses did. How could Joe be so narrow-minded; wasn't he a sophisticated man of the world?

Someone waved to Sidney, and having made his point to his daughter, he wandered off to get tips for his column.

People in New York were certainly much more cosmopolitan than the people here. Hollywood was like a small town.

Five minutes later, as we started up the steps to her dressing room, I caught a glimpse of Marilyn examining herself in the mirror. Exasperated, she wiped off her newly applied lipstick, talking to herself, "Come on, face, give me a break."

Steffi and I trooped in. "Sorry, I look like shit—oops, sorry." She covered her mouth. I realized she was apologizing for cursing in front of us. I'd heard it before, even if I didn't say so. It was sweet of her, but I didn't think I was *that* young. Gazing at her beautiful face, not classically beautiful, but radiantly pretty, I was baffled. How could she be dissatisfied with the face that was launching a million dreams?

As we stood in front of three full-length mirrors, I peeked around Marilyn, trying to catch a glimpse of myself to see how I looked. Her golden image filled all three mirrors, which was probably just as well. Next to her, with my unmade-up freckled face and long, lanky, light brown hair, I knew I'd seem pallid, puny, and dull. She asked me about my acting career. It thrilled me that Marilyn knew who I was.

When we were leaving, she leaned down, her lips close to my ear. Her voice wasn't whispery; it was intense. "I really admire your father, I've heard such wonderful things about him. He's so brilliant with actors, you must be so proud of him." I was, but Pop was Pop to me, just an ordinary genius. She didn't notice I was blushing because she was gazing into space with a faraway look, as if divining the future. "I'm going to come to New York and study acting with him. It's what I want to do more than anything." I thought, Sure you are, there's about as much chance of that as a snowstorm in July in Hollywood. But it was thoughtful of her to say it.

She wanted to talk privately with Sidney now. He was one of her best friends as well as one of the main cocreators with her of the brilliant publicity stories that flooded the press; they'd get together and dream up items. One of Sidney's brain-children was the poignant story about the lost and found white piano.

Marilyn had told reporters, "My happiest hours as a little girl were around that piano." Supposedly it had belonged to Fredric March. She'd gone on to say that her mother had to sell the piano. She, grown-up, had found it, bought it, and kept it in storage until she had a home of her own to put it in.

"Tell them you dragged it around with you from one place to the other," Sidney improvised.

"Even when I didn't have enough money to eat, I borrowed money to keep that piano in storage," Marilyn said, improvising on his improvisation. It was strange, because her life didn't seem to need embellishment.

Climbing down from her trailer, I turned to take one last look. She and Sidney were lost in conversation. With their heads together, they looked like conspiratorial spies. I wondered if next month I'd read in *Photoplay* what they were making up.

How would it feel to be Marilyn Monroe and have the world at my feet, to be beautiful and adored by millions? I didn't exactly envy her; she was like an alien from another planet. We had nothing in common except being females and actresses. Although she could never fit into my world, I was thrilled that I'd met her in the flesh. As I looked back, her three mirror images shimmered, glitzy, gaudy, larger than life. She was gorgeous, the American dream. I was sure I would never see her again. . . .

STEFFI

My father had a good eye. He'd picked out the unknown, Betty Grable and Carole Lombard. Since he didn't drive, they'd chauffeur him around and he'd plug them in his column. He must have liked blondes. . . . Marilyn was special. People suspected hanky-panky between them, but he always looked on her as a daughter.

My father was extremely self-protective, and so was she. They didn't like their friends to know each other. Their friendship was outside our family. He introduced us but didn't want me to become close to her. They were very alike. My father knew every doctor in town. He wrote his column from an office at Schwab's Drugstore. He was a hypochondriac who knew every pill manufactured. Marilyn would call him up for recommendations of doctors.

I loved my father. He was a genius and funny, but he was also paranoid and neurotic, like Marilyn. That was part of the attraction.

When she went with Joe, she was afraid of his friends. Frantic, she'd come to my father: "They're after me." She was fearful and fascinated at the same time. Dad had hung out with Dutch Schultz. He wasn't afraid of DiMaggio.

All those years he made me listen in on her phone conversations. I never knew why. It was only Marilyn's calls. One morning early, I answered the phone. "I have to talk to Sidney, this is Marilyn."

"I don't care who it is, it's three o'clock in the morning." I was afraid my father would kill me if I got him up. She kept calling and I kept saying, "He's asleep!"

Finally I woke him. I just hadn't realized how desperate she was that Joe was doing whatever he was doing to her. It was the only time she came to the house in all those years. When Dad left with her, he said to me, "If anything happens, remember who I'm with if I don't get back." The drama, my father loved the drama, just like Marilyn. That's what drew them together.

That trip to Hollywood enthralled me. The dusty sound stages, the emotions, the glamour. The grand illusion, Marilyn's grit and sweat, which emerged as a smiling face and dancing feet. The romance—"Frankly, Scarlett, I don't give a damn! . . ." "Heeeathcliff . . ." Would my real life ever measure up to reel life?

By December of that year my head was in the jaws of Leo, the MGM lion. John Houseman had cast me in my first picture, *The Cobweb,* about a mental institution. It had an all-star cast. I'd ridden on Jimmy Dean's motorcycle, fast. Sipped my first champagne slowly. Opened my first bank account. My burgeoning affluence would soon give me independence. I'd be able to do *anything* I wanted, if I could just figure out what *anything* was.

That year for the holidays, Cheryl Crawford, a friend of the family who had cofounded the Group Theatre with my father and Harold Clurman, gave me a copy of a recently published book by a fifteen-year-old Dutch girl who had died in a concentration camp. Her youth and humanity had survived the degradation and horror of war.

"Read this," she said in her deep, man's voice, her face phlegmatic. "It's a part you could play." I was thrilled that she considered me an authentic actress, and I suspected that she might want to dramatize this book. I ended 1954 reading *The Diary of Anne Frank* and laughing and crying with a young girl my age who seemed to be able to articulate all the things I felt but couldn't say about life, parents, dreams, the craziness of the world. "I still believe that people are really good at heart," she had written. So did I. When I wished on the new moon or over my left shoulder on the first evening star, I always wished for peace on earth, and then I wished that all my wishes would come true.

That New Year's Eve I agonized over my desires. Did I want children and a family like all my friends in school? Like Anne Frank, I didn't if it meant being like my mother, whose whole life was lived for my father and who kept putting her dreams and opinions and projects on the back burner to cook his. Did I want to be a great actress like Eleonora Duse, who had died alone of pneumonia after being accidentally locked out of the theater she was appearing in on a cold winter's night in Pittsburgh? Could I be like Marilyn and have a huge career and love, or was happiness a great passion, like that of Héloïse and Abélard or Romeo and Juliet? Only I wasn't thrilled with how they all wound up—I wanted to be in one piece, no body parts missing, not cloistered and alive. Whatever I was going to do, I wanted it to be special. When Anne Frank wrote, "I thank God for this gift of writing, of expressing all that is in me, because I want to go on living after my death," inside me a small voice whispered, "Yes, yes, yes, me too." I didn't want to be left out or miss anything. I wanted to be part of that vast exciting universe out there—ideally before my death.

The tabloids promised Marilyn and Joe were going to get married. I was glad she would be happy and have babies who wouldn't be waifs. Whenever someone else was happy, it made the odds of my happiness greater.

"Be patient," Mother counseled. "Life is like an ocean and you can't make a wave of the ocean come in any faster than it wants to."

Ashamed, I admitted to myself that world peace had taken a backseat in my bedtime prayers. Top priority now was for that onrush of the future, my destiny, to catch me up in its arms and carry me across the threshold of my new life. In the meantime I stuffed myself with pints of coffee ice cream until I didn't care about the future.

As the months slid by I felt very grown-up in some ways but still a baby in others. I still read movie magazines but hid them inside more intellectual material like *War and Peace* or *Remembrance of Things Past*. I wasn't ashamed to read movie magazines, it just didn't seem to fit my new image. How could people take me seriously if I didn't show them I was? Besides, would my father's daughter subscribe to *Photoplay*?

Marilyn must have been going through similar dissatisfaction with her image because at the beginning of that year 20th Century-Fox suspended her for refusing to do *The Girl in the Pink Tights*. That provoked an uproar in Hollywood and then Marilyn topped herself by eloping to San Francisco with Joe DiMaggio. Maybe we Americans didn't have monarchies, but we had our own homegrown plebeian kings and queens.

The studio congratulated her and retracted its suspension, putting her back on salary. On her honeymoon in Japan, she was mobbed. Afterward, in Korea entertaining our troops, Marilyn caught pneumonia after singing in a low-cut dress in freezing weather. Joe must not have had a great honeymoon, but Marilyn looked like she loved it. Later, in an interview for Sidney's radio show, she revealed her feelings about entertaining before a live audience: "For the first time in my life, I felt I belonged, that people saw me and accepted me, liked me. . . . For the first time I felt like a movie star." The high had been so exhilarating, it actually made her consider doing theater. I knew just what she meant about belonging; it was wonderful.

As well as Sidney knew her, he was baffled by some of her

behavior. One day he agreed to drive with her to a little town outside Palm Springs ". . . to visit my father," she confided. He was surprised, because supposedly she didn't know where her father was or even which of two men was her real father.

As they neared the dairy farm that was their destination, she stopped to buy a newspaper, explaining, "It has a story about me, I want to show it to my father so he'll know who I am . . . what I've been doing."

Sidney waited in the car as she disappeared into a house hidden behind trees. Shortly, she reappeared, deeply upset. She drove in silence until finally she burst out, "That son of a bitch told me he wanted nothing to do with me."

Later, Sidney was talking to Marilyn's coach Natasha, who described accompanying her on exactly the same journey, dialogue, newspaper, and all. Over the next ten years MM made repeated trips to that destination with different friends. No one was ever invited in. So no one was sure what the truth was. Who did she see? What did they say? Was it her father?

Another time not long after she'd returned to the States, she quizzed Sidney, "Guess who I'm going to marry?"

Taken aback, he reminded her, "Marilyn, you just got married."

Blithely she stated, "Yeah, I know . . . but I'm going to marry Arthur Miller."

She seemed to have the same disease my mother did: a compulsion to predict. Mom made prognostications about the future all the time, based on intuition and information she seemed to glean out of the air. The scary thing was how often her predictions came true.

I loved following Marilyn's life in the papers and through Steffi. It was such stuff as dreams were made of . . . I empathized with her. She wasn't distant like Greta Garbo or haughty and pretentious like Joan Crawford or foreign like Ingrid Bergman. I felt she was like my friends and me, that we shared common dreams. She aspired to do more, to be more, to improve herself. She took ordinary black-and-white life and reflected it back to us in Technicolor, in epic proportions. Yet she kept it accessible. As famous as she was, she remained human.

Besides, since I'd met her, I had this sense of propriety about her life.

I was talking to a friend. We were contrasting Marilyn and Joe's personalities. He was neat, she was messy. He was reclusive, silent; she was social, talkative. He was Latin, Italian; she was from English-Scottish stock. I said I was sure she and Joe would be happy "because everyone knows that opposites attract." They retorted, "Only if you don't like yourself." Could that be true? If so, I'd have to find and fall in love with someone just like me. On the other hand, what if being with someone just like me was painful, drove me crazy—or worse, bored me?

"Bored, he bores me." This was the reason Marilyn would give to Sidney in explaining why she left Joe nine months later. She'd loved him, she'd had great sex with him, but he'd bored her. She hated to be bored. Was it as simple as that?

At sixteen my dreams were adrenaline-fueled, "dreams of passion" inspired by the poets and novelists I'd read—Tolstoy, Dickens, Keats, Shelley.

Most of my dreams were borrowed. In them I was Marilyn, Anna Karenina, Mary Queen of Scots, Elizabeth I. As soon as I had time, I promised myself, I was going to sit down and make up my own dreams. Maybe they'd turn out to be what I'd dreamed in the first place and discarded as impossible.

My passion that year went into my acting career. My studies to be a commercial artist were over, paintbrushes replaced by makeup ones. The science fiction mystery novel I was writing, *C for Sibelius*, was forgotten in a drawer, which was probably just as well. My ballet career had swan-dived. I was too short for George Balanchine anyway, at whose school I'd had a scholarship. My toe shoes were tossed for the Cuban heels my mother let me buy (still no stiletto spikes, but I was working on it).

My father's reputation as a teacher was exploding, thanks to the films of Elia Kazan and the success of the members of the Actors Studio. Some he'd trained, some he'd inspired, others had worked with teachers who'd emerged from the Group Theatre. As Marlon Brando, Geraldine Page, Eva Marie Saint, Jimmy Dean, and others became known, interest in the studio grew. Pop, its artistic director, had a vision of a new realism, based on technique, discipline, and the ability to elicit and control real emotions and behavior.

This "sudden" success came after many lean years, when Pop's pride had been trampled. After his triumphs with the Group Theatre, his gifts had been neglected in Hollywood, where he'd been under contract at Marilyn's studio—20th Century-Fox. Now of course, with success and credit also came criticism and jealousy. My father was accused of encouraging every personality problem of the actors he trained. If they drank, were temperamental, mumbled, or were egotistical, he took the blame. I knew better, because at the Actors Studio I constantly heard him yell, "Speak up, we can't hear you!" or, "If you can't do what the director asks you to, get out of the business. If he asks you to climb up a wall, do it, and then go home and justify it." Torn T-shirts and mumbling became the trademarks or stigma of studio actors. Many of the younger ones couldn't afford clothes fancier than jeans. Then because many of the parts in which they were successful portrayed characters like that and they were so good, the actors were confused with their roles. Marlon in *A Streetcar Named Desire*, for example. Even non-Method actors suffered from this stereotyping: Marilyn, the dumb blonde; Bill Holden, the macho man; Cary Grant, the assured lover. All illusion. Acting was creating real thoughts, feelings, and behavior under imaginary circumstances, just like life. Becoming a myth sure seemed to lead to "mythconceptions."

Mother drummed into me that I must be the most profession-al, uncomplaining, responsible actor ever invented. "You're a Strasberg," she told me, and whatever I did would be attribut-ed to my father. This engendered mixed feelings in me. If Pop got the blame, he'd also get the credit. What would I get?

The pleasure part was that as an actress, people acknowl-edged me differently. It was delicious and frightening. I was no longer just "little Susie," Paula and Lee's daughter. My younger brother, Johnny, felt very left out. We'd been close before, and I tried to pay attention to him, but he seemed so changed and so young at twelve, it was as if we lived in two separate worlds. He made underhanded remarks, little zingers, expressing his growing hostility and alienation from the family. I pretended I didn't hear. He and my mother were the ones in the family who spoke out. I took after my father, who avoided confrontation whenever humanly possible.

When I appeared in "The Marriage," the first color televi-sion series in America, my mother held my face in her hands and shook her head in wonder. "Thou art thy mother's glass, and she in thee brings back the lovely April of her prime." Hopefully I would live up to her expectations, but my father's opinion meant more to me than anyone else's in the world. The ultimate goal of my life was to win approval from him.

Summer on Fire Island brought a bad suntan and my first romance. He was older, in college, and as we lay on a sandy blanket, looking up at the stars and tracing the Big Dipper and Orion's belt with our fingertips, I became aware of parts of my body I hadn't known existed. I was still a virgin when the summer ended, but I was living.

A confusing thing started to happen. In my roles I was permitted to release all kinds of emotions that were unaccept-able in real life. I cried, screamed, laughed, loved, and died, winning applause for it. Then I had to return to the compara-tively gray world of normal life. But all my feelings, all my passions, were awakened, and I didn't know what to do with them, where to put them.

I took to disappearing into my closet, where Sweetie Pie, our cat, the most neurotic cat in America, had taken to hiding, too. Wrapped in darkness, I created this ritual. I'd save old socks, a torn nightgown, a ragged towel. When I reached a point where I couldn't hold in my tears, anger, or frustration, I'd retreat to the neutral darkness and safety of my closet and rip, tear, and bite the things I'd kept. I'd cry and scream silently until I felt better or was too exhausted to feel worse. My father was the only one who could get angry or emotional with impunity in our house. Often his rages ended with him getting a nosebleed, Mother terrified he'd have a heart attack.

Mother released her emotions by getting hysterical or threatening suicide, usually to my brother and me. My father would flee the apartment to go on a compulsive book-buying spree. Repeatedly Mother would threaten to visit a nunnery in Connecticut, implying she might not return. Later she'd tell friends, "I don't have time to think myself into despair," but that was wishful thinking on her part. Johnny and I were unable to move her when she became depressed.

Our household revolved around my father, his moods, his needs, his expectations, and his neuroses. He was teaching people how to act, but nothing compared to the drama in our house.

Toward the end of the year, I was asked to read for a new play. Someone was finally doing *The Diary of Anne Frank*, and I was reading for the part of Anne. I prayed to God, "Please let me have this part and I'll be a wonderful person." I made all sorts of promises to God as if he were running "Let's Make a Deal" in heaven. My desire to play the role wasn't a career gambit. Anne Frank's spirit had moved me so profoundly when I'd read the book, I longed to be part of it. "Dear Lord," Michelangelo had written, "free me of myself so I can please you." In a project like *Anne Frank*, that might be possible. To go beyond myself . . . The thought was thrilling.

My mother had taped a sign to the icebox: "Anything the human mind can conceive of is possible." Tacked next to it was the Mayo Clinic diet—egg whites, steak, and grapefruit— for my mother's perpetual battle against her weight. I "conceived" myself getting the part.

The day of the reading, I wanted to be so good so desperately that I got hysterical and couldn't find the stage door of the theater. Like a confused laboratory rat in a maze, I ran round and round the block, finally stumbling in the right door. Totally out of contact, I had no idea how the reading had gone. My suspicion was I'd been terrible. Finally I'd found something worth fighting for, and I'd messed it up. Happy Thanksgiving.

All I read about in the New York tabloids was Marilyn shooting *The Seven Year Itch*. One scene she did without any retakes or forgetting her lines. Her character talked about liking shy men, not macho ones and Marilyn identified with this. Afterward she said, "It was a real scene with real people, I could act like a human being. . . . That was the first time I felt really clean before a camera."

A few days later she did another scene, with a fan blowing her skirt over her head while she stood on a subway grill. It hit every paper—twice. Apparently DiMaggio was offended by it, which figured. Since he was uptight when she ran to kiss him, I could imagine how he'd react when her underpants were showing. It was pretty risqué, except she didn't seem lascivious or dirty, just playful. I thought, If my legs looked like hers, I'd do the same thing.

She was so generous to Joe in the papers. "I'm just a pretty girl who's soon forgotten, but Joe's an all-time great." Would this prophecy come true? I hadn't forgotten her.

The romance of the century didn't last out the year. Joe and Marilyn were divorcing. She was claiming mental cruelty.

The romance of the century didn't last out the year. Joe and Marilyn were divorcing. She was claiming mental cruelty. Weeping and dressed in black, in mourning for her marriage, she was helped into a car. Hordes of hungry photographers and newsmen grabbed at her as Sidney and her lawyers protected her. It looked staged. But her tears were real.

The next thing I read was that she'd disappeared. Her studio, 20th Century-Fox, put her on suspension for the second time in a little over a year. It was better than the radio serials I'd loved: "Stella Dallas," "Backstage Wife," "The Lone Ranger," and "The Shadow."

It was romantic, dramatic, alive, and it wasn't acting, it was for real. "Mister Sandman, send me a dream . . ." "Hey there, you with the stars in your eyes . . ." "Whatever Lola wants, Lola gets . . ." But would Marilyn? Would I? Would any of us?

I ended the year daydreaming about my future and anxious that it wouldn't happen fast enough, whatever it was. At least since I didn't know exactly where I was going, I couldn't get lost, and I was on my way. . . .

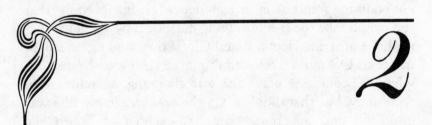

THE YEAR 1955 WAS A GOOD ONE FOR BROADWAY: it produced Arthur Miller's *A View from the Bridge* and William Inge's *Bus Stop*, the latter starring Kim Stanley. She and Geraldine Page were the two greatest American actresses. Martin Luther King, having led boycotts against segregated buses in Alabama, became leader of the desegregation movement. Rock-and-roll music was attacked as being immoral and disgusting. Charlie "Bird" Parker died of a drug overdose. Churchill resigned. Arthur Mitchell was the first black dancer with a major ballet company in New York. "Love Is a Many Splendored Thing," from the movie with Jennifer Jones, was playing everywhere, but not for me. Almost seventeen, I'd been kissed, but I wanted my great love.

Marilyn had surfaced, hiding out in New York City with Milton and Amy Greene. She'd formed a production company, with Milton as her partner. He was a photographer but had never done any movies. Some of her friends, like Sidney in Hollywood, were angry with her for being impulsive and not choosing someone more experienced. It intrigued me that she would take the risk of ruining her career by alienating her studio. Katharine Hepburn and Gloria Swanson never fought like that. Of course, they hadn't played the parts she did, but what else could she play? She was charming, adorable, sexy, and funny, but that didn't mean she was an actress. She was beautiful, and apparently she had courage. I hoped she wouldn't slip and fall on her ass again.

The press went crazy over her leaving Hollywood. People joked about her acting talent, saying she was trying to be "a Bernhardt in a bikini." None of that stopped her, she took New York by storm, as she had Hollywood. People like Carl Sandburg and Isak Dinesen and Truman Capote wanted to meet her. Her magnetism attracted people from wildly diverse backgrounds, from politicians to poets and physicists. Reading about her, I was grateful for my family and background and new career. I dreamed on about the great things I would see and do and say, so maybe all those fascinating people would court me one day, the way they did Marilyn.

The main quarrel I had with fate was, it was sneaky. Even a storm played fair; it gives you warning, a flash of lightning, a distant rumble, a heaviness in the atmosphere, a pain in a toe as the pressure drops, a cloud on the horizon. Not life.

It was one of those early spring days when there's a kick in the air. It's nippy and hot at the same time and you don't know what to expect . . . from the weather, either. I'd gotten home from school early. With her usual dramatic flair, Mother waved her arms, motioning me to be still when I came into the house. My mother's penchant for drama had increased since she'd been blacklisted. All her creative juices flowed into our lives.

"Shush"—finger to mouth—"Daddy is working, he's coaching someone."

"Who?" I whispered, impressed, because my father never coached anybody one on one; that was my mother's job. Pop had only worked privately with one actress—Jennifer Jones, who'd been too shy to perform in class. Pop adored her dark beauty and luminous sensitivity.

"I don't want them disturbed."

She still hadn't told me who it was, so I tried to figure who could be important or special enough for my father to give up some of his rare quiet time. Laurence Olivier, Greta Garbo, perhaps a politician who wanted coaching or some unknown he'd discovered. I wondered if it was a girl and if she was younger than me. I hated not knowing, so I tried to eavesdrop, as my mother was doing. She hugged the entrance to the living room. Since we were both talking to one another in whispers, we could only eavesdrop in the pauses. Tricky, but not impossible.

My mother had developed this habit of eavesdropping because she said it was necessary for her to know what Pop was saying to people, since he often wouldn't tell her. I understood her frustration because I was usually dying of curiosity. One part of me hated that she was so intrusive and inquisitive, because I figured if she was doing it to Pop, she was probably doing it to me.

"If I don't know what's going on, how can I help?" Mother said, justifying herself to me. My mother had cause for her anxiety. She was extroverted, communicative, and social. My father was the opposite, introverted, secretive, silent, enigmatic. If Pop were a gambler, he'd play his cards very close to his chest with a total poker face. Sometimes I imagined someone could drop dead having an interview with him and we'd never know until the stench of the rotting corpse got strong enough to be inconvenient in his life. Then he'd call Mom so she could mop it up.

Mother had this burning desire to help everyone and anyone, with anything, whether they asked for help or not. My brother, Johnny, who was almost fourteen, was constantly telling her, "Butt out of my life."

"I'm sure he doesn't mean it," Mom would say, laughing.

I'd keep quiet. I knew he did.

So Mom and I stood there. We also served who only stood and waited.

As long as he was in there, that part of the house was off limits. The living room was also my father's study. It opened onto the dining room, which my mother had done in red flocked paper because "red arouses energy, gives you an appetite, and makes you hungry, or angry, so of course it's death for a bedroom." She was into color interpretation, the emotional impact of color on mood.

I heard my father's voice coming closer. He was laughing, in a good mood. I was relieved. My father's moods were the weather vane of our family. As he turned, we followed.

Our apartment was long and narrow; half the windows faced a courtyard. Dusk began to insinuate itself. The smoky light gave everything a chiaroscuro effect. The rich smell of that night's pot roast, cooking with onions and potatoes, filled the house. A Mozart record was playing softly in the living room.

Marilyn appeared in the darkness, like the sun in the morning. She was just . . . there. Surprised, I gave my mother a dirty look to say, You should have told me. She smiled, satisfied. All I could think was, Boy, everybody wants to be an actress. Then I remembered that Marilyn had told me she was going to study with my father. She'd meant it.

With the blondness of her hair, the blueness of her eyes much bluer without makeup, the pearlescent paleness of her skin, she gave the impression of being surrounded by a halo of light. She was laughing, and Pop was laughing with her. He liked her.

Before Mother could introduce us, Marilyn said, "Hi, I'm Marilyn Monroe. You may not remember me, but we met in California," as if I or anyone might forget her.

When I was three my parents had taken me to meet Tallulah Bankhead. She'd made a grand entrance announcing in her whiskey voice, "Dahling, I'm Tallulah Bankhead."

Puzzled, I'd gazed at her and asked, "Why?" There was no reason to ask "why" of Marilyn. I was old enough to get it.

Mother's voice interrupted my memory, "Oh yes, Susie told me you'd met . . ."

I told her everything. I didn't need a diary, I had my mother.

My father took Marilyn's arm, and she glommed on to it. This surprised me. He never took anyone's arm, they took his.

She seemed very fragile—not fragile breakable, but fragile "handle with care." We all followed my mother into the kitchen. Funny, with her blond hair, blue eyes, and translucent skin, she could have been my mother's daughter. With my light brown hair and hazel eyes, I resembled my father.

It didn't seem possible. Was this vibrant, shy, shimmering mermaid who somehow managed to undulate on her high heels—this fresh-faced, clear-eyed, normal-size girl—the same overblown, sexy, exotic creature I'd met a little over a year ago in Hollywood? How could she have changed so totally? I was stunned by her transformation. In comparison, I'd hardly changed at all.

My father seemed even more taken by Marilyn than he'd been by Jennifer Jones. He was leaning over the kitchen table, helping her get the best cut of meat. I wondered if I'd look good in the full-skirted, small-waisted dress she had on and how I'd look as a blonde. I'd been blond until about four, when I'd gone darker. Then my brother had arrived, with white-blond curls that made people gurgle over him as though he were an adorable little girl. If a four-year-old can snarl, I did: "He's a boy, a little boy, see? . . ." I'd point to his diaper, which I was willing to take off to convince them. This was no boy.

After dinner Mother did the dishes, Johnny disappeared into his room, and Pop went to put on another record. Everything in our house happened to music. Our lives were a drama scored by Beethoven, Bach, Mozart, Vivaldi, Schubert, and Wagner. Marilyn asked about school and what parts I had done since I'd been in California. She said what pretty long hair I had, she'd always wanted to have silky hair like mine. I decided she wouldn't be here that long. Jennifer Jones had gone back to her husband, David Selznick, and California rapidly, as would Marilyn. So I paid more attention to what she said. She was funny and bright, and it turned out she was a Gemini, too, like me, which pleased my mother. "Gemini's the brightest sign, always young, always learning, seeking knowledge."

"That's funny," Marilyn said. "My first charge account was at Martindale's Bookstore. I love books." She looked at the ones in our kitchen. "I even took a course in literature, but, God, has he actually read all these books?"

"A lot of them," I replied. Pop was reading a book now and seemed engrossed. But you never knew. He had the capacity to listen to music, read, and hear whatever you said.

"Some are in languages," I explained, "like Japanese, he can't read, so he has people come to the house to translate them. He taught himself to read some French and Italian and German when he was a kid. He knows where every book is."

"Wow," she said.

"Believe it or not," I confided, "there's nothing for me to read in this house, they're all so esoteric and special. He doesn't read novels or anything like that, so I have to buy my own books."

She mused, "How could one man read all these, how does his head hold it all? It doesn't look that big, but it must be filled up there." She laughed and pointed to her forehead.

She gazed in wonder at the walls covered with old and new volumes on every imaginable subject from science to slavery, from psychology to politics, music, art, painting, dance, religion, costume, and customs. Anything could and did relate to the theater, at least the kind of theater Pop dreamed of. He'd once turned angrily to some author who was upset that my father was talking with the actors about the theme of his play. The author wanted equal time, I think, and my father snapped, "This theater is not about your play, it's about ideas." And there they were on our walls, all the ideas that had practically ever been thought for thousands of years.

I was glad Marilyn couldn't hear what my mother said about these volumes: "These damned books, all our money is in them! You'll have the greatest library in the world, and we'll starve to death."

We talked on about clothes and what books she'd read, many of the ones I was reading, like Rilke's *Letters to a Young Poet*. I forgot she was almost thirty years old. She seemed like one of my girlfriends, maybe a little more fun, a little freer, and much more interesting. . . . What things she could tell me about the world.

That night after she'd gone and I'd done my homework, I practiced walking like her in front of the mirror, only since I had no shoes as high as hers, I had to do it on tiptoe. I decided it was imperative to get high heels, Cuban heels were for teenagers.

JOHNNY

The first time I met her I remember she came out of the living room and Pop said, "This is my son," and my first impression of her was that she was different from most of the people who came to the house. I'd watch all these people trading their most human qualities, betraying themselves for success at all costs, to become rich and famous, and afterward, when it was too late, they'd realize they had lost the best part of themselves along the way, but she, she was like me. When I looked into her eyes, it was like looking into my own, they were like a child's eyes. I was still a child. You know how children just look at you. My feeling was she had less ego or was less narcissistic than most of the actors who never really bothered with me. She was just another person to me, another one from that world I felt cut off, excluded, from. She was nicer, real simple, no make-up, and she really looked at me as if she saw me. It wasn't that I wanted people to look at me, but I knew the difference when she did. I knew everyone said she was the sexiest, most sensual woman in the world. Not to me. I thought there was something wrong with me for not feeling that from her. I'd felt it from other women who came to the house. I was pretty sexually frustrated then. She was so open, so loose, and her sensuality as such was so totally innocent, nothing dirty in it at all, and the first time it was just like talking to an ordinary person, only realer than most who came into the house in those days. She was quiet, too, I remember, like an animal is quiet, and I was like that, too, survival tactics. She seemed smart, but not in an educated way, instinctively smart, nobody's fool.

My father started giving her free private acting lessons at the house. She was too shy and terrified to come to class. My father made his living from his private classes. Each one had about thirty students of varying ages and degrees of experience, from beginners to stars. The Actors Studio was another entity. It was a nonprofit studio. Pop was supposed to get paid but they usually didn't have the money to do that. You auditioned to get in. Thousands did, though they took in only a handful of new members yearly. Membership was for life. You didn't ever have to work if you didn't want to, and no one paid. At the studio there was no set routine of work. In the private classes everyone started with certain exercises and escalated to more complicated work. The studio was a gymnasium not a school. It was a place to experiment, to fall on your face, without worrying about the pressures of the commercial work place, to take risks, to play parts you might never be offered.

Pop and Marilyn decided that she would observe at the studio, work with him at home, sit in on the private classes and eventually do the exercise work and scenes with the other students. Observer privileges at the studio were a courtesy that was extended to foreign or already established actors. Some came once, like Laurence Olivier; others came often.

My father had gone out of his way for both known and unknown artists before, if they were needy, financially or emotionally, and if they were talented. He said that often the depth of the emotional problem was correspondent to the degree of talent. He was fascinated with the transmutation of antisocial behavior into creative work. Because of this, he was accused of doing therapy. One student and friend remarked, "Lee, you should have been a therapist."

He shook his head. "Why, darling? I have more freedom in my work."

He sent numerous actors to psychiatrists, and many doctors sent their patients to class because they felt his work helped theirs in analysis.

He felt Marilyn had to go into therapy before he could work with her. She'd seen doctors before only on a hit-and-run basis, emergency room therapy with no continuity. Now she agreed to commit on a long-term basis.

After a day of teaching, my dad was usually too exhausted to talk, and even when he wasn't exhausted, he wasn't exactly a magpie. Now, three times a week after work he and Marilyn disappeared into the living room. Soon I'd hear laughing or weeping, sometimes an outburst of anger, a diatribe against her studio or someone who'd betrayed her trust. She was very unforgiving during these bouts, it was all black and white for her. People were either for her or against her, there was no middle ground. If she even suspected they were against her, and she could be very suspicious, she'd go wild. I don't know if "those bastards . . . sons of bitches . . .," and so on were ever told off in person, but if they were, I doubt they would have ever forgotten it. And she didn't stutter once.

Her scatological language fascinated me. My parents rarely cursed in private. You didn't say certain words in public, it just wasn't done. Others could do it, but we didn't, except my brother, who refused to obey the unspoken rules. "Hypocrites!" he'd yell at my parents. "Goddamned hypocrites."

Marilyn's vocabulary included words I'd never even heard of, and she wielded them like a sailor, with no embarrassment. She had quite a temper when she lost control. It didn't faze my father, perhaps because he was always battling his own prodigious rage, which more than matched hers. He seemed to have a calming effect on her. Her tirade would evaporate and, as if nothing had occurred, they'd be speaking quietly about very personal matters—men, her mother, her feelings of worthlessness or hopelessness. It was such a stark contrast to the way she behaved with me, I could hardly believe it was the same woman.

When I overheard snatches of these sessions I'd get excited with a sense of being part of something forbidden. As if I were a sieve, I'd feel her emotions run through me. If she cried, tears came to my eyes.

On the other hand, I was ambivalent about the tenderness I heard in my dad's voice as he consoled her. When I'd gone to my father to talk about something personal in my life—my fights with Mother, my need for more freedom, a young man I'd been dating who never called anymore—he closed up. "Darling, I'm not concerned with that except as it relates to the work." It was true, mine weren't life-or-death problems, but they felt that way to me, and he acted as if they were so trivial he couldn't be bothered. I wanted to cry out to him, "I don't care about the work. I'm young, I want to have a good time. I don't want to suffer or be in pain, I want you to help me. I want you to hold me." The words lodged in my throat, and I couldn't say anything.

Another thing confused me—given that my middle name was confusion. It confused me to observe the attention and time my father devoted to Marilyn. It began to dawn on me that there was some connection between them that went beyond the work. She was so different from the classic actresses he spoke of with glowing admiration, the actresses he admired—Rachel, the great French tragedienne, whom I looked like; Eleonora Duse, whom he'd seen and whom he believed was the greatest actress that had ever lived. He advocated willpower and structure and discipline. Marilyn seemed such an unlikely disciple. Her work and life seemed the antithesis of everything he stood for to me. Was he in love with her? I didn't think so. But he was practically a stranger to me. In some ways our entire family were intimate strangers. I wondered if my mother was jealous of the time he gave to Marilyn.

"She's not your father's type, you know," Mom confided.

"My type is Jennifer Jones, that dark-haired, fair-skinned beauty," Pop affirmed.

"It's her talent he loves," Mother assured herself. "She's so incredibly talented." Then she wondered whether I should darken my hair and eyebrows for a more glamorous look. Eventually I did and, when I saw the photos of myself, dark and dramatic, I realized with a shock that I resembled a young Jennifer Jones.

Someone who'd known Pop from the Group Theatre days was reminiscing to me: "There were two things we knew about Lee. He loved baseball and Alice Faye." Alice Faye was a blonde like Marilyn, like my mother. Maybe my father didn't have a type.

Even when Marilyn wasn't physically present, she often monopolized the conversation. My father was unaccustomedly verbal about her. After dinner one night he told us, "She has this phenomenal sensitivity, her instrument is incredibly responsive. Despite the bad mannerisms and habits she may have acquired in Hollywood, and with all the abuse she was subjected to, they haven't touched what is underneath. It's difficult because you have to look past what she looks like to see what's hidden. She had to hide it or she'd have been too vulnerable to survive, and she's so eager and willing, as if she's a flower that's been waiting all this time for someone to water her."

There was this strange constriction in my throat as he continued. Was it boredom, or was it resentment? He never talked about me with that look in his eyes. He wasn't finished, either; he went on to say, "After Marlon, she has the greatest talent, raw talent, that I've ever come across, except in her it's just not at all developed. But she has the desire. And if she has the discipline, the will, she can do it."

Early one evening Marilyn had finished a particularly grueling session with Pop. We were waiting for dinner, which we ate around six-thirty, and she'd borrowed some of my makeup to fix up her face because she'd been crying. She was unusually relaxed and pleased about whatever they'd done. We were in my bedroom, and I sprawled on my bed, watching her apply my rouge and mascara, the only makeup I used.

As she began to talk to me, she seemed to be talking to herself, too. Her voice was hushed but clear. "I thought your father would be so forbidding, I was terrified the first time I was alone with him in there. But he wasn't scary at all. Gadge [Elia Kazan, the director], a lot of people told me he was scary, but I think they just didn't want me to see him. Susie, the best thing that ever happened to me was when your father took me seriously. I've always wanted for people to see *me*, not the actress, the real person. Your daddy does. He treats me like a human being. I was so sick of being treated like a poster babe or a broad out there. Everybody laughed when I said I wanted to play Grushenka in *The Brothers Karamazov*, like I was a dummy. They were the dummies. If they'd bothered to read the book, they'd know she was this sensual girl, a barmaid. I could really have played her."

She turned to look at me. "You know why I make fun of myself? So I'll do it before they do. That way it's not so bad, doesn't hurt so much. It's either commit suicide or laugh." She had this pensive look on her face, as if she were figuring something out.

Daylight was fading fast, and she switched on the lamp near the mirror. "And you know, since your daddy's given me his stamp of approval, other people are suddenly changing their tune. Only I'm not sure they believe it like he does."

Inside I was dying. I'd been one of those people who'd looked down at her aspirations. Thank God she couldn't read my mind.

In a stream of consciousness her voice flowed on. "I worked with this woman in California for years. She taught me, educated me, like your father, gave me books to read, but even she thought I was a dummy. He doesn't, and the most important thing is, with your father for the first time I feel it's okay to be me, the whole kit and caboodle, you know, the whole mess.

"I never dared to even think about it before—who's got time to think when you gotta survive? But now I want to be an artist, pardon the expression, a real actress. I don't care about the money and the fame, although I'm not knocking it, but like the man says, 'Life's not written on dollar bills,' right? Since I came here to New York, I feel I'm accepted, not as a freak, but as myself, whoever the hell that is. I'm kind of just finding out."

She was so open, her face flowing with fervor and longing, I felt glad for her, and I wondered if this was what my father was drawn to—this longing of hers.

She turned off the makeup light, and then, almost as if she'd made a discovery, she continued. "You know, for the first time in a long time I feel that something good is going to come out of my life . . . and I'm beginning to think that the something good is me. I know your father's really going to help me. You don't know how lucky you are." I assumed she meant to have a father like that, and I was a little embarrassed on general principles and just nodded agreement.

It was dark in the room now, and we sat, unable to see each other's faces, lost in our own thoughts. Faint notes of some lyrical strains of flute music drifted in the air. The sweet-sour aroma of red cabbage and brisket made my mouth water.

Listening to her had reminded me of this story about an agent who sold a producer on this actress, saying she'd stop the show if he cast her. On opening night she did stop the show and got a standing ovation. The agent turned to the producer triumphantly. "You see, I told you she was great, and now I believe it."

Marilyn seemed like the agent before the ovation, hoping for the best yet not convinced.

It amazed me that she was so much older, had achieved so much, yet she was just as insecure as, maybe even more insecure than, me. She had won my complete admiration for one thing: she wasn't scared of my father, not even a little bit. I determined I'd watch her closely so I could learn her secret.

3

THE ARRIVAL OF MARILYN AT THE ACTORS STUDIO brought
it into the public eye. Everything she did attracted such
intense interest: where she shopped, whom she dated,
where she was studying, that glaring spotlight that is felt
by a handful of celebrities. Some found it possible to live
fairly private lives. For MM, no matter what she did, it
was impossible. People were just fascinated by her. Paul
Newman was becoming a star, but he didn't attract the
same kind of obsessive curiosity as Marilyn or Elvis. It
wasn't just personality or talent. I couldn't figure out
what it was, but I sure would have liked to have it. . . .

Marilyn's arrival in our lives was a double-edged
sword. Father's celebrity rose; he became more famous,
almost infamous. Before MM, people had been admiring,
worshiping, indifferent, condescending, or respectful,
but in some normal context. After her arrival people's

attitudes toward my dad became inflated, as did everything connected with MM. Pop's new high visibility made him a much easier target. It was very difficult for me when anyone was critical of Mom and Pop. It was all right if I was, because I loved them, but it made me feel embarrassed and furious when anyone else dared to judge them. It was especially difficult because of Pop's orders not to defend him or Mother or the work. I pretended I didn't care and suffered in silence. Critics were many and often vicious. When he publicly affirmed Marilyn's talent, he was called soft in the head, a star fucker, an opportunist (he had reaped no financial rewards, as he never charged for her private sessions, and in the classes she paid the same thirty dollars a month, as everyone did). Actually it turned out my father was risking more than he was gaining.

All the years of my father's career he had one vital need: to be respected. If you couldn't give that to him, he wasn't interested in you. The issue of respect was so important to him that he'd endure a confrontation, whether it was over Johnny's lack of respect for him or a student's for the work. Marilyn's presence brought him the possibility of losing the respect he'd worked so hard for over the years. He was staking his reputation on his belief that Marilyn not only had talent, but that with all her problems, personal and professional, she could mobilize herself to develop into a fine actress. It wasn't a responsibility he took on without much deliberation, and he did it because he responded to something he perceived in her, something that moved him to his depths.

"Jealous," Mother proclaimed. "They're jealous." Mother was crazed about the criticism, and so was I. Tears sprang to my eyes, ready to overflow, if anyone even sneered about Marilyn, her attributes or her talent. And sneer they did. "Don't defend your father," Mom said, "they're not worth it. You leave it to me. You and your father are artists. You just have to do the work, we'll have the last laugh." So Mother once more led the cavalry charge against anyone who dared question my father. She was as fierce as a mother lioness defending her young.

"She's going to surprise everyone, but it takes time. They're like vultures waiting for her to fail. Why are people so mean-spirited? You'd think the other actors would know better. . . ." She'd shake her head mournfully. "Why doesn't talent come with kindness? Susan, learn from this. You have to please yourself, you can never please *them*." She heaved a deep sigh.

How could she not know it wasn't them I was concerned with? The only one I wanted to please was Pop.

At first my father had seemed oblivious of his detractors. When it was obvious he could no longer tolerate or ignore the criticisms people were leveling at him, he ignored them anyway. He had a rule that he impressed upon me later when I had to deal with situations that became public or humiliating. "Susan, if it's true, ignore it because it's true; if it's not true, ignore it because it's not true."

So instead of defending himself, he would tighten his lips and walk away, silent, seething, infuriated. He'd say, "I'm not interested in anything but the work, let them talk," but his pride was hurt. He'd turn up the music louder than usual.

"Daddy knows and Marilyn knows," Mother said. "That's all that counts." In front of him she kept quiet, but when he wasn't around she defended him, explaining his motives, attacking anyone who was a doubter, and exhorting Marilyn and me to bigger and surely better things. "This too shall pass. They can't keep making fun of us," she predicted, and although the ridicule or envy should have passed, somehow it never did. . . .

That spring I read for director Joshua Logan for the role of Millie in *Picnic*. Millie was a tomboy adolescent, a young writer stuck in a small town in Kansas with her mother and beautiful older sister. This got me a screen test for the role, which I won.

Before my mother and I left for Hollywood and locations in Kansas, the Actors Studio had a benefit for the opening of *East of Eden*. Marlon and Marilyn were ushers. She was as excited as a debutante at her coming-out ball, which meant she was also exceedingly anxious. She fortified herself with champagne and constant reassurances from everyone that she looked beautiful, that she didn't have to do anything other than be herself. As the photographers went into a feeding frenzy, I hid behind my mother and father. I wasn't hiding from anyone in particular; I was intimidated by all the lights and noise and hullabaloo, and worried I'd do something wrong. I seemed to worry a lot. I remembered first really worrying about whether my dolls liked the biblical and historical names I'd given them and it had snowballed from there. Marilyn was the opposite. Her trepidations seemed to vanish with the lights and action, and she handled it all with panache, though I noticed her clinging to my father's arm whenever she wasn't clinging to Marlon's. So she clung to his arm as I clung to the back of his jacket, just in case he forgot me.

In the last scene in the movie, I cried so hard that I was uncontrollable. In the midst of my sobbing, I caught a glimpse of Marilyn's face. There was one tear running down her cheek, but otherwise she was impassive. The scene that had demolished me was the one about "how awful it is not to be loved, it makes you angry and cruel and violent. . . ." Watching Marilyn, I wondered if she empathized with that.

Marilyn gave me advice about little things to do with makeup for the film. "Put a dab of Vaseline on your cheeks and lips."

"I don't think they want me to have any makeup," I said with a sigh.

"They'll never know," she said, and proceeded to show me how to put on makeup so it looked like no makeup. I was grateful because I was terrified I'd look ugly playing the plain tomboy. I'd agreed to wear my own glasses on camera, but I was determined to put on mascara underneath. When she'd finished I was sure I looked at least five years older. She took me in to show my parents. My father just nodded, but Mother said to him, "She's a great beauty." I was eternally grateful to Marilyn.

Kim Novak and William Holden were cast as the young lovers, Kim at the insistence of Harry Cohn, who owned Columbia Pictures. She was a young actress he was grooming to replace Rita Hayworth, who'd walked out on him, and he wanted to make her the next Marilyn.

With money that I'd saved from my TV work and movies (the rest had gone to my parents, who, between my father's growing book addiction and our upgraded lifestyle, always seemed to need more money), I went to Jax, the store Marilyn recommended. Amy Greene, with whom I too had become friends, had first taken MM there. I bought three of everything: pedal pushers, shirts, and full-skirted dresses with crinolines and fitted bodices with scoop necks. "I'd give anything for your neck," Marilyn said. "It's so long . . . and your chin."

Surreptitiously I looked at her chin and nose. Steffi had told me Marilyn had undergone plastic surgery to correct her chin and nose. I didn't know anyone else who'd done that except Ruth Gordon, who'd had her bowlegs broken and reset straight.

"I'd give anything for two more inches in the leg," I said. "I'll trade you."

"It's the high heels," she said. "Get high heels and always keep your shoes the same color as your stockings, black with black, nude with nude. It makes you taller, get it?" I did and immediately went shopping again.

"Try lemon for your hair or beer. It's even better, you know, for the highlights on camera. If it doesn't work, you can drink it . . . as soon as you're legal, of course."

"I've had champagne," I bragged.

"You're never too young or old for champagne, remember that," Marilyn said, laughing.

"I'd love to have some man drink champagne out of my shoe one day," I daydreamed aloud.

"Think of the smell." She popped that balloon.

"I'm really nervous about this movie."

She said, "You've gotta be kidding, you've done stage and live TV in front of an audience, *live*. After that, a camera's easy. I'd die in front of a live audience."

"What does Pop say I should do with this part?" I asked my mother later.

"Go ask him," Mom said.

"He's really busy, Mom." I made excuses as my stomach started to go squishy with fear.

"There's no one in there now. Go talk to him, ask him."

"He's tired, Mother, he's listening to music. I can't inter-rupt."

"Everyone else does. You're his daughter, go in there."

I couldn't, I wouldn't, and when I finally worked up my courage and did, he asked me to read something from the script. "I—I'm not ready," I stammered. "I'll do it tomorrow."

"No, darling, do it now."

Trapped, I thought. What if he hates what I'm doing? I knew I had a bad habit of saying the wrong thing at the wrong time and then talking fast to cover up. Except with Pop, when words would fail me. I began to cry.

"What is this, darling?" God, but that "darling" could be a slap or a caress. "Is this the way you're going to play it?" He thought I was an idiot; I ran out of the room crying harder.

"You give all that time to some mediocre actor," my mother screamed at him, "and nothing to her. She feels you don't want to. She's your child, you have to take responsibility, she needs you. She doesn't want it from me, she wants it from you."

I hated being the cause of their fights. Afterward my mother would remind me of the danger she'd been in. "He'll leave me, and I did it for you," she'd sob.

Once they had a big fight about my brother and me.

He said, "Don't you tell my children things about me."

She said, "What do you mean, *your* children? They're *my* children, not yours."

Flatly he said, "I made them, they're mine."

Her voice rose, incensed. "They're not yours. You had nothing to do with it. I did it all. I practically put it in. . . ." And I didn't listen to the rest because I was sick to my stomach by then.

Even Mother didn't comprehend that I didn't want his coaching or his critique of my acting or his professional advice. He gave that to every actor who came into the house and had the nerve to ask him. I wanted him to take me somewhere, maybe the museum to see the Egyptian collection, the way he had when I was a little girl. We'd lose ourselves in the intricate delicacy of the pharaohs' jewels and the stone walls of the pyramid. He'd talk to me about things I only half-understood, and we'd get an ice cream or a hot dog. He loved New York hot dogs with mustard and sauerkraut. I wanted him to hold my hand, to be my father the way he'd been when I was his little golden-haired "Princess Blintzes." There was no way I would ever ask him for this. Never a gambler, I'd already risked so many no's. So he didn't and I didn't.

"I don't want to ask, and what if he says no?" I said to my friend Marty, a student of my dad's. "He's my father, I shouldn't have to ask. *She* never has to ask." We both knew who she was.

My mother and I left Johnny, the cat, Lee, food supplies, the maid, instructions to various students to visit, and a part-time secretary and took off for the wilder shores of California. "This will be good for Johnny," Mother mused. "He'll get to spend some time with his father." And Marilyn was to continue her private sessions, doing the exercise work with my dad at the house.

JOHNNY

I really felt alone and unloved, unapproved as the family star was rising higher and higher. I was more and more isolated. You and I had been close before, now suddenly you were gone, working. When you were home, you didn't have time for me anymore. When Mom went off with you, she wanted me to have a relationship with Pop, but it was hard for anyone to have a relationship with him if you weren't a book, a record, a cat, or Marilyn. He was really fascinated by her, but that's like saying about someone who is so fascinated by animals that they put them in a cage so they can study them. In that sense you could say he loved her. He did have this great generosity in his work, although usually he never considered the needs of anyone else before himself. His gift to Marilyn, his great gift, was that he took her seriously in her work, and even personally, too, up to a point. Marilyn was there more than anyone before had been. Lee adored her; at least he seemed to do anything to please her. She loved champagne, he got champagne. He didn't react like that with other people. His relationship with her was more complex than with the others. And at least she didn't ignore me.

At sixteen I was the youngest person on the set. At night I'd lie awake reading, doing homework, listening to the rest of the cast partying in the nearby rooms. Ostracized by my age, I felt like an outsider—almost an alien.

Bill Holden got drunk and hung by his fingers out of the

window of his tenth-floor suite. That gave director Josh Logan, who was watching and acrophobic, a scare.

Watching Bill on the set, I was perplexed. He had won an Academy Award. He was a family man. He'd had parents and an all-American background, the complete opposite of Marilyn's history. Despite that he was almost as insecure as she was. After every take he'd look for reassurance about his looks ("I'm too damned old for this part") or his acting ("Christ, I'm like a monkey in this"). Although his behavior was impeccably professional with the cast and crew members, he wasn't so kind to himself. At night he drank excessively. In the day he beat himself up emotionally. How could this mature, respected, successful, handsome, bright, lovely man be so lacking in self-esteem? Was he born like that? He wasn't an orphan like Marilyn. Had he inherited the trait? Was it the business we were in? Was self-deprecation an occupational hazard? If it came with the territory, I was in trouble.

Josh was brilliant and supportive of me. He loved everything I did. I adored him. He also had tremendous mood swings. One day he screamed at me, attacking me in front of thousands of extras because I'd been late, never asking why. Later, when he found out the studio car had broken down, he apologized. But I was devastated by then and never felt the same way about him. There were so many people not to trust, it was hard to remember. Years later I found out he was a manic-depressive and eventually had had to regulate his moods with lithium. Then I forgave him and felt terrible for not having understood.

Kim, at twenty-two, was only six years older than me and also having problems. Harry Cohn, the head of Columbia, wanted to control her life. It was said of him that you had to stand on line to hate him. Kim was having an affair with a musician, a married man, the same one Marilyn had been madly in love with years before. It seemed the world was awfully small. On top of this, Kim was inexperienced as an actress and insecure about her looks. Every morning she spent hours in makeup. Her legs were prone to be heavy, and they spent more time making up her legs than my face. She was beautiful; no one would be looking at her legs anyway. In the swimming scene I tried to convince Josh to let me wear a pretty swimsuit, lowcut like Kim's. "It's a hand-me-down of hers," I rationalized. He said no. Furious, I bought the most hideous suit I could find in Kansas, cutting my nose off to spite my face.

In one scene Kim had to cry. She begged Josh, "Pinch me." He hesitated. "I'll bruise you."

"You've got to, I can't cry otherwise." When he finally gave in, she kept saying, "Harder, harder, harder . . ."

Off to one side of the set, my mother and I watched. Mother turned to me and shook her finger. "You see, that's why Marilyn came east; she's smart. I hope this girl decides to study. If not, she could wind up one big black-and-blue mark. That's not what we mean by suffering for your art."

I had a big scene where I had to lash out at Kim as my older sister. "She gets all the attention. Madge is the pretty one, Madge is the pretty one."

"Don't worry," Mom counseled me, "if it doesn't happen, we'll find a substitution for you."

In *Remembrance of Things Past*, Proust says, "The smell and taste of things remain poised a long time like souls, ready to remind us, waiting and hoping for their moment . . . and bear unfalteringly, in the tiny and almost impalpable drop of their essence, the vast structure of recollection." This is the natural, spontaneous process of acting. A scene triggers your imagination, some memory is unlocked, and you respond. If it doesn't, you go to the storehouse of your life and choose some specific experience or object to call up the desired reaction—an event, a face, a voice, a piece of music. You substitute this remembered object or person for the one in the script. Making love to an actor you hated could be horrible without this personalization. Sometimes it could be horrible even with it.

"Let go," Josh encouraged me. "She's really upset." We rehearsed a little, and when we did the take, he printed the first shot.

"That was wonderful." Mother was unusually effusive with her praise. "What were you thinking of?"

"Nothing," I lied.

"You're just an instinctive actress, it's in the genes. I think you got it by osmosis."

I hadn't really lied. I wasn't thinking of anything, deliberately, but when I'd cried out, "Madge is the pretty one," and looked at Kim, Marilyn's face had flashed before my eyes.

On May 22 I turned seventeen. I blew out my candles with one breath. Next year, if even half my wish came true, things would be different. I was so lonely I cried myself to sleep that night.

As the film ended, a ferocious tornado destroyed a nearby town. It was terrifying and tragic, yet reassuring that God was still better than Hollywood at that kind of thing.

Back in Los Angeles, I made a list with Steffi. "What I want to be like when I'm famous": elusive like Garbo, "there" like Marilyn, difficult like Marlon, sexy like Ava Gardner, cool like Grace Kelly, and talented like Duse and Bernhardt.

Marilyn made lists, too. Steffi remembered one, of interesting men: John Huston, because he'd cast her in *The Asphalt Jungle* on the first interview; Marlon, because he was so sensitive and one of the finest actors in movies; Arthur Miller, because she'd read his novel *Focus* and because he'd been so nice to her when they'd met; Jawaharlal Nehru, because he was attractive and had ideals; and Jerry Lewis, because he'd been kind and protective to her when she appeared with him.

Not to be outdone, I made another list of an all-men's party we'd give. Marlon made both our lists, but only mine had Albert Einstein.

The week after this I again read for *Anne Frank* for the authors and with Joseph "Pepi" Schildkraut, who was to play

Anne's father. After the reading Pepi kissed me and said, "Hello, Anne."

"God works in mysterious ways," Mother said with tears in her eyes to match mine.

Anne Frank—to be her voice, to embody her spirit, to express her joys, rebellions, love, and ideals. This wasn't a part, it was a privilege.

That same month, on Marilyn's twenty-ninth birthday, *The Seven Year Itch* opened in New York to wonderful reviews and box office receipts, the best kind of present an actress can get. Everyone was ecstatic but Marilyn. "I hope it's the last of those kinds of parts I'll have to play. If I thought I had to keep on wiggling in crummy movies, I wouldn't want to work in movies anymore. I could go back to working in a factory if I had to. It wasn't so bad, sort of fun . . . pretty boring," she admitted wryly. "It's a good thing I wasn't a Method actress then. Imagine living that part, a dopy blonde? I've had my moments, but never that bad. Of course, Lady Macbeth wouldn't be so great to live, either." The misapprehension that Method actors lived their parts was so prevalent that my mother finally instructed me, "Just tell them if it were true that you lived your part, you'd have been dead the first time you played Juliet."

The family had rented a house on Fire Island for the summer. Friday afternoons we'd arrive on the ferry. We formed a little caravan, pulling red wagons, with bells attached, loaded with books and food. Johnny, me, Pop in his baseball cap, his shirt in the hottest heat buttoned to the top button, and Mom with her umbrella, large sun hat, and dark glasses, her skin too fair for the hot sun. I wore a hat and dark glasses just like my mother, but I'd absolutely refused to carry an umbrella. She'd hold hers over me as I pushed her away—"Mother, leave me alone, everyone will stare at me!"

"What do you care? You're an actress, this is for your part,

you have to stay pale. Anne didn't go outside for two years."
Grudgingly I gave in.

Marty Fried, one of my father's students, was along to help
out, and instead of sun he was soaking up all my father could
teach him about music and books and theater.

Marilyn was there, sharing my bedroom, drinking champagne, laughing, running barefoot with no makeup on, followed by the neighbors' kids, dogs barking, radios blasting,
"Sugar bush, I love you so . . ." There were a lot of theater
people on our part of the island. They were sophisticated,
which meant they stared at MM from a distance instead of
staring up close. But there was no one, old or young, who
wasn't fascinated to see her.

"Doesn't it bother you?"

"It would bother me more if they didn't know who I was.
As long as they don't attack. They don't mean to be, but they
can get scary, almost like they want to take home a piece of
you for a souvenir. But they're the people who made me a
star."

"You have to read Anne Frank," I urged her. "She says so
many things that were ahead of her time."

She looked so wistful. "What is it?" I prodded.

"I'd love to do a part that would mean something like yours,
that people would really get something from. You're so lucky.
No one will ever let me. Besides, my looks are against me. I'm
too much one type."

I looked at her, with no makeup on, hair straggling around
her face, nose sunburned and freckled. She didn't look sexy or
glamorous to me. I suggested, "You could do a part like this,
the way you are now, show people you can be different."

"People get used to you one way. I can feel their hostility
when I try to change. People get nervous when you change.
Anyway, they don't think I can do it. Change, I mean."

It crossed my mind that she was too vain to let people see

her like this, but she didn't seem bothered by it now. Maybe she was too scared to give up "Marilyn," her Hollywood creation.

"My father and mother talk about it a lot, all the really interesting parts you can do, like . . . like *Rain*, playing Sadie Thompson or *Anna Christie*."

She agreed with me enthusiastically. "Your father says the only good Sadie Thompson was Jeanne Eagels, and that Joan Crawford and Gloria Swanson were terrible, but he thinks I'd be good." She brightened. "There are some people who want me to fail. I can't wait to see their faces."

"Who?" I inquired.

"Oh, certain people, who shall be nameless. But the sons of bitches will know who they are." Then she totally changed the subject, which she did often, following her own inner train of thought. "It's hard when you grow up an orphan. It gets so you don't expect anything good, like a habit of expecting the worst. You're so lucky to have your family."

"Uh-huh," I agreed. She related everything back to her past. She carted that past around like Mother Courage did her cart.

Neither my father nor Marilyn went in the ocean. She said she couldn't swim that well. So she'd get wet, but not over her head. And in all the years we spent at the ocean, my dad never went in past his ankles. He loved walking by it, listening to it, but he didn't swim. Annie Bancroft, who lived next door, asked him, "Lee, why don't you ever go in past your ankles?"

"Because, darling," he admitted, "I don't want to get involved." I suspected he was scared of the water, so while he and Marilyn watched, I'd run into the high surf and swim so far out I'd panic that I'd drown. "Come on in," I'd cry out, waving, smiling. "It's great." I felt I'd proved some point.

Burning with excitement and my mind racing with anticipation, I was unable to fall asleep at night. Marilyn was restless, too, and we'd lie in our single beds in the dark talking about life and love and listen to the waves. " 'Out of the cradle endlessly rocking,' " I quoted.

"Poetry," she said. "I write poetry sometime."

"So do I. Walt Whitman was a Gemini, like me."

"Like us," she corrected me.

One night she was rambling on about her childhood. There'd been much champagne and dancing earlier. I could dance formally, ballet, but not free form like her. She was like a child. She followed her feet, she didn't look at them the way I did mine. So I wouldn't dance when she was around. That evening she'd been the center of attention. She'd filled the room with her full laughter, sensual movements, and high spirits. My father loved it; he had this smile of pleasure on his face. He got that smile around children and animals. Marilyn made him laugh, even surprised him. She'd beckoned to him seductively, shaking her hips, tempting him to dance with her.

My mother watched. My mother had been a modern dancer. She didn't dance anymore because her increasingly heavy body embarrassed her. Instead she pushed me: "Dance with Marilyn."

"Mom, I don't want to, I'm tired tonight."

"Johnny, you dance with . . ." He'd already slipped out the back door and was nowhere to be found.

Marilyn was telling me a story about one of her foster homes and how rough it had been. I was only half listening because I was dreaming about what my life would be like after Anne Frank. Besides, I'd already read those stories in the movie magazines. She'd tell them the way people repeat jokes. Only she didn't say, "Stop me if you've heard this one." All of a sudden she fell silent, and I thought she'd realized I wasn't listening, so I said, "Yes?" as if I wanted her to go on. But she was quiet for a while. We listened to the surf as the moonlight streamed onto the dark stained wooden floorboards.

Finally, in a small but clear voice, she said, "Maybe it wasn't all as bad as that; maybe I just took it too hard." I had no idea what she meant.

Here I was, immersing myself in the spirit of Anne Frank

and sharing a room with a woman who outwardly represented the antithesis of everything that Anne stood for. Anne was simple, unglamorous, self-aware, and concerned with the larger world. Marilyn was dazzling, glamour incarnate, sex personified, and self-centered. Yet people weren't all that different. Beneath Marilyn's facade of Hollywood razzle-dazzle was a lovely woman who cared. She was for the underdog. She had concerns for the world like Anne; she just couldn't articulate them. I felt almost disloyal to Anne's spirit, because though I admired and respected her, it was Marilyn who fascinated me. She was the person I wanted to be like. How could I be a sexy Anne Frank? Then I remembered that even in hiding, Anne's collection of movie star photos had hung on the wall. It had been one of her prized possessions. Surely she, of all people, would understand and forgive me for my vacillating sense of values. After all, even Pop was fascinated by Marilyn, and he was a genius. There had been a chorus line of beautiful, intelligent, talented women, famous and unknown, around him: Nancy Berg, Julie Newmar, Inger Stevens, Caroll Baker, Anne Bancroft . . . None had elicited anywhere near the response Marilyn did. I was determined to figure out why, if it killed me.

DOROTHY MONET—Friend of the family, writer, and artist

I had left the convent when I was seventeen years old to come to New York City. I met Harold [Clurman] and then started going out with Clifford Odets and met your parents. These men were always fascinated by any woman the other fell in love with. I became very watchful and observing of this crowd and what made them tick. At first your father was very interested in me—I think it was that Svengali thing—but when I didn't want to be an active part of the studio and the class, he wearied of me.

The way they treated each other. Harold, for instance, was very condescending. He and your father always treated Clifford like an idiot savant. Anyway, here they were trying to revolutionize the American theater, and yet they came from a very, very parochial group of Eastern European stock with a very strict morality connected to it. They did not allow themselves to be overt or wildly eccentric, as people would tend to be twenty and thirty years later. These men were sheepish, guiltful about the very things that were making them artists. Anyway, if you weren't Jewish like me, you already had it made because they all had this problem. I once asked Harold, who, of course, had been married before to Stella [Adler], but now only dated Christians: "Harold, why are you always going with these little Catholic girls?" And he said, "Well, because there's no such thing as a gentle Jewish woman," and I said, "Harold, what about the Virgin Mary?" There was this underlying, unconscious anti-Semitism, so Marilyn Monroe was the epitome of all their masturbatory dreams. This poor little adorable waif who was as un-Jewish as she could possibly be. There was an overriding ambition shot through all these people. They neglected interpersonal relationships. They were rushing headlong to be famous. For your father, it wasn't fame; he wanted to be acknowledged. For your mother, it was more complicated. She called me around the time Marilyn came into your household. She was really in trouble, and I went to see her. Paula was desperate. She was sitting swathed in black, propped up against the headboard in her bedroom, like a Buddha. She loved to have visitors in her bedroom, but this time she was very miserable and wretched. We talked and talked for a long long time, and when we stopped I realized that nothing would satisfy her. She was so pain-

fully dissatisfied, and I thought, Why? Her children are well, her husband's got a job, what does she need?

One morning I awoke early. The sun was just coming up and filling my room with golden-blue light. I could hear the gull cries just beyond the dunes that sloped from our house down onto the beach. Marilyn's bed was empty. I thought she wasn't in the room. Then I saw her standing in front of the window, nude, leaning with her head pressed to the window-pane, a melancholy figure. She had been so still, I thought she was part of the shadows. She was lost in some private reverie. Rather than speak and break her moment, I stared. In the morning light her body was lovely and her pale curves empha-sized. There was something lush about her. I'd never looked at another woman's body before. I wondered what men thought when they saw her, what they felt when they touched her. Her flesh looked resilient, like a child's, smooth and soft.

She turned quickly, before I had a chance to close my eyes. I felt myself blushing and blurted out, "Marilyn, I'd give any-thing to be like you." I thought of this blue-eyed, blond-haired, full-breasted pagan goddess dancing in the moonlight, drunk on life and Dom Pérignon.

"Oh, no, Susie." She was horrified, half whispering so as not to wake anyone, half-husky with emotion. "Don't say that. I'd give anything to be like *you*. People respect you."

Respect, that word that meant so much to my father, too. Even Anne Frank complained that no one respected her. Who cared about respect? I wanted freedom, success, love; she could have respect. You only got that when you were old.

My mother had astrological charts done for Marilyn, me, and Anne Frank. "If it was good enough for both Roosevelts and Galileo and Copernicus and Benjamin Franklin, it's good enough for me." She threw her hands up in the air. "I knew it!" she crowed. "You and Marilyn and Anne are all Geminis

with Leo rising and Pluto in Cancer in the twelfth house." I
had no idea what that meant, except that there was some
supernatural link among the three of us, some meaning that
only my mother and the stargazer could interpret.

My father bristled, lodging his silent protest by walking out
of the room. "He doesn't understand," my mother moaned. "It
scares him. Lee, it's synchronicity, like Carl Jung. . . ." But
he'd gone.

"Mother, maybe it's just a coincidence," I suggested gin-
gerly.

"Aha, it's way beyond the numerical probability. Anyway,
they say coincidence is God's way of remaining anonymous.
There are no accidents, it's all *bershert*." Her face glowed with
her convictions.

"What's *bershert*?" Marilyn asked. I didn't know, either.

"It means it's meant to be, it's God's will."

"Gee, Paula, I'd like to believe in that stuff, but it's a little
farfetched. That's my skeptical side talking. . . . There's no
proof."

"Just like Anne Frank says." I was obsessed with Anne.
"She's got two sides, and the bad side keeps coming to the
outside and the good side goes on the inside, and she's trying
to switch them around."

Mother gave me a look. "Susan, that has nothing to do—"

"Did she do it?" Marilyn interrupted.

"Well, she was working on it when she died."

"I'll probably be doing the same thing when I die," Marilyn
predicted. "You know, the whole Jekyll and Hyde thing?"

My father called out, "Who wants hot dogs and who wants
chicken?"

He would barbecue on the weekends in his boxer shorts and
baseball cap. Standing over the coals, he attacked the meat as
he did a scene; they had to be just so. His weekend tan ended
at his shirtsleeves and neck, the rest of him was white.

We entertained a continual stream of people, and our refrigerator was kept full to overflowing. "This is a Jewish icebox," a friend commented.

Marilyn personalized this, as she did most things. "It's like the Jews are the orphans of the world. Maybe that's why I feel so close to them."

Salads, corn on the cob dripping with butter, baked potatoes with sour cream and chives, cream cheese and lox with bagels and bialys for Sunday morning brunch, and my father's famous ice-cream sodas. Like everything he did, there was a discipline to his method. First the milk, then the soda, followed by the syrup, then stir. Next came the ice cream and the rest of the soda. It was like a scene, filled with hot apple pies, boxes of cookies, Zabar's salamis, Sacher tortes, and Danishes.

"I'm trying to lose weight," my brother screamed when my mother thrust these rich temptations under his nose.

"It's just baby fat, it'll go by itself. Unless you've taken after my side of the family. If I smell a piece of lettuce, I gain," she explained to Marilyn.

"I don't think you're fat, Johnny." Marilyn's compliment drove him from the house with a deep blush. It didn't take much in those days to drive him out.

My mother and Marilyn would sit in the bedroom and have long conversations about "Arthur"—"Arturo." Arthur Miller and Marilyn were involved in a heavy romance, but he was still married, so they spoke in veiled references and whispers. They loved the secrecy. So did I. I wanted to be a part of it.

As Marilyn became more and more comfortable with us, new facets of her quicksilver personality emerged.

One weekend, on Fire Island, she had decided she was going to cook for us. She was a simple cook. She liked carrots and peas, for the aesthetics of the colors on the plates. This night she was cooking chicken. Sipping champagne, Marilyn put on an apron and danced into the kitchen. There was a scream. We all ran in. "What—are you all right? Did you cut yourself?"

She pointed accusingly at the counter. Her body trembled. "It looks like a chicken."

"Darling . . ." My father walked over to it, looked, and affirmed, "It is a chicken."

"It looks like a bird, Lee." This in a wail.

"It is a bird. At least I hope so." Pop ignored her hysteria.

"Sit down, Marilyn." My mother ran to her. "Breathe, relax." She demonstrated a long "Aaah."

"Just a second, darling, let her talk. So it's a bird, and . . . ?" Pop waited.

"And I can't cook it if it looks like a chicken. The poor thing was alive and they killed it, it had a mother. I can only cook it if it's cut up in pieces so I won't recognize it. Is that crazy, Lee?"

"No, darling, it's just very sensitive."

Mother, who was erratically involved in the vegetarian diets of a man called Gaylord Hauser, Garbo's diet guru, said, "I can eat anything as long as it doesn't have eyes to look at me."

We all chopped the hell out of that chicken till it looked like nothing that had a mother.

Marilyn had an intense identification with animals. "I like them more than a lot of guys I've met," she commented. "It's sort of an insult to the animals to say that we're like them."

When she'd gone to the zoo to study the animals for an exercise in class, Marilyn had loved the seals, but she'd really identified with one particular lioness, June, who'd gotten familiar enough to let her reach over and pet her tail. At closing time Marilyn lingered. As the fading light of the day played hide-and-seek behind the skyscrapers, Marilyn would be the last person out the gates. She was so fond of June and empathized with her so much, she was reluctant to leave her. "She'll be all alone in the dark, she'll be so lonely." She couldn't separate her fears from June's; lions loved the dark, it was people who had problems.

After our chopped-up chicken dinner, as we fell asleep, she mused, "I don't know what's wrong with me. When I was a girl they had this aviary in one of my foster homes and I'd go in when no one was looking and put out watermelon rinds to feed the flies. There were all these flies that would have starved if I hadn't, and I'm not even that wild about flies. They say it makes you a gentler person if you don't eat meat. But wasn't Hitler a vegetarian? . . ."

"Good night, Marilyn, sweet dreams. God bless you."

Silence. The waves shook the earth beneath the house. "Do you believe in God?" I asked.

"I'd like to"—Marilyn was wistful—"but people sure give him a bad name, don't they? I guess I do believe, not in some guy in a beard, but in something."

"Anne Frank says it doesn't matter what you believe in, as long as you believe in something. Not a religion or dogma, but something."

Marilyn was quiet, then, "My problem is I believe in a lot of things some of the time, but not everything all of the time, and the rest of the time I believe in everything a little. . . . That's sort of like Lincoln, '. . . all of the people, some of the time . . .' What did I say?" Her voice had gotten drowsier and drowsier. She was asleep.

I'd dropped out of the High School of Music and Art, where I'd majored in art, but I still carried around my paints, brushes, and some pads in case I got inspired. One rainy summer day I spread newspapers on the floor and got out my paints. I was engrossed but noticed Marilyn watching me with a wistful expression. I asked her, "Do you want to try?"

Excited, she said, "I'm not very good but thanks." I handed her the brush and my small pad. She dipped the brush into the black paint. "You can use the colors," I offered.

"I like black and white." Sketching intently, she used the brush like a pen. Her tongue stuck out the corner of her mouth like a kid's. Quickly, without stopping, she did two paintings.

One was of a child, the other of a woman. The child was in a raggedy dress, one dark stocking falling down her leg. She had a black face or a mask over her face. One eye was clear. In the background, very hazy, was what appeared to be a house in some trees. The pathetic figure looked very sad, like a little orphan girl. "Lonely," she commented when she finished it.

The woman was full-bodied, feline, done in long strokes, not filled in. Her face was catlike, full dark lips and eyes, hair, a cat-woman, free, sexy, sensual, gay. "That one should say, Life is wonderful, so what the hell," she said, laughing. She looked at the little girl again. "Maybe it's a self-portrait? Like a Rorschach, whatever it's called. It's very Freudian, isn't it?"

By now everyone in the house was gathered around us, analyzing her sketches. "They're wonderful." Mom hugged her. "See how much perception you have when you're not thinking about it too much. Spontaneity . . . We'll get you some paints."

Pop gave his enigmatic "Yes, darling." While they praised her, I thought, I'm the one who trained to be a commercial artist. I slipped away, unnoticed.

Her sketches were revealing, but they weren't Picassos. Later I asked her if she wanted them. "Oh, no, Susie, they're yours, you keep them, you're the artist. Thanks for helping me." She made me feel guilty. Mother framed them for me and eventually I hung them in my room alongside Clifford Odets's "welcome home" flowers and my Rembrandt etching.

There was a song in *Annie Get Your Gun* that went, "Anything you can do, I can do better . . ." She liked painting; we both wrote poetry; we read a lot of the same books, both skipping the parts that bored us; we bought clothes at the same store. We were two Geminis with Leo rising, and both of us were alternately shy and outgoing. Her twelve foster homes clearly outweighed the ten schools I'd gone to as my family moved around. She'd been sexually abused when she was young, by an older man in one of her foster homes. No one had believed her then, and there were still skeptics because the details of the trauma changed each time she told it. It just seemed like emotional instead of artistic license to me. She kept trying to improve her life by making it more dramatic, more terrible, or more wonderful. She'd also recalled being smothered by a pillow as an infant. People said it was impossible for her to remember that far back but I'd seen actors in class doing affective memories, strong events from the past that were recreated by going through the sensations experienced and remembered by the body: what you saw, felt, heard, tasted, touched. Bypassing conscious recall, you went directly to the event. Some actors were able to recollect things that happened at birth, even in the womb, so I knew it was possible. Most people never talked about those things, except maybe to a priest or a psychiatrist. I thought Marilyn was really brave to tell the world things most people kept hidden in shame. Nobody talked about things like that.

Whatever I'd experienced so far in my life, she'd experienced more . . . more intensely.

And then there was her overwhelming and demanding curiosity . . . Where did I get my makeup? What kind was it? Where did I buy my clothes, where did I go for facials, what music did I listen to? I felt like those natives who don't want you to take their photographs because they think you're stealing their souls. It may have been paranoid, stupid, illogical, but I felt she could devour my life with those hungry questions.

"Susan, Susan . . ." Mother stroked my hair. "Imitation is the sincerest form of flattery."

"Let her imitate someone else, I'm not telling her anything else."

Then the guilt about my lack of generosity overwhelmed me, and I showered her with information she didn't even want. She'd give me that wide-eyed gaze. "Gee thanks, Susie." I was sure she could read my mind. Soon after that a photographer expressed surprise when I asked to see his pictures before they were printed. He thought I was awfully young to be so cautious. "Well," I'd explained, "Marilyn does it."

Back in the city, Sunday brunches had become a ritual. We didn't have to invite people, they just came.

On one crisp autumn afternoon, when the leaves were beginning to fall outside Pop's study window and Central Park was a moving carpet of red and gold, Marilyn and I wound up alone in my parents' back bedroom. Like the other rooms, it was covered with books. We were conversing about nothing of importance. Marilyn was idly looking through the titles of my mother's small collection of reading material: books on the tarot, astrology, diet, psychology, science fiction, and science, plus a Catholic selection with many metaphysical titles. Every now and then Marilyn would say, "Hey, I read that, too," as delighted as if she were going through my mother's drawers and discovering secrets.

"Oh, my God," she gasped, plucking one book from the shelves.

"What, what is it?" I jumped off the bed I'd been lounging on and rushed to see. She held it up.

"*Look.*"

I looked. "So? . . ."

"It's the *Kama Sutra*," she said, reading the gold letters on the worn cover. I must have looked blank because she explained, "This is the classic dirty book, only it's not dirty because it's Oriental and they're very classy about this kind of thing, not puritanical like Americans are." I still looked blank. "It's got hundreds of drawings of all the positions of how to do it, you know f— uh, make love." I was now hanging over her shoulder, trying to see for myself.

"Oh, my God," I echoed her earlier exclamation. "How could anybody do these? You'd have to be an acrobat . . . well, not all of them."

"If any of the guys I'd been with had done this, they'd have had a heart attack. How come I got the ones with no imagination?"

"I could do that one." I pointed to a drawing, rather graceful, tiny, but exquisitely detailed in its depiction of the human anatomy. "I'm pretty flexible," I bragged.

"Have you ever been . . . you know, with a man?" She was very tactful.

"You mean, like—" I gestured with my hands, bringing them together.

She nodded her head up and down for yes, and I nodded my head side to side for no.

"We gotta try this." She giggled. "If you find some guy who does these, let me know."

"What if someone comes in? There's no lock." I was chickening out.

"I got it. We're rehearsing, improvising."

"Who's going to be the man?" I asked. She looked at me. I looked at her. "You're taller," I blurted, "and older."

She acquiesced gracefully. "Okay. Boy, is this a switch."

We got down on the floor, and after battling with our full skirts—thank God they weren't tight ones—we began to go through the book by the numbers, so to speak. "The highest number I ever got to was sixty-nine," she said.

"Where's that?" I looked in the book.

"Never mind," she said.

We twisted and turned, a leg here, an arm there. "This could put someone in traction," she gasped at one particularly difficult position, laughing and giggling. I was alternately horrified and thrilled. We flipped through the book.

When we heard footsteps coming down the hallway, Marilyn leaped up and tucked the book under her arm nonchalantly. "Education interruptus," she said. "You have to swear not to tell. I don't want your parents to think I'm corrupting you."

"Cross my heart and hope to die, stick a needle in my eye, Girl Scout's honor. Actually I was only a Brownie."

"It's enough, I believe you," she said.

The door opened. "What are you two ladies doing back here? The party's up front."

I was thrilled with my new knowledge. I'd been too inhibited to tell Marilyn, but I had never even masturbated, except to lie in the tub in a dark bathroom, covered by bubbles, and touch myself under the water cautiously. When I had gotten wet with excitement lying with the boy on Fire Island, I'd thought something was wrong with me. Now I was relieved. Marilyn had acted as if sex were natural, nothing to be ashamed of, as if it were actually fun.

I couldn't help thinking that between what my dad was teaching her and what we'd read, I liked what she was teaching me better. We'd certainly cemented our friendship.

A brave fellow student visiting once for Sunday brunch brought something for Marilyn to see. He unwrapped it. She looked at what lay in her palm and then looked closer, bringing it up to her eye. Upset, she said, "Susie, look at this, look what they've done." I looked. It was a ring with the nude calendar photo she'd posed for when she was a struggling young actress. Embarrassed, I handed it back. The student was all shaky. I gave him a dirty look for upsetting her. "See," she cried.

"No, what?" I squinted again.

"My eye, they've smeared my eye."

"That's awful," I murmured, trying to muster some indignant feelings. She burst out laughing, and in relief so did we.

"I don't think there's any room to sign it." She giggled and gave him an autograph on a piece of loose paper.

I was impressed that she was so natural about something as shocking to me as a nude, naked, unclothed calendar. I could hardly look at myself naked in the mirror when I was alone.

Maybe being physical wasn't as disreputable as I'd thought. When Marilyn and I went shopping together, I was no longer as embarrassed as I had been that she wore no underwear and stripped naked before the saleswoman.

We were meeting my parents for dinner at friends. I wound up in charge of accompanying Marilyn. She was running late as usual, and I knew the way, so they went on ahead. She was totally made up and ready to go. "Just let me take another look, the light's not so great."

"You look beautiful," I reassured her, trying to rush her.

"Just a sec," she called.

After ten minutes I went into the bedroom. All the makeup was off and she was redoing it. I watched, fascinated, as she shaded her face with pancake, did her Garbo eyes, white over the lid, shadow in the crease, false lashes. I couldn't wait for a part where I would wear all that. When she finished she turned to me. "How's that now?"

"Gorgeous," I said truthfully, although she had put on a much heavier makeup this time.

She stared into the reflection in the glass. "It's too much," she stated. I nodded. She cleaned her face and redid the whole thing. This time she used as much makeup, only it looked as if she didn't have any makeup on at all. "I'll show you how," she offered sweetly when I admired it.

"Not now," I urged.

"This is better, isn't it?"

I would have agreed if she'd looked like a clown, but it was better and we were three hours late. I think she'd hurried because of me.

Anne Frank and her family had hidden successfully in an attic for two years with friends until they were betrayed and arrested by the Nazis. Anne died two months before the end of the war in a concentration camp. As an actress how could I capture her suffering? "You can't act the war; you have to act her life, not her death," my mother said. "You have to act the personal things happening to her. Imagine what it would be like to not be able to talk and move." That was difficult. Talking was my most constant activity. Mother made me go for days in silence to get the feeling. My father spoke to me in inspiring terms about the play. He asked me questions, but it was Mother who really did the day-to-day work with me. I wanted him to do with me whatever he was doing with Marilyn. "You don't need it," Mother said, but I heard her complaining to him. "You have to spend more time with her. She's your daughter, she needs you." I never heard his answer. Either he was speaking softly, or he hadn't bothered to answer.

It was humiliating that he had to be begged. No matter what, I would never sink to that.

My attention turned to my stage family as we began rehearsals in a dark, dingy rehearsal studio in downtown New York. I began to feel more alive than ever before in my life, although alive wasn't exactly it—I felt more myself. . . .

The Little Bastard, he'd named it. *The Little Bastard* was destroyed in a head-on collision, and Jimmy Dean was dead at twenty-six. He had gotten the new Porsche the day before and was on his way up the highway going to a race. That same day, outside Googie's, where it was parked, the distinguished English actor Alec Guinness had seen Jimmy with his new baby. Although a total stranger, Alec had felt compelled to go over and beg Jimmy not to drive the car for a while. In reply, Jimmy had laughed.

My father never took death well. It was one of the few things he got personal about, no matter how hard he tried to remain objective. At a session of the Actors Studio, his voice crackling with emotional static, Lee told us Jimmy had been killed. Someone had called him from California within minutes of the accident. He didn't cry, but Mom did, and I did.

Months later my father spoke about Jimmy's death. It wasn't

planned; he simply lost control. He was talking about the new place the studio had moved to, a former church, and the fact that they had a permanent place now and he wanted people to take more responsibility. Then he burst out, "I will say it, the hell with it. I saw Jimmy Dean in *Giant* the other night. . . ." He began to weep. I didn't know what to do, Pop weeping. He went on, voice choked with the vehemence of his feelings. "What I cried at was the waste, the waste, the talent and the work that goes into getting it where it should be . . . and then what the hell happens . . . the senseless waste, the senseless destruction, the waste of your lives, that strange behavior Jimmy had, a lot of you here have. I cried because of our helplessness. . . . I haven't the slightest idea what the hell to do about it. It isn't temperament. As soon as you reach a certain place, there it goes, the drunkenness and the rest of it, as though now that you've made it, the incentive goes and something happens that to me is terrifying. You can tell some-body, Go to a psychiatrist, go there, get help. Such a waste . . . You fight in the beginning, but once you get where you want to be . . . you've worked to have enough money and security so you can sometime or other do what you really want to do. The sometime never comes. Instead something else comes along and takes it out of you, takes it out in chunks of heart and soul and talent and mind and incentive and initiative. . . ."

As he spoke, I looked around the room surreptitiously. Some people were weeping, some were nodding agreement, others seemed lost in their own thoughts. Marilyn looked as if she were a million miles away, that strange, "nobody's home" look she'd get in her eyes. For a welcome change, I didn't identify with what he was saying. I didn't drink, I was disciplined, with a little help from my mother, and I was never going to work for the money. I could never be wild like Jimmy or late or drugged like Marilyn, and listening to him, I was sure that he'd realize soon that I embodied those qualities he stood for and held up as admirable. He'd recognize me and realize that he'd made a mistake thinking they, the others, all the adopted children, would do anything but disappoint him. I would make him proud. I'd be all the things he wanted them to be.

As my opening night approached I walked around reassuring myself and everyone else, "After all, they can't shoot me . . . can they?" On the day, Mother cleared my dressing room of flowers, gifts, and unopened telegrams. "Nothing matters but what happens onstage," she reminded me.

Marilyn was early to the opening night of *The Diary of Anne Frank*—unheard of; she was never early. "Darling," my father said to her when she complained that she could never be on time. "Darling, you don't have to be on time. Be early." Her escorts that night were Delos Smith, Jr., our newfound friend from Hutchison, Kansas, who'd come east to study with Pop, and Marty Fried, a young acting student, ex-boxer, and orphan, who drove his own cab to make a living while he was training. He knew Marilyn from class and Fire Island.

DELOS SMITH, JR.

Your mama put me in charge of getting her there, not on time, early. Mama knew she'd distract the audience if she made an entrance. "I'll kill her if she's late," she said. "Delos, it's up to you." Marty and I went to get her. She didn't take one of those four-hour baths that night. She was ready and dressed simply, no sequins to flash when she shook her behind. We were so early they were just taking the dustcovers off the seats. We were seated up in the balcony. Your mother wasn't taking any chances, this was your night. We sat up there and didn't even go down for the intermission. Marilyn cried her eyes out at the play. She didn't say that much about you, she was jealous of you, she wanted your family, your parts. When everyone praised you, she got very quiet. But she muted her light that night. When she wanted to, she could get attention from anyone. She'd just do that walk and they'd become like pigs in heat and she'd shine. I thought she must use fluorescent makeup, the way she'd shine.

Afterward in the dressing room I cried and then burst into great gales of laughter. Marilyn was very quiet, taking pictures with me for the *Life* photographer but staying in the background as much as she ever could, and afterward as she entered Sardi's I heard her exclaim to columnist Earl Wilson, "Wasn't Susie wonderful?" Waiting for the reviews, I got to sit next to my father, with Josh Logan on my other side. Marilyn wasn't even at our table. She was with other close friends of the family at the back table, and she wasn't in sequins. We were both dressed in black dresses. Mine was a high-necked, short-sleeved black velvet dress; hers was a scooped-neck, black sheath. If I had thought about it, I would have been grateful to her for keeping such a low profile; but there was no time. I was basking in the warm glow of the approaching spotlight of stardom. I felt loved. I felt I belonged. More important, I knew Pop was pleased with me, finally.

EXCERPT FROM "FATHER OF THE STAR,"
by theater writer Lewis Funke,
Pageant magazine

One day shortly after seventeen-year-old Susan Strasberg had made her sensational Broadway stage debut as the inspiring heroine in The Diary of Anne Frank, *a neighborhood tradesman greeted her father with the remark, "Congratulations, Mr. Strasberg. I see that now you are made." Lee Strasberg smiles as he recalls the incident and notes* with some amusement, "Once it was that Susan was my daughter. Now I am her father."

The tradesman's ignorance of Strasberg's own lofty position in the theatre, however, is nothing new. Strasberg simply is not known beyond the confines of show business. Yet, the incontrovertible fact is that he happens to be just about the top teacher of actors and directors in this country. According to those who know, Strasberg has had a more profound influence on actors and directors, in motion pictures and the legitimate theatre, than any other man.

Marilyn Monroe, in her quest for serious acting honors, was sent to him and Elia Kazan, director of ... On the Waterfront and ... Death of a Salesman, publicly bows in his direction. Kazan says, "I went to him green out of the Yale Drama School in 1932. He taught me the nature of acting and many insights into its processes. He stimulated me and opened vistas of what the theatre had been and was in other countries and above all what it might be. If it had not been for his influence, I would have been a different director."

Strasberg is a squarish little man with graying hair, penetrating eyes, and the demeanor more of a Fourth Avenue bookseller than a high priest of Thespis. He speaks in a low-pitched voice, chooses his words with a semanticist's care, and, unless he is especially stimulated prefers a shrug to extended conversation. Teaching is his way of life, and like all great teachers, he is dedicated to his subject and his students. He has absolutely no temperament for publicity and little use for the tinsel, blandishments, and chichi sophistication of Broadway. He would rather go sleepless in an effort to solve a student's personal problem or console a veteran actor in distress than spend 15 minutes with a gossip columnist who could spread his fame.

Nevertheless ... he has steadfastly insisted on maintaining a normal family relationship with his wife, Paula, *who once was an actress herself; his daughter, Susan; and his fifteen-year-old son, Johnny. Nothing gives him greater pleasure than to pass either an evening at home with them listening to recordings of musical masterpieces, or an afternoon at the Polo Grounds rooting for the Giants. . . . "Children," he says, "must feel that they are important in the family unit. They must have a sense of continuity, identity, and normalcy."*

Brooks Atkinson, the . . . drama critic for The New York Times, *reviewing her performance as Anne Frank, wrote: "Miss Strasberg has a heritage that any young player might envy. But that does not account for the incandescence that shines through her acting, nor for the grace and selflessness of her characterization." Strasberg himself, more in a vein of incredulity than immodesty, says, "In my wildest dreams I would not have dared dream that she would have such talent. Although she had no formal training, she nevertheless seems to have a natural instinct for the theatre and an inborn sensitivity for the characters she plays. I'll never forget that opening night. When she came out on the stage I was amazed. I couldn't help feeling that she was like a young tree, planted there, belonging there, full of life, buoyancy, and utter radiance. And when she did the sleep scene in the second act I was overjoyed. The rhythm of her performance was like a piece of music—it's something you don't teach an actor. He has it or he hasn't."*

However, Strasberg recalls her Broadway debut with mixed reactions. As an actor and director he had been through his own opening nights and had, of course, shared Mrs. Strasberg's jitters when she faced premieres. But this was different. Mrs. Strasberg says, "I can't remember ever seeing Lee the way he was that night. You could feel his excitement in the house, in the air. For all of us even our breathing seemed different. Susan kept wondering whether she could repeat what she had been doing during the pre-

Broadway run and whether she would be able to remember her lines. Lee, meanwhile, trying desperately not to show his own nerves, kept reassuring her that all she needed was faith in herself. He told her stories of how all the great stars of the theatre have opening night tensions, and he explained to her that without them she could not really be a first-rate sensitive actress. The important thing . . . was how she harnessed those tensions and used them to her advantage."

After the theatre . . . at Sardi's . . . when Mr. and Mrs. Strasberg walked in with Susan [Johnny had stayed home to study], she was given a standing ovation. . . . The morning paper reviews arrived . . . Susan was the bright new star in the theatrical firmament. Someone rushed up to Strasberg, clapped him on the back, and said, "Isn't it wonderful? You must be so excited."

"No," Strasberg remembers he replied, "not excited. Relieved."

He says now, "I just couldn't share in the general excitement that night. . . . I knew what had happened to Susan . . . life for her suddenly had changed; suddenly, at seventeen, she was being pushed into all the responsibilities a star has to her public, to her colleagues, to the playwright, to her art. I couldn't help wishing that she wouldn't have to give up so many of the everyday pleasures to which a girl her age is entitled."

"Once or twice, if you're lucky in your career, God touches you," Pepi Schildkraut had told me when we began rehearsals for Anne Frank. And God had touched us. The applause, the attention, the reviews, the worldwide recognition, were all exhilarating and new to me. The stillness was even better— the performances in which we'd come out to take a curtain call and no one moved, no one coughed, no one applauded. Silence. The audience merged with the actors to become one ensemble family unit caught in the radiant glow of the spirit of this one little fourteen-year-old Dutch-German Jewish schoolgirl across time and space. Her presence was so real to me that I'd talk to her before I went onstage, asking for her help.

Every night I got to dance onstage with my make-believe father as he held me in his arms. I accused my stage mother of smothering me. Every night I cried out, "Everything I do is wrong and everything she does is right." "She" was my older sister in the play. But as in *Picnic* I couldn't help thinking about Marilyn when I said those lines. Every night I fell in love with Peter, my make-believe love. The freedom I experienced onstage, the fullness of expression I was permitted as Anne, began to make my offstage life seem lopsided. My inability in life to express myself, to be outspoken, honest, like Anne, although it got her in hot water sometimes, was bothering me. I knew art was supposed to imitate life, but I longed for my life to imitate art. I wanted to dance with my father, to tell him I loved him, as I did with my stage father.

That winter, to publicize *Picnic*, Kim Novak and I were asked to do a scene on "The Ed Sullivan Show." As she'd never done live theater before, Kim was understandably nervous. In the scene, I had much more dialogue than she; that was in the characters in the play. The day of the appearance she threw a fit, breaking a mirror in her dressing room. Afterward she sat tearing a rose apart, sobbing, "I'm tearing this flower apart like I'm destroying my life." It amazed me that she could cry so much in life and not a tear on screen. She got her way. Josh and the producers took her to dinner to calm her down, and when they came back my part was cut in half. She was so beautiful, why did she want my lines? Why did these beautiful girls want anything I had?

"Unprofessional." My mother delivered her verdict. "Amateurish. It's bad enough what they say about Method actors. Don't react; you have to be better than she is, Susan. Set an example."

"Yes, Mother," I said obediently, thinking, Let Marilyn set the example. Why me?

For Christmas Marilyn got her divorce from Joe DiMaggio and a big new 20th Century-Fox contract. She had beaten the studio against all the odds, the first contract actress to achieve that kind of victory. The girl they'd treated like a piece of property had freed herself. Her courtship with her idol, Arthur Miller, was out in the open, though he was separated but still very much married. "He's so gorgeous; I love to cuddle with him. He's the most beautiful man I've ever seen, isn't he?" What could I say? "And he's so brilliant. He and your father are the two most brilliant men in the world." She hugged me. I was ashamed to think, Well, there's Einstein and Jung and a few others, too, so I didn't say anything. Like my mother, she was unstoppable in her enthusiasm.

I'd started the year hiding behind my parents at an Actors Studio benefit. I ended the year at another studio benefit, this one for *The Rose Tattoo*. I wasn't hiding anymore in my first low-cut, formal evening dress. I decided I was going to get up and dance if it killed me. I'd watched Marilyn enough, so I knew exactly what to do. I began to chugalug champagne, and by the third glass, when a student of my father's asked me to dance, I practically grabbed him. He was a great Latin dancer and I relaxed in his arms—I had to, my head was spinning— and let him lead me in this wild tango right in front of the table where my parents were seated. The photographers went crazy, and everyone stopped to watch us. But as I whirled around in a dizzying spin, I searched for my father's face. I wanted to see that look of pleasure he'd had when Marilyn danced. I saw him. He wasn't smiling. He wasn't even watching me. I danced faster and faster, until my feet were so swollen

I couldn't dance anymore. Moira Shearer, I thought as I fell asleep. I'd felt like Moira Shearer in *The Red Shoes*, dancing till I died. . . .

The producers of *Anne Frank* wanted to make me the youngest star on Broadway in the new year. My parents felt it was "too much, too soon" and might put terrible pressure on me, that it would be much better to wait till the next show. I went crazy. "He doesn't think I'm good enough . . ." I wailed to Mother.

"It's not that, Susie. Daddy's just thinking of your future."

"I could be dead tomorrow, this is my future," I heard myself cry like a spoiled child.

EXCERPT FROM "FATHER OF THE STAR," *Pageant* magazine

Right now, Strasberg is most concerned with helping Susan maintain a sense of balance and perspective in the face of sudden fame. He says, "Those who rise by a continuous and logical development to the point of stardom usually have learned in the process how to solve the problems of stardom. But those who are not so well prepared can go crazy. It's like candy . . . the whole box can make you sick."

After the opening of The Diary of Anne Frank, *he hesitated at first to permit official recognition of Susan's stardom and the placing of her name in lights on the theatre's marquee alongside that of the veteran Joseph Schildkraut. When he finally did consent, it was with the stipulation that Susan continue to take curtain calls with the company instead of alone. "That's the way you started in the show,"* *he explained to Susan, "and that's the way you ought to go on—a regular member of the cast."*

Fortunately, he thinks Susan is psychologically prepared to meet the situation.

I met Richard Adler at a party. He was older by almost twenty years, sophisticated, smart, attractive, nice, and the cowriter of two successful musicals. We began dating. He cooked me eggs after the show, tucking me into bed. The only other man who'd cooked for me was my father; of course, he cooked for everyone. Someone asked him, "Lee, why are you in the kitchen cooking so much?"

"Because this way I don't have to talk. If I make small talk, sooner or later the other person asks, 'So, what do you think, Lee?' It comes down to me pontificating, so I cook."

When I remembered the sweetness I'd felt lying under the star-studded nights on Fire Island with my first boyfriend, the surf pounding a rhythmic beat while waves of pleasure had streamed through my body, I'd get this melting sensation in my stomach and thighs as if I were disintegrating. I was almost eighteen, almost a star, and still a virgin, but I had high hopes for the new year.

So did Marilyn. She was busy making plans to launch her new company, working in class, seeing new friends, getting ready to embark on her new life. She had two men standing by ready to transform her: Arthur, as a woman; my father, as an actress.

_4_

THE DIARY OF ANNE FRANK WON the 1956 Pulitzer Prize and the Tony Award. My name went up in lights on Broadway. Grace Kelly married Prince Rainier, an event predicted a few years before by her psychic, who had told her she'd become a star and a princess. She'd believed the part about stardom but said, "Don't be absurd. How could I be a princess?" Eisenhower was reelected with Nixon as vice president. Martin Luther King, Jr., became the leader of the desegregation movement growing across the nation. Castro landed in Cuba. A young singer called Elvis Presley was shaking his hips, waking a nation, and begging, "Don't be cruel . . ." and "Please don't step on my blue suede shoes . . ." Maria Callas made her New York debut, the _Andrea Doria_ sank off Nantucket, and New York won the World Series over Brooklyn. Two women—"Baby Doll" and "My Fair Lady"—dominated public consciousness. Rocky Marciano retired undefeated while Doris Day sang "Que Será Será."

DREAM—Hollywood, 1991

A woman, enormous, gigantic, like Gulliver in Gulliver's Travels, appears like a goddess, not human. It is Marilyn, lying on the ground, bound with ropes tied to stakes in the earth. She is a prisoner. Suddenly she awakens, looks around, and decides to break the bonds that hold her. She begins to struggle to get up. There are all these babies and little children covering, clinging to, her body. As she moves, they begin to fall off. She doesn't mean to, but she is crushing, stepping on, them. They are being killed or maimed. I am helpless, unable to warn the children or the woman. One part of me is wondering who the children are—Marilyn's childish side or her unborn children, the ones she's aborted or miscarried. Unless, could they be Johnny and me?

Picnic came out, and Bosley Crowther of *The New York Times* called me a genius. I was afraid he'd confused me with my father. People called me Anne Strasberg; they'd confused me with Anne Frank. I spoke at the United Nations with Mrs. Roosevelt. I started to receive awards. I was eighteen; I felt I didn't deserve all this yet. I was beginning to feel this pressure and responsibility to live up to everyone's expectations. If they'd tell me what and who they wanted me to be, I was willing. I was an actress, I could be all things to all people.

Marilyn said, "I can be anything they want. If they expect me to be innocent, I'm innocent. There's lots of cards in my deck, so to speak. I give them the one they want. Of course, you've gotta watch out not to get confused."

If she could do it, I could.

I tried it. Witty for a press interview, intellectual for a family friend, sensitive for others, sexy for suitors, romantic for photos. I must have gone overboard. In my longing to be accepted, I began to pose a little, affecting a more ladylike voice, wearing a lot of lace. My father commented, "What are you doing, darling? You are lyrical; for God's sake, don't act lyrical."

He didn't understand. I was doing the "As You Desire Me" dance, steps choreographed by Marilyn.

Marilyn, Anne Frank, and I shared this burning desire to be taken seriously, to let people know we weren't dummies. I watched how Marilyn did it. When she wasn't an expert on a subject but wanted to be, she got hold of someone who was and picked their brains. After she'd gone through enough information, she was pretty knowledgeable about whatever it was: painting, music. She might miss the details, but she got the gist. Whatever it was, she might not be able to dive in, but she could wade like crazy, in politics, religion, literature. She collected experts—one on the stock market, one on poetry, one on the world situation. They were all men at the top of their respective professions. She drank the best champagne, she thought with the best.

Her class attendance was consistent whenever she was in town. Her romance with Arthur Miller flourished. Her New York friends, the Norman Rostens, the Greenes, her various floating friends, actors, writers, gofers, all approved.

She compartmentalized her friends. Somehow we never seemed to all get together—except for the Greenes. Amy was a friend of mine too, now. We heard about her other friends because she mentioned them, often to complain about them: they were "neglecting" her, "using" her, "didn't understand" her as well as my family did. I wondered if she complained about us to them.

She talked a lot about Arthur's family: his children, how

the children must never be hurt as she had been (she also had this concern for DiMaggio's son), his parents. She was crazy about his father, not so crazy about his mother. "That's natural," my mother commented. "She has a mother who's"—her voice lowered to a whisper—"schizophrenic."

It irritated me when Mother got so melodramatic. "Mother, why are you whispering? There's only us."

She was unstoppable. "You never know who's listening, and Arthur isn't divorced yet, and think what could happen." She never did say what, and I didn't ask because I believed her, even when I thought she might be making it up. My mother's prescient ability to pull something out of the air that then happened scared me a little. "Olivier is calling me this afternoon," she announced. "It's important I talk to him." I wondered if she was making it up to impress. I knew she barely knew Olivier; why would he call her? He did. When he was announced, she panicked. "Don't tell him I'm here, I don't know what to say to him. I'll call him back." It drove me wild.

My mother was like an actor. She told lies that became the truth, like the boy who cried wolf. Other times she was modest and humble about her accomplishments. Which person was the real one?

She finagled, wheeled and dealed, for a lot of people, not just Pop—actors she'd adopted, friends, and friends of friends. She'd change their names to fit on a marquee, buy them new shoes or a dress, feed them, care for them if they were sick. When Marty Fried had hepatitis, she insisted he move in so he wouldn't be alone. A matchmaker of people—not for marriages, for art. She had many friends outside the family circle: George Cukor, Alfred Hitchcock, and George Weidenfeld, the English book publisher. She'd threaten, "I'm going to go off and do something alone . . . produce a play . . . write my book. Someday you'll see."

I wondered if she'd never followed through with her own

ambitions because of the influence of her generation, her upbringing. She'd been brought up to do things for the men in
her life, yet she longed to do something for herself, and didn't.
It was one more confusing paradox. There were so many. I
was beginning to worry that if I couldn't accept the paradoxes,
I'd have to get off the earth.

I planned to attend my dad's private acting classes as soon
as all the excitement, publicity, recognition, and attention died
down. Secretly I hoped it never would. I'd finished high school,
almost. Actually I'd dropped out in my last year. Having no
time to study, I was afraid that if I took the finals and flunked,
it would be too humiliating. Anyway, I figured I already knew
things they'd never taught in the twelfth grade. I attended
the Actors Studio, as did Marilyn, on Tuesday and Friday
mornings, along with half the actors on Broadway.

When Mother pushed me to start class, I looked for excuses
not to. My father normally didn't take anyone in his classes
under eighteen because, he said, "it's like trying to tune a violin
that doesn't have all its strings."

"He didn't mean you, Susan, you're his child." Mother was
adamant. "He wants you to come." But I didn't want to go, I
didn't know what to expect there. I had the feeling that in class
my father's critiques might not be as effusive as the critics', and
I knew I wouldn't be teacher's pet.

Besides, there were parties, photo sessions, interviews,
lunches, and charity appearances, and six days a week I went
to the theater by five-thirty to get ready for the eight-thirty
show, twelve o'clock on matinee days. My mother insisted on
this discipline. "Aside from this," she said, "you can do whatever you want." When? There no longer seemed to be time.

I turned down Greta Garbo. She had seen Anne Frank two
or three times and invited me to her home. Unfortunately it

was between shows on a Saturday. "You have to rest between shows," Mother reminded me. "Don't worry, she'll ask you another time." Discipline came first. I respectfully declined, and she never did ask again. It occurred to me I could wind up refusing my whole life. I was young, healthy, I didn't need to rest, I needed to kick up my heels with my friends the way I once had.

Milton Greene, Marilyn's partner, signed Laurence Olivier to direct the movie of *The Prince and the Showgirl*, a light play by Terence Rattigan. In London it had starred Vivien Leigh, who was married to Sir Laurence. The original offer had been for him as costar, and he had insisted that he also direct. Marilyn agreed and gave away many of her hard-earned rights so that, for all intents and purposes, Olivier was producing *her* project. My father told us that "Olivier works so differently from the way she does. I doubt that he'll be sensitive to her problems. She has the talent, but she still doesn't really know how to act. If he puts pressure on her . . ." What he meant was that he didn't think it was such a good idea, but he didn't want to take the responsibility.

Mother planned ahead, a battle plan for the filming in England, when she would be by Marilyn's side as her coach. She reassured Pop, "Larry will adore her, Lee. They're both Geminis, and if he can deal with Vivien and all her problems, he certainly should be able to handle Marilyn. Besides, you'll join us in England when shooting begins and talk to him so he understands her. Why wouldn't he listen to you? He'd have to be an egomaniac." My father's response was his "We'll see, but I'm right" shrug.

First Joshua Logan was going to direct Marilyn in *Bus Stop*, William Inge's play about a singer from the West who meets up with a naive cowboy who falls madly in love with her. Although Marilyn was a blond showgirl again, this part had more dimension and character than the adorable but semi-mindless blondes she'd played while under contract.

She was nervous and excited about returning to work. "It's a business out there. Here maybe I can be an artist, but out there it's all money. Every time you go in front of the camera, you've got to deliver." Marilyn almost shuddered. She really seemed afraid.

But she was prepared. She'd taken her time, planned her moves years before she actually did anything. Michael Chekhov, her first teacher in Hollywood, also a student of Stanislavski who had broken away and developed his own system, had told her, "You can do anything. Don't let them trap you into what they want." He'd also told her she could be a great actress. She had gotten trapped in the image that had catapulted her into stardom. Making this transition now to becoming an "actress" was her raison d'être. She was as single-minded as a Zen archer aiming at her career goals.

Mom pushed me to be more ambitious. "Look at Marilyn; even when you're a star you have to work." This was not the way to handle me. It made me want to do nothing. Hadn't my mother heard of child psychology?

Finally Marilyn did her first exercise in class, a "song and dance." My dad had developed it to deal with inhibitions and expression that was often tied up when the actor got in front of an audience. Most actors just sang "Happy Birthday" because they were afraid they'd forget the words. Marilyn picked a harder song. She stood up there alone and began to "sing," "I'll get by as long as I've got you . . ." Well, the tears began to pour down her face. She kept her concentration, not wiping them away. She was sobbing and singing, and when she finished everyone in the room wanted to run up onstage and hold her. She beamed a luscious smile through her tears. There were still some skeptics—"Well, that's not acting"—but she had won over some of her toughest critics. These kids were snobs. They looked down on movie actors. *They* were in the *theater*.

Next she did her first scene in the private class. She'd been watching for over a year. It was from Odets's *Golden Boy*.

Nervous, obsessed with her debut, she queried, "Do you get scared before you go onstage, Susie?"

"Kind of. I wasn't in the beginning, but ever since I got such good reviews, I throw up before I run onstage," I admitted.

"Gee, I'm not that bad yet. But if I could have a little shot before I go on, that'll help me, I think."

Shot? "My mother would kill me if I had a drink."

"I didn't say I was going to do it, just that it might help," she explained. "I don't ever drink when I work. I just hope I don't break out." Sometimes when she was nervous, she'd erupt in hives. Other times she'd relapse into a childhood stutter.

Marilyn's great fear was that under pressure, in front of people, she might freeze as she'd done on movie sets. Some people thought she was dumb when she was just plain terrified.

She was scared. Even my father was nervous, though with his phlegmatic manner it was hard to tell. Attendance was on and off in the classes. That day the room was full, SRO. Everyone had brought along their "show me" attitude. They were going to see if Pop had sold out his ideals for fame and notoriety with the greatest sex symbol in the world.

She was playing Lorna Moon, a woman who wants desperately to change from her old life of conniving and hustling because she has fallen in love. Marilyn started slowly. The scene opened on a stifling hot day, and she created the heat of the day so well, she actually began to sweat. When you try to sweat and you're nervous, you can't. Emotions and sensations are funny. Like a small child, if you try to force them, they run away. But when you coax them, intrigue them, ignore them, and concentrate on something else, they won't leave you alone. They jump in your lap.

The initial jealousy and resentment of the other students melted as the scene began. She moved around, doing bits of business. This was a Marilyn no one had ever seen on the screen. This was the girl who roomed with me on Fire Island.

Her movements were natural, graceful, not the exaggerated sexy walk she was famous for. She was a real person. When she spoke, there was nothing to dispel the humanity and simplicity of that impression. She gazed at an imaginary road before her. "Look at all those cars. . . ." She was gutsy, vulnerable, charming, sad, in love, desperate, soft, with an edge . . . no whispering or breathiness, just *herself*.

An actor, overhearing my father praise Spencer Tracy as a natural Method actor, said condescendingly to Pop, "I just saw him in a movie. He was good, but he was just being himself."

"Who else should he be?" my father snapped. When the actor went on, "But he didn't study—" Pop interrupted, "Darling, a wonderful actor with no training is better than a bad actor with all the training in the world."

My parents believed that the most difficult thing to be was yourself. Most people are trained from childhood to hide behind a thousand masks, lying, pretending, ignoring. An actor has to be capable of the full range of human expression— emotionally free and spontaneous, yet self-aware, revealing the wonderful and terrible things that make us truly human and unique. It was another paradox: the more personal you were, the more universal you became.

"Being private in public is what the actor does," my father used to reiterate. "The career grows in public, but talent develops in private." We were all great artists at four in the morning before our mirrors. Delivering in public was the trick.

The scene ended. Before his critique, Pop couldn't resist turning around to the roomful of students and asking, "So, was that excellent or not?" She'd proven herself that day before one of the toughest audiences she would ever have. She was justifiably proud of herself afterward, like a kid who'd crossed the street alone for the first time. It was obvious my father was proud, too. He also looked relieved.

"You were wonderful," I told her. I meant it. I didn't mind her being wonderful, I only wished my father looked at me the way he did at her. At least Marilyn couldn't play the same parts as me. That would have been really awful.

My name looked good up in lights, one hundred and eighty bulbs of "me." I was thrilled, although I knew that one day in the not-too-distant future, when the play was over, those letters would be used to spell someone else's name. When I got to work the street was usually deserted, and I'd stand underneath the sign, looking up as the lights came blinking on in the gray dusk. S . . . U . . . S . . . My mouth hung open in awe, the way it did when I saw fireworks—aaaaah . . . oooh.

Some nights I gazed a little longer at those tiny dancing electrical circuits that came alive only at night. Twinkle twinkle little star, how I wonder what you are. Do you live up there where everyone can see? When you're switched off, will you turn back into me? The evening after Marilyn did her first scene, I stood staring longer than usual. I had no idea what I was feeling or thinking. My thoughts were zinging by too quickly to catch them.

"SHE DID IT ALL BY HERSELF,"
by Marcia Benton, *Movie Magazine* interview

"What about Marilyn Monroe?" I said. That was the first time I ever saw Susan annoyed. She positively bridled. "What about Marilyn Monroe?" she demanded.

"Well," I said weakly, "do you like her?"

"Miss Monroe," Susie said, accenting the "Miss"—for dignity, I think—"is very nice. A very fine person. I'll tell you something about her. I first met her in Hollywood when she was making a picture . . . and they took me over to see Miss Monroe do a number. Afterwards we were introduced. Then we met again in New York . . . the first thing she said to me was, "You may not remember me, but we met in

Hollywood—' and of course I had been planning to say exactly the same thing!"

It turned out that Marilyn had shared her room when she went out to Fire Island with Susan and her family last summer, and Susan thought she was very nice to live with. Also sensitive, and talented. She had only seen her once in the movies, in How to Marry a Millionaire, *and she thought she was very good. Considering that her other favorites are Olivier and Brando and Leslie Howard and Garbo, Garland, Vivien Leigh, and both Hepburns, that's putting her in good company. . . .*

I'd nominate Susie for one of the best kids I know, and one of the wisest. Even sitting in Schrafft's, watching her eat a horrible combination of lobster bisque and a hot pastrami sandwich and cole slaw and hot chocolate, I figured her for pretty mature. . . .

My elation at becoming a star was wearing off. I was disturbed that my performance was becoming forced. I was having difficulty maintaining the high emotional level I'd started out with, but the audience didn't notice. Mother and Father did.

My older beau began talking about commitments. I wasn't even eighteen. I'd commit next year, though what I'd commit to I wasn't sure. Whatever my mother told me to, probably. . . .

Things were busier than they'd ever been in the Strasberg house. I'd expected that with my father's success he'd have more time for the family. Instead he became less accessible than before—to us, at least. To outsiders, adopted family, the door was always open. The phone was answered, even at two in the morning. If an actor needed help, he got it. My father was inundated with requests to speak, to coach, to teach, and to be interviewed, and he was deluged with young actors, writers, and directors, known and unknown, who wanted to work with him. "Make me great," "Make me a star." Some threw themselves at his feet, literally. He was their guru.

I couldn't do it. I watched it all, and I couldn't fight the crowd to get a seat at my own kitchen table, to compete for a plate of food I'd paid for. My mother, however, would save a chair for me or make someone move when I entered the room. She'd become my agent, negotiating with Pop for time for me. It was so humiliating, I wanted to cover my face and run away from home. Only where would I go? Even when it hurt, it was so *interesting* at home.

I watched how wonderful my father was with some of his students. Carefully he'd unroll his rare antique Japanese scroll that told a story in beautiful pictures. He'd explain how the Japanese had invented the first movies with these sagas, which had closeups, crowd scenes, fade ins and outs. I heard his advice to a lovelorn actor, a struggling actress. Sometimes I caught myself wishing I wasn't in the family so I could enjoy it the way outsiders did.

We moved to a larger apartment on Central Park West. It had ten rooms with a view, high-beamed ceilings, and a mock fireplace. The decoration and style was basic *books*. Eight rooms, including the kitchen, were lined with my father's book and record collection. The rest was mine. I was paying half the rent and household expenses. I had a two-room suite in the middle of the apartment, a small sitting room, bathroom, and large bedroom. A decorator friend of Mom's helped me furnish the rooms with antiques. The sitting room was for entertaining and interviews. While Pop held court in his study, I would hold smaller court in mine. I was thrilled. I felt so grown-up. I'd gotten my own place and stayed home at the same time.

White and violet were the colors I picked. I was going to do all white until I realized it might seem as if I were copying Marilyn, whose apartment was white on white, including the white piano. The bedroom was violet drapes, blackout curtains underneath so I could sleep late, violet bedspread, one long mirrored wall, built-in closets for my rapidly expanding wardrobe. "More mirrors than me," Marilyn exclaimed. Violet? Was I inviolate?

Mother no longer had time or needed to cook her goulashes and stews. She was cooking up deals and future productions and coaching Marilyn, me, and, in her spare time, other actors who came to her for help. She'd teach Pop's classes if he was busy lecturing. She orchestrated all our lives, and we could finally afford a full-time housekeeper and a secretary Pop and I shared.

I wasn't sleeping so well. I had nightmares, waking in a sweat, just like the scene in the play when Anne dreamed that the Nazis were coming to get her, only there was no one after me. I wandered around the house, raided the refrigerator, sat in front of the windows overlooking the park, watched the lights of the city going off and coming on. It was busy out there. My head was filled with thoughts and dreams. It was busy in there, too. Maybe insomnia was normal for an actress. Marilyn had it, too.

I was becoming aware of the other side of Marilyn. She was getting into the habit of coming over in the middle of the night when she couldn't sleep. "The Geminis are restless tonight," Mom joked, but she wasn't laughing. Marilyn's sleeping pills often didn't work. She'd call friends who often couldn't talk at three in the morning. Then she'd come home, to our house. When Father and Mother had told her she was welcome anytime, they'd meant it.

She arrived, unmade-up, hair messed, dressed haphazardly, nothing matched. She was unrecognizable. Her mood shifted from distraught to depressed. Her speech was extremely slow for a girl who was usually so quick with a quip. Trying to help, I offered her books to read, but she went for the champagne. "Have some hot tea and milk," Mother pleaded, massaging her tense shoulders. Marilyn leaned her head on Mother's ample bosom and sipped her tea. She got Lee and tea and sympathy.

Then she went for the champagne with a glass in hand. I followed with my glass. Mother grabbed the bottle and put it back in the refrigerator.

"I'll sit up with you, I can't sleep, either," I offered.

"No thanks, honey, that's really sweet. It's okay, I'll be okay." She didn't want my company, she wanted my father's.

Sometimes she arrived earlier, before she opened the pill bottle. Those nights my father went into the bedroom with her and talked to her until she nodded off. She got Johnny's bed, he slept on the couch. "She just wants to be held, she wasn't held as a child," Pop explained. "If I hold her, she can go to sleep without pills. I won't give them to her, she's got to stop the pills. . . ."

One morning, on one of my sleepless-night prowls, I'd raided the refrigerator, tried reading, counting sheep, deep breathing, nothing had worked. I walked by my brother's room. Johnny's door was open, and in the faint light from the street lamp outside, I could see my father, in his blue and white striped seersucker pajamas and his old wilted wool bathrobe, sitting on the side of the bed, holding Marilyn cradled in his arms. I moved closer to the doorway, staying out of view. He was singing softly to her, "Go to sleep, my dusky baby, sleep and dream of angels maybe." A Brahms lullaby, my lullaby, the one he'd sung to me when I was a little girl with white-blond hair and big eyes. He was gently caressing her golden hair. Her eyes were closed, her head lay trustingly on his shoulder. A slight smile softened her lips.

"What about me?" I cried to myself. "I can't sleep, either."

Another night late after the show, I was puttering around in the kitchen when I heard sounds from the hallway. Carefully I peeked around the kitchen door. Silence. Nothing. Then I saw a movement at the far end of the long, red carpeted hall lined with theatrical posters and paintings by John Garfield, Clifford Odets, Zero Mostel, Henry Miller, and others. A white figure was crawling down the hallway on its hands and knees. It was Marilyn. A loose robe fell open over her nude body; luminous, she seemed to glow in the dark. She was only going across the way from my brother's bedroom to my parents', but she was moving slowly, sluggishly, on all fours. Her progress seemed interminable.

My impulse was to rush to help this loose-limbed, lost being, but I didn't want her to know I'd seen her like this. I was afraid she'd be embarrassed or, worse, angry. She finally reached the door, raised her hand, and began to scratch on it, like a puppy that's been locked out. "Lee . . . Lee," she whimpered. I decided that if my parents didn't hear her, I had to help her. I couldn't stand seeing her like that. Just as I started toward her, the door opened and my father appeared. He was half-asleep, but he lifted her up and took her back to Johnny's room. She'd taken too many pills again. She would forget and take more and then remember, too late. Hiding in the shadows at the end of the hallway, I watched them disappear. I felt like a spy, an intruder in my own home.

The more I saw Marilyn and my father together, the more confused and resentful I became. She broke all the rules, all the rules I was expected to follow. She said "Fuck it" to a lot of things. She wasn't professional. She was late. She popped pills and drank excessively. She lost contact with reality. She was unpredictable, explosive, impulsive, easily distracted. He didn't yell at her. He totally accepted her. No matter what she did, he constantly validated her.

Their unlikely friendship, their mutual attraction and response to one another, shook up my whole frame of reference. I'd been trying so hard to be good, as in "Good girls don't ask, they just take what they get," to be correct, to do the right thing, to control myself. I'd gone to all the lengths I could think of, and for what? She did everything wrong as far as I could see, the opposite of what I was doing, yet around her Pop was vulnerable, paternal, and permissive. Around me he seemed withdrawn, impersonal, forbidding, and critical.

What was I doing wrong? If someone had told me, I'd have changed. Why didn't he give me permission to be myself as he did her? Let him love me whatever I did. Let him validate me as he did her. Unconditional love was good; I wanted some, too. It was turning out that Marilyn and I had more in common than I could ever have imagined. We were both looking for acceptance from a teacher and father . . . mine.

GERALDINE BARON—Director, teacher, actress

I was nineteen or twenty when I met your dad. I was very intimidated but he was so gracious and humorous I got over that. We were at a Fourth of July party at Shelley's house in Malibu. He was wearing a blue blazer and so was I. He looked me over and said, "You and I are the only ones here who are properly attired."

I studied with him for fourteen years. He was the most loving, generous human being I've encountered. There was this lovely actress in one of his master classes. She didn't get to do her second scene because your father had talked so long about the scene before. So he told her he'd take her first, next class, in two days. She burst into tears because she was leaving town. "When are you going?" he asked. She said tomorrow and he said, "Do you have time tomorrow?" It was his day off but he came in and saw her scene and worked with her for two and a half hours. He didn't charge her, no one else knew. The love your father had for actors!

And his patience. One actor came year after year to class and he was hopeless, terrible. I thought, this is wrong, why is Lee taking his money? But your father kept working with him and he was still impossibly bad. After seven years of this something happened to that man, it was extraordinary; he works now as an actor. He's not a star, but he works and he's happy because of what your father did for him.

Your father was so simple but so profound and he was like Carl Jung. He was a man who saw things other people couldn't see. I wouldn't say he was shy. If he had something to say, believe it, he said it, but he was a gentle man. People said he was explosive but it was only in trying to awaken the actor. Like Buddhist teachers do, he could strike you awake with his words. Everything he did had a purpose; to help awaken an actor by whatever means necessary. In all the years I never saw him wrong. And he was both poetic and precise.

I think your father was a great master; he even taught you with his use of silence. Some people thought he wasn't capable of communicating, that he was antisocial, but he was just never frivolous in his conversation. He was above that. He was so loving, not in a sentimental way, in a real way. I'm still changing from what he taught me. His work was the pathway to discover myself; he gave me myself.

Our family doctor gave me sleeping pills, Placidyls. They smelled awful. I only took one. At first they were like knockout drops. Later they didn't always put me out. Instead they made me giddy and my whole body turned to jelly and I felt wonderfully silly and soft. I would sing out loud to myself, "Sleep and dream of angels singing while the humming bees are humming, making honey for my baby . . ."

I danced alone in front of my mirrors the way I had when I was a little girl, the apple of my father's eye. Or had I made that up?

Marilyn mentioned that if you punctured a sleeping pill with a needle, it worked even faster. She was a walking pharmacy.

She seemed really knowledgeable about the pills she took, and I got the impression that she not only knew what she was doing, but had been doing it for a long, long time. "Listen," she told me. "I'm a war veteran of the night. If I haven't tried it, it doesn't exist. Just ask me if you want to know anything. It's kind of the Monroe *doctrine*. Dr. Monroe . . ." She was pretty tipsy when she said this.

STEFFI

Schwab's used to call my father all the time because he was so close to Marilyn. She was really young then, just coming up. Jack Schwab was worried about her. They all liked her. "What should I do, Sidney? She's in with another prescription, she's taking too many." And my father would say, "What can we do? If you don't fill it, someone else will."

DELOS

With the pills, she'd take five; it took five to sedate her. Seven could be lethal, so she was living, for years, two pills away from the lethal dose, and sometimes she got to it. There was a death wish, thanatos. She was always saying to me, "Let's kill ourselves." She'd write it on my notepads in class, and I had the feeling, That girl's not going to live. I didn't know if the folks could put her together again. Later, gallant knight Joe couldn't do it. We gave copious advice, your mother particularly. We thought she listened, then she went ahead and did what she damn well pleased. She paid no attention to warnings. I felt the wish to die. The death wish was strong because it represented freedom, escape. Sometimes she had this great bubbly beauty, but dank un-

derwater like she was more submerged than we were, other-
worldly, as if she were drowning. She told me that when
she went to the psychiatrists, she couldn't tell them the truth
and instead would never get that far past reciting her life
story. She was suicidal on and off and terrified that she'd
become like her mother and in physical pain as well, chronic
physical pain. Female problems and the pills had to be
damaging her chemical balances. I'm not ordinarily a pessi-
mist, but my prognosis was death. Your father would get
furious with me when I told him I didn't think they could
help her enough. He wouldn't accept it. He hoped the work
would release some of her darkness that had built up; it was
so powerful you couldn't ignore it. But he felt that if she
could break some of those negative conditioned reflexes
through the work, she'd get better. Your father was afraid
of death, he wouldn't face it. His mother's, his first wife's,
the young one he was in love with who died of cancer in
her early twenties, his sister, his little brother . . .

Often, after her private lesson, Marilyn would stay for dinner. We sat around the kitchen table listening to music, our
faces glowing like jewels in the warm light from the fake Tiffany lamp over the glass table. We were like a normal family.
We'd laugh at my father's stories and jokes. He'd act them
out, a little hammily, illustrating them with his hands, moving
his body like a mime.

Marilyn's favorite was the one about a professor of religion
who's giving a course on "great religions." The only research
the professor has to complete is on Judaism. His subject is
"What Is the Talmud?" He's having difficulty understanding it.

He mentions this to his friend Sol, who owns the Jewish
deli where he lunches every day. Sol says, "Since we're friends,
I'll tell you what the Talmud is, but first I'm going to ask you

three questions, Professor, and when you answer them, you'll know 'What Is the Talmud?' "

The professor agrees. "I'm ready."

Sol says, "The first question is as follows: Two men go down a chimney, one man comes out dirty, the other man comes out clean, which man washes?"

The professor is taken aback. "Sol, is this a joke? What kind of question is this? I'm speaking about a college course, not a joke."

Sol assures him he's serious, so the professor says, "Well, it's simple, the dirty man washes."

"No, no, no, my friend." Sol shakes his head. "After all, the dirty man looks at the clean man and thinks he's clean and the clean man looks at the dirty man and thinks he's dirty, so . . . the clean man washes."

"Aaah," the professor says, "I see. Interesting, go on."

"The next question is as follows: Two men go down a chimney, one man comes out dirty, the other man comes out clean, which man washes?"

"My friend, you're making fun of me. This is a serious business, religion."

"Professor, please, would I insult you? I'm serious."

"You convinced me through logical deduction that it's obvious, the clean man washes."

"Please, Professor, think. After all, they don't just look at each other, they look at themselves, they examine their clothes, and the clean man sees he's clean, the dirty man sees he's dirty, so . . . the dirty man washes."

"I'm beginning to see this has to do with a philosophical attitude, very good. What's the next question?"

"The third and final question is as follows: Two men go down a chimney, one man comes out dirty, the other man comes out clean, which man washes?"

The professor is really upset now. "Yes, you've convinced

me that my thinking was remiss. I understand that it's the dirty man who washes!"

Sol shakes his head sadly. "Professor, please. Two men go down a chimney, one man comes out dirty, and the other man comes out clean? How is that even possible?"

The professor is furious. He yells, frustrated, "Oh, this is too confusing, I don't understand anything!"

"That's it! You've got it. That's the Talmud!" Sol says triumphantly.

"That's my life," Marilyn empathized. "I can't figure out if it's them or me who should wash."

One evening Marilyn seemed in a daze. She sat with her head propped up on her hand, eyes at half-mast, looking exhausted. Suddenly she keeled over onto the kitchen table, kerplunk, her head half on the glass table, half on her arm. As she lay there, we all stared at the back of her blond head buried in her arms. I was stunned, my mother was frozen in shock, even my father's composure was shaken. Ethel, our cook from Jamaica, who'd worked for a rabbi before she'd come to us, was tough but compassionate. She broke the silence with a sigh. "Lord, that girl sure am sick."

Galvanized into action, the family got her undressed and into bed. My mother was in tears. "She's sick, but it's not incurable, Susan, we can help her." Like me, my mother thought she could save the world, change it, make people over into what she knew they could be if they would be, if only . . .

I was saddened. I'd seen many actors like this, but Marilyn was the only one I'd become close to. She was like my sister and I felt so terrible that I was unable to help her.

With some of the others, Clifford, Franchot Tone, my father would let them have it, not yelling, just steady, angry assault. "This is what you do repeatedly, darling, you don't listen, you insist on repeating this kind of behavior. . . ." It wasn't just what they were doing to themselves; he abhorred what they were doing to their talent. That to him was a crime. He felt they had a responsibility to their gift the way you do to a child.

With Marilyn he was tender, understanding. "She can't handle certain kinds of criticism or anger directed at her. She takes it as rejection. She's not able to deal with it yet."

He was disturbed but optimistic. Although I thought his "yet" carried more hope than faith.

How many creative people had I seen like this—drunk, despairing, suicidal, homicidal, manic-depressive, paranoid? Laurette Taylor, Clifford Odets, Montgomery Clift, Franchot Tone, John Barrymore . . . on and on. Too many; their capacity to suffer seemed to be directly equivalent to their capacity for pleasure and their ability to experience life fully, yin and yang. I assumed that this was the price real artists paid for their talent. Van Gogh, Beethoven, Nietzsche, Nijinski, Tennessee Williams, Cocteau, Sartre, Camus, Hemingway, Hesse, T. E. Lawrence, Rilke, Zelda and Scott Fitzgerald, Dostoyevski, Tolstoy, Gauguin, Keats and Shelley, Strindberg, Ibsen, Rimbaud . . . a roll call.

There were great artists who had the ability to lead normal or at least outwardly acceptable, conventional lives by society's standards: Shakespeare, Strauss, Renoir . . . But they were in the minority. Why were so many unable to find any peace or happiness? Some were even admired for their excess, unless it killed them. Why were there so many "outsiders" in the creative arts? Maybe, I thought, normal wasn't necessarily good; it was just what the majority of people were.

Garrick and Kean were both great actors, but Pop's voice was more excited when he described the daring and craziness of Kean. He became so expansive when talking about him. My father preached: Commit. Create! Explore the widest, wildest realms of human expression, no matter what. Yet he held himself under such tight rein, pulling against the tidal waves of his own passion and anger. Could he be identifying with these rebels?

One of Marilyn's ambitions was "I want to be wonderful." So did I. I also wanted to be happy. Did wonderful and happy come on the same menu? If they didn't, how much was I willing to sacrifice for my art?

If you had to suffer to be good, then maybe what was wrong with me was that I hadn't suffered enough yet. Marilyn had such a big head start on me, how would I ever catch up? Another puzzle was, were the best actors talented and then crazy or crazy and then talented? Some artists avoided therapy or change, afraid it would neutralize the tormented aspects of themselves they drew upon to create. I wondered if that was true . . . or if it was an excuse not to grow up and take responsibility. The thoughts of youth were long, long thoughts, and they didn't engender a good night's sleep.

My father taught at the Actors Studio for love, not money, because as he affirmed, "There are actors all over the world who regardless of their circumstances, professional or personal, regardless of whatever difficulties they're facing, whatever problems or changes, there is one thing they can rely on and that is, that at eleven o'clock on Tuesday and Friday morning, come rain, shine, or snow or what have you, there is a session at the Actors Studio and in that session, *work* is being done. The fact that actors can count on that, that they know that exists, can help them get through . . ."

There was standing room only at the Actors Studio. People who hadn't been around for years showed up. The word was out that Marilyn was doing a scene from *Anna Christie* with Maureen Stapleton. Marilyn was playing Anna, the part Garbo had played in the movies. She was so terrified, I didn't know how she was going to get herself up there. She also knew as many people were there to see her fail as succeed.

This was a command performance before the royalty of New York theater. It was also a trial by a jury deeply prejudiced against the defendant. Many of the people in the room that day looked on Marilyn as the symbol of everything they fought against—Hollywood superficiality, the star system. Many even condemned her for being a success, for being beautiful and sexy. When she came to the studio, sitting hidden in the back row, hand propping up her head, intent on the scene, like a sponge absorbing everything she heard and saw, some of the people thought her simplicity and humility were affectations.

"If they'll just give her a chance. Everyone deserves a chance." My mother was fanning herself with one of the numerous fans in her collection. She used them winter and summer, not when it was hot, but when she was hot. She'd get these spells, dizziness, hot flashes, and whip out a fan from Japan, China, or France. At one point she used battery-propelled fans. The large purses Mom carried held flashlight, fan, food—in case anyone got hungry, war was declared, or an emergency arose—vitamins, smelling salts, aspirin; it was a supermarket, pharmacy, deli grab bag. . . .

My mother, too, was nervous. She looked around, counting the house, who was there, who hadn't come. My father's feelings were hidden behind an impassive expression. I envied him this ability. Whatever I felt showed on my face, especially if I tried to hide my emotions.

I knew Marilyn was a wreck. Petrified she'd forget her lines, she'd still refused Maureen's suggestion to leave a book with her dialogue in it on the table where she'd be sitting. There would be no retakes today. Just thinking about it made me scared; my heart was thudding in sympathy for her.

When she came onstage I thought she was sick at first; she seemed tired, worn, disillusioned. Her hands were trembling when she picked up a glass. The scene was set in a bar. Then I realized that all these things were required by the character. If she was afraid, her fear was Anna Christie's—she was using it. Through the character's despair, Marilyn had a luminescent glow. Her work was simple, real, moment to moment. It was particularly poignant when she had to talk about the father who'd abused and betrayed her. You could feel the depth of her feelings, though she didn't overdramatize them. Her voice was clear—not loud, but she could be heard.

The scene ended. There was silence. Then the studio burst into applause, a rare phenomenon. Applause was frowned on here. Those who didn't applaud her acting applauded her courage. Kim Stanley, the great actress who'd done *Picnic* on Broadway, came up to Marilyn and apologized to her for doubting her talent. She had been lovely in a classic part. She still had detractors, people who held her in contempt or were envious or who just didn't like her. But she had shown she was a real actress. And she had won a greater battle: she had conquered her fear.

My father was restrained but generous with his praise. He handled her as though she were the most precious of jewels. I tried not to be jealous.

"Thank God it's over," Mother gasped. "I thought I'd have a heart attack, I was so nervous."

She received compliments as if she'd given birth to Marilyn.

My birth announcement had proclaimed, "At last the Golden Girl arrives" (a play on Clifford Odets's *Golden Boy*). There was a new Golden Girl in the family.

Marilyn was desolate afterward, inconsolable. "I let your father down."

My mother went around asking other people, "Tell her, please, she doesn't believe me. She was wonderful, wasn't she? We're so proud of you! This is only the beginning."

"I was lousy," she insisted. She was so hard on herself.

Another challenge was just around the corner.

The McCarthy committee had called Arthur Miller to testify. If he didn't name names, he'd be in contempt and risk a jail sentence. If he named names, like Kazan or Sterling Hayden or Clifford Odets, his career could go on. But Arthur's plays were a voice for freedom of expression. He'd never name names.

Marilyn was frantic. "He could go to jail for a year, we could be dead in a year." She was right—we could have died that night, then, an earthquake, a car accident, a heart attack; everybody was dying all the time. Except me, I was young, I knew I'd live forever.

Marilyn raged: "The bastards, I won't let them do it to him. He's got to tell them to go fuck themselves, only he can do it in better language." Arthur had anger, she had passion. Whether he intended to tell them to go fuck themselves or not, she was like Saint Joan urging the dauphin to fight. She was a warrior goddess, awakened and full of piss and vinegar. She was thinking only of him, not herself, of the principles involved.

My dad suggested, "Paula and I will talk to Arthur if you'd like. We've been involved in this kind of thing. Maybe we can be objective since we have no ax to grind here." My father was apolitical, liberal but noncommittal.

"It's not fair. I grew up with 'not fair' for a roommate, but not anymore. They can't do this to us, I won't let them," MM insisted.

I believed her.

When Marilyn's studio heard that she was considering backing Miller publicly, they called her to threaten or cajole her not to do it. "Professional suicide," they warned her. "Your fans, the public, will reject you, your career will be seriously jeopardized. Maybe over." She'd heard this before: the nude calendar, her leaving for New York.

That was all she needed. "Those sons of bitches can't tell me what to do anymore." The more they threatened, the more determined she became to go ahead. "What's my career against his if the people turn against me? This is America, and I'm standing with the Constitution and Jefferson. If it's good enough for him, it's good enough for me."

Spyros Skouras, head of 20th Century-Fox, visited her and Arthur to put in his two cents worth. Marilyn cried, kissed him but remained constant.

Mother, after being blacklisted herself, was ambivalent. "Marilyn, these people are serious. They've ruined lives for less than this. Look at my career as an actress, ruined, Julie Garfield, dead at thirty-six, Larry Parks will never make another movie. If you're a writer or director, you can change your name, they don't need to see your face. But an actress—these are the best years of your career you're coming into, nothing should jeopardize that. Even though I think you're right, is it worth it to take the risk? Arthur's problem is from before he met you, it doesn't really concern you; let him resolve it."

My impression was that Marilyn had dragged Arthur to my parents' house when they showed up for a "family conference." Arthur obviously didn't like my parents. Whether it was competitiveness or that he wanted total control over Marilyn or just personality differences, I couldn't figure out. There seemed to be two kinds of people: those who went for control, like my father and Arthur, and those who went for approval, like Mom, Marilyn, and me. Of course, it wasn't that simple because sometimes you went for approval in order to get control, and vice versa.

Pop and Arthur had so much in common; I couldn't understand why they didn't get on. They both gave off the same forbidding, shy, intellectual demeanor—not shy exactly, but closed. When they were around Marilyn, they both opened up. Unfortunately, when they were around her together, they both withdrew again.

It wasn't a very successful meeting. Miller indicated that he resented any advice on his private business. Marilyn would have liked them all to be friends, but it wasn't to be. As Arthur became more embroiled in Marilyn's business affairs and less in his writing, the rift between them all got wider.

Watching MM with Arthur on one side and Pop on the other, I was amazed at how she could be so subservient and helpless and yet wind up dominating everyone.

She'd said in one of her half reveries, "When you're an orphan, you kind of have to learn how to get what you need to survive." I noticed that although her mother was still alive in an institution, she'd referred to herself as an orphan.

She was at her best here, like a soldier who rises to the occasion of war. Even when there was peace, her life was like a war zone. When nothing was happening in her life to distract her, she'd get restless, hyper. She had tremendous energy, which came out in herculean bursts of activity, followed by total depletion and depressions. There were more mountains and valleys in her life than in the Himalayas. Whenever she had something to devote herself to, she was much more together.

In the end she did what she wanted to, as usual. She told the press the truth—"I support Arthur one hundred percent"—just as she'd told the truth about the nude calendar, almost. She'd said it was to pay her rent when it was actually to pay her car payments. "People who've never lived in Hollywood don't realize your car is as important as a place to sleep, so in case they didn't get it, I changed it a little. What your daddy calls artistic license."

Marilyn claimed, "I don't know much about politics." She knew a lot more than I did. She'd read books, asked questions, gotten answers. She just didn't trust herself.

She told me, "When I met Arthur, he awakened my interest in government." She'd always been drawn to fight for the underdog. In the early fifties MM had arranged to have Ella Fitzgerald booked at the famous Macombo nightclub in Hollywood. The owners had agreed to this only when Marilyn, then at the height of her new fame, promised she'd sit at a ringside table every night.

Mom quoted the saying by Rabbi Hillel, part of which is engraved on the sundial at Yale University: "If I am not for myself, then who will be for me? And being for myself alone, what am I? And if not now, when?" Marilyn wrote it down.

Simply dressed, hair windswept, arm in his, Marilyn and Arthur appeared on the steps of his lawyer's house. The attendant publicity generated sympathy for Arthur. Arthur didn't name names, and eventually the committee decided not to jail the future husband of the quintessential American dream girl. Together they'd weathered the crisis. Marilyn had shown herself to be a woman of principle.

Mom remarked, "You know, Susie, people still think she's a joke, but there's no other star I can think of—sex symbol, smex symbol—who has put herself on the line like this for her beliefs."

I didn't need convincing. I thought she was terrific. I wondered what I would have done in her place. She had a lot more courage than I'd suspected. I started to tell her that I thought she'd done something admirable. She cut me off and said, "People look up to him; it's like with Joe. Young people really count on them. I didn't want anything to hurt that."

"She's at her best when she's not thinking about herself," Mom explained. Weren't we all?

After she left Washington, Arthur announced to the committee that the reason he wanted to go to England was "to attend a production of my play, and be with the woman who will then be my wife." The press went crazy. Marilyn, back in New York, was besieged. Arthur had not formally proposed to her. "Gee, I was surprised, too," Marilyn confessed. "We'd talked about it. But then, pow . . ." Arthur was learning from Marilyn. He'd become a master of the media.

DOROTHY MONET

I remember I went to a restaurant right after Arthur had come back from Washington. She was sitting there with him and a few other people, and we were all so admiring of him that he'd taken this position. I ran over to him and said, "Arthur, you were wonderful. You don't know how good this makes me feel." And he stood up and we embraced, and all of a sudden I looked past him to where she was sitting, and she was so woebegone. I've never seen anyone look so woebegone. . . . I interpreted it to mean she was thinking, I would like to be admired like that. I'm nobody.

So, there you all were, you and your family with this creature in your midst, this woman who was the embodiment of sexuality, and yet it was so phony and fake. I doubted she'd ever had an orgasm in her life, this poor creature. And you were real live people who were being sacrificed on the altar of this myth, and your parents were adoring and cultivating and nursing. You seemed to accept this idea that she was this great, splendid creature. Parasitic, she was parasitic. They take take take. They demand, they live off the juice of other people. Even the greatest actors do that to some extent. Even at its best, it's part of the job. You inhabit this creation of somebody else. And yet Marilyn was adorable. I adored watching her. And you, you were the most beautiful child, exquisite and so sweet, you were so ingratiating, too ingratiating.

Lee was a very depriving father. I saw all these artists, Clifford, the others, masquerading as parents, and I felt they didn't have a right to reproduce themselves simply to create extensions of themselves. They needed to realize they were creating another separate person. It seemed a cardinal sin to me not to nurture and, worse, to denature a child. Artists are narcissistic people who have children to add to their own nature for their own growth.

Your mother was amazingly vulnerable about the whole McCarthy business. It surprised me. She was very concerned about what you felt and that in the future you would have some impression of what it was all about if you ever questioned it.

Look, they—your father, his contemporaries—were very strange, and they were not allowed to be strange in the way people, celebrities, are allowed to be strange now. In those days it wasn't just that they'd come out of the Depression. They were very close to their Jewish roots, and they had this Jewish morality. They were supposed to be good family people, and they were really mavericks, suddenly proclaiming themselves professional artists.

I remember watching you get up to do a scene in the studio, and I wondered how you had the courage to do it. Pit yourself against Daddy's favorites and make yourself seen.

Marilyn and Arthur had been victorious, but the stress she'd been under had taken its toll. She was hospitalized with bronchitis in Los Angeles, where she was preparing to do *Bus Stop*.

Pop, Johnny, and I celebrated my eighteenth birthday. Mom, with Marilyn in California, called. "I would give anything to be with you, my darling girl." She sent me to Dr. Finger, our family doctor, for one of my gifts, a diaphragm. "I want you to be free, Susan, to know whatever you want to do is all right as long as you don't hurt yourself or anyone else and don't get pregnant!"

While Marilyn was filming, Arthur was in Nevada, getting his divorce.

Every evening Marilyn and Mother called to talk, sometimes for hours, to Pop. Though Josh Logan was one of the few directors she felt fairly safe with, Marilyn needed reassurance. On bad days she felt Josh was favoring Don Murray, the young actor opposite her. She worried that Hope Lange was too blond, so Hope darkened her hair. This was standard star self-protection. Mother and Marilyn worked out together like an athlete and his coach. My father's work dealt with training for the long run. Mother's work was moment to moment, a line reading, a gesture, if necessary, a piece of business. Coaching is result-oriented. There's no time for anything else on a set.

Lee and Paula made suggestions about how to play "Cherie." After talking with both my parents, Marilyn was able to follow her instincts, utilize their advice, and assert her creative ideas. She and Josh picked a costume for Cherie. "It's too nice. Wouldn't it be older ... even ripped? She's got no money, right?" Josh loved the suggestion.

They decided that since the girl worked at night and slept in the day, she was very pale. Milton Greene worked out a look with white makeup. Josh loved that, too. The studio hated it. This was not the old Marilyn. They didn't care if it was the character. Who did she think she was, Katharine Hepburn? An actress?

This was the first job my mother had done with Marilyn. She'd worked with Tallulah Bankhead, the most temperamental of actresses, and a director who referred to actors as "cattle," Alfred Hitchcock. He'd adored Mother. She treasured the drawing, his famous profile self-portrait, he'd given her.

That was then, this was now. Josh said he adored Mom, but he forbade her to come onto the set. She hid in the dressing room. She wore black, as if that would make her invisible. It did the reverse. My mother was the "point man" for Marilyn the way she had been over the years for my father. A point man is the guy in the army who goes first and takes all the fire. The general and the troops follow. Sometimes the general stays at camp, like Pop in New York.

Josh adjusted to Marilyn's eccentricities as an actress. He left the camera running before and after each take to catch Marilyn's wonderful improvisations. One day, when she was late, he rushed her physically into the street for a sundown shot. He adored and respected her talent. She responded with some of her best work. Ironically, prior to filming Josh hadn't wanted Marilyn. He'd called Lee, who convinced him that she was more than capable of doing the role.

In one scene on the bus, Cherie talked about this place she longed to go. Marilyn was particularly proud of her work in it. Mom explained to *Time* magazine writer Ezra Goodman, coincidentally a friend of Steffi Skolsky's, that "these words of the writer don't mean anything to Marilyn, so as an actress she has to make them real for herself." Then she added, "God knows that longing for something is very real to Marilyn. Her whole life she's been longing, so I had her substitute by thinking about a place that meant something to her personally. She never told me where; actors have to keep their own secrets. When she did this scene, her eyes filled with tears that poured down her face. . . . People are going to be surprised by her."

Mother knew Pop would be pleased, too. His training was paying off already. Mom needed my father's approval as much as I did.

"Susie," Mother predicted, "it's the kind of scene she'll get an Academy Award nomination for. Nobody's ever seen her like this, an actress with range."

Mother was used to actors, charming, manipulative, needy, insecure, frightened, sensitive, demanding. Her life revolved around them. When Marilyn became temperamental or ill, or when she overindulged in champagne, she'd coax and comfort her and make SOS calls to Pop about what to do. Sometimes she begged him, "You tell her, it's better if it comes from you . . ."

At this point in time Mother didn't know if she'd become a part of Marilyn's entourage or even if they'd work together again. She took it one day at a time. She didn't take the director's or Marilyn's problem personally. As she said, "If I didn't murder Tallulah Bankhead, I can survive anything."

When Ezra first arrived on location to interview Marilyn, he found the task more difficult than he'd anticipated. "She's locked in her dressing room working with Paula Strasberg," they told him day after day.

One afternoon, still waiting for his audience, he ran into my mother, who was so bored she was shopping in the ski store for presents, even though she knew no one who skied.

"They told me she was with you," he exclaimed.

"And they told *me* she was with *you*," she replied. It turned out Marilyn had been closeted for days with Milton Greene. So Ezra and Mother wound up having coffee and waiting for Marilyn, which was a bit like waiting for Godot.

He asked Mother for help after he finally got his interview. He wanted to talk to friends of Marilyn's, and she had told him, "Call Marlene Dietrich." So he had, and she'd said she'd barely met Marilyn. He asked Mother why Marilyn had done that.

"You have to understand, Marilyn never had any friends, she never had time to make friends. She probably gave you Dietrich's name more as someone she'd *like* to have talk about her." But Mother confessed to me later, "I don't know for sure that was why she told him that, maybe too much champagne, but I tried to put myself in her place and make her look good."

Mother thought that Marilyn, with her sixth sense, might have intuited that Ezra was one of the few reporters less than enchanted with her and that his piece might not be very sympathetic.

He'd documented Marilyn's many love affairs. He'd uncovered new material on her early history that showed the degree to which she had taken creative license with the facts of her upbringing. She'd borrowed some of her stories of abuse and the number of homes she'd had from a young girlfriend of hers, although she had enough horror stories of her own. This girl said about her: "After a couple of foster homes you become cagey, cynical, and you know how to get the most out of

people. You call your story 'The Girl from the Broken Home.'
Marilyn isn't in this business for fame or glory. It's a release as
necessary as becoming an alcoholic or a drug addict. She's
looking for a mother, father, family, all rolled into one. . . ."
Ezra wanted to show a different Marilyn from the studio's
version, or hers.

Mother defended her. "Let's face it, one rejection to a highly
sensitive person is like a thousand to another. After that first
betrayal . . . does it matter?"

In pursuit of the real Marilyn, Ezra took Mother and Steffi to
dinner. He plied Mom, who didn't drink, with some disgusting
sweet rum drink to loosen her tongue, but to no avail.

It was all much ado about nothing because *Time* edited the
piece till they had an upscale movie magazine version.

"How could he learn the truth about a girl who's such a
good liar?" Mother laughed. "As if there's one truth, anyway.
All those facts he collected may have less to do with the reality
than her fantasies." Mother spoke from experience. She was
also a woman who more than once had molded the truth to
suit her dreams.

In the pinch, Mother had done what everyone around MM
did—she'd protected her as if she were a little girl. There is a
child who lives in all of us, but Marilyn's lived so much closer
to the surface. That little girl of Marilyn's seemed to absorb
and carry the burden of all our collective abandoned children.
Even I felt like her mother sometimes.

Josh was effusive in his praise of Marilyn's luminosity and
brilliance—"genius like Garbo or Chaplin, mystery." By now
people weren't laughing as hard. She was winning some grudg-
ing respect, but why was it so difficult?

In June *Bus Stop* was completed on time, and Marilyn and
Mom flew home with not a moment to spare. Marilyn just had
time to get married before she left for England to shoot *The
Prince and the Showgirl*.

Marilyn and Arthur were married twice. A rabbi officiated

at one service, at the house of Kay Brown, Arthur's friend and agent. The other was with a judge. "One time for each Gemini twin." Marilyn insisted on converting to Judaism, although Arthur wasn't that religious. Later she referred to herself as "an atheist Jew," saying, "I believe in everything a little, and if I have kids, I think they should be Jewish. Anyway, I can identify with the Jews. Everybody's always out to get them, no matter what they do, like me." She had also wanted to please Arthur's family, now hers. Over the next year she'd pepper her conversations with Jewish expressions as if reaffirming her conversion. "Hi Bubuleh, oy vay, what tsures."

I felt she was driven by deeper motives when I saw the books on philosophy she read and the psychics and card readers she'd run to when she got in trouble. She seemed to be searching for some spiritual roots she'd been deprived of. She was so skeptical of all organized religion from her childhood contacts. Most of the religious people she'd known were "devout hypocrites," although she liked the ideas embodied in the Christian Science church, of which she had been a member as a child with her favorite aunt Ana. Years before she had joked, "When Jane Russell tried to convert me to religion, I tried to convert her to Freud." She said of herself, "Spiritual maybe, but the thing that's scary is most people who tell you they're religious are the worst."

"When you're in love, the whole world is Jewish." Mother was rapt. "They're so much in love, Susan. I hope you find a man like that. He treats her so wonderfully, I've never seen a man treat a woman as tenderly as he does her. He really values her for herself." She emphasized the words *tenderly* and *values*, drawing them out like incantations. "I always thought Arthur was a little puritanical and cold. Well, he was, but he's so changed with her; he's opened up, he's so affectionate. He really loves her."

There was a look of longing in her eyes as well as admiration. As a husband, my father was much like what I'd heard Arthur had been like before MM—withdrawn, not physically affectionate, self-centered. I had never seen Pop be tender with my mother, who was so physical and embracing. I knew he valued her, but I wasn't sure if it was for herself, the woman, or for what she did for him. She took care of him. She certainly valued him. I speculated about their relationship. They'd made love. Johnny and I were proof of that, but now? . . . It was funny. Mom touched too much and Pop touched too little. The dichotomies of life were so bewildering. Walt Whitman was right: "Do I contradict myself? Very well then I contradict myself . . ." Or was it just us?

Shortly before the second wedding ceremony, Marilyn turned to my mother and father. They were driving somewhere, and she announced out of the blue, "If it wasn't for the work, I'd throw myself out of this car." How could she say something like that one minute and be laughing and gay the next?

She reminded me of my mother, perpetually dissatisfied. "Dear God," I prayed, "don't let me be like that when I get as old as them."

Just before the wedding, a woman reporter was killed when the car she was in crashed while chasing Arthur and Marilyn in their car. It was a senseless tragedy.

"This is an ill omen," Mother worried.

My father snapped, "Please, darling, be logical."

Marilyn was horrified and had to be reassured it hadn't been her fault.

Unable to attend the wedding because of the play, I made my mother give me a blow-by-blow description. Marilyn had looked like a "real bride," and Arthur had outdone himself with her, cuddling and kissing. "He didn't look like a Grant Wood today." Grant Wood was a primitive painter who did portraits of grim-faced American farmers. "You'll be next, Susie, you'll see."

How did Marilyn do that, loosen Arthur up like that? She

did the same for Pop. Was it something she did deliberately, or did it just happen spontaneously? Could I learn how to do it?

Months later Marilyn showed me the wedding ring. It was engraved, "A to M, Now is Forever." I tried it on. It was too big. "Marilyn, forever is so romantic. . . . I can't even imagine forever, can you?"

She looked thoughtful before saying, "I guess it isn't as long as we think it is, 'cause I feel like I was at Fox forever, and when I get the blues it feels like I'm in hell forever. I don't think you can 'think' forever, it's more a feeling. . . ." We agreed that although forever was ephemeral, after you found Mr. Right, happily ever after definitely existed.

It had to; we'd bet all our dreams on it.

In coming east, taking a leap into the darkness of the unknown, MM had finally found her "key" light. That's the light in shooting a film that's yours, set up for you, aimed at you. All you have to do is be aware, feel it, and hit your mark. If you miss, even by an inch, you wind up in shadow, if not total darkness. She was lit up now, surrounded by men who adored and responded to her on a level beyond what she'd imagined: one of the world's top playwrights and the most renowned acting teacher in the world. These men of acknowledged intellect reflected her image in the mirror of their eyes: "You are the fairest of them all." She seemed alternately delighted and terrified by the respect they gave her.

I couldn't blame her. I was beginning to feel that life was dangerous. Just getting out of bed in the morning could be an act of courage because there were no guarantees of anything. Whoever you were, whatever the reviewers said, whoever loved you, the universe didn't seem to care. Fate didn't seem to care. Did we really have any control of our lives?

Doing Anne Frank eight times a week was becoming exhausting, not just physically but emotionally as well. I felt I died at every performance. I had been getting the flu over and over again, and I was beginning to feel trapped by the relationship I was in. My beau, now my fiancé, was ready to settle down. He talked about getting married. I was ready to break out. I wanted an all-encompassing passion, a love I'd die for—what I'd dreamed about when I'd embraced my pillow the year before. I'd caress it, pretending it was "him," the love of my life. I'd been freer and more passionate with my pillow than I was now with a real man. My father's favorite saying was a quote from Browning: ". . . a man's reach should exceed his grasp, or what's a heaven for?" So maybe it was natural that my fantasy exceeded my reality, but I wasn't about to give up without trying.

A young woman student of my dad's complained to him about her life and problems. He turned to her and replied, sounding annoyed, "Darling, what makes you think you have a right to be happy?" It seemed he was talking to me.

Marilyn, who had fame and success and love and beauty and talent, didn't seem very happy or even to expect happiness. "I didn't have it that much as a child, so I didn't get used to it or expect it, so it's not like a habit where I need it. . . . It would be nice to have it, though," she admitted.

That wasn't good enough for me. I'd shoot myself if I had to live like most people or my parents, who settled for less. I was never going to get married if it was like that. If people lived lives of quiet desperation, I was determined to at least live a life of noisy desperation. There had to be more choices out there. When was my real life going to begin? Maybe this was just the rehearsal for when I turned twenty-one in three years.

"You've got to get away from him, away from the play for a few weeks, and rest, relax. You'll join us in London, alone, we'll talk about this," Mom insisted. She had been so crazy about my fiancé in the beginning. Now she was plotting to get rid of him. "You need to experience life before you settle down. The only place you're going to be a child bride is on-stage."

By the time I arrived in England, a few weeks after shooting had begun on *The Prince and the Showgirl*, there'd already been trouble. Mom and Marilyn had called in the big gun, code word "Lee." He'd arrived just before me.

Father had been right when he'd questioned Milton Greene's hiring of Olivier. Sir Laurence and Marilyn were like water and oil. It was her company, her project, and she had hired him. Somehow, in the negotiations with Milton, Olivier's company had wound up producing *her* film. To add to that, he was condescending to her the way they'd been in Hollywood—worse, or it sounded worse with an English accent.

Olivier had talked to other directors who'd worked with Marilyn. Josh had given him detailed instructions about how to handle her. When my father arrived in London, Larry (he insisted modestly on being called Larry) had called and come up to our suite at the Dorchester Hotel to talk to him. My father told him the same things that Josh had. "She's very talented but has no technical training yet, and can be easily thrown off, not because she doesn't want to do it, but because she will panic and freeze when she doesn't know how or is unsure." My father suggested that Olivier's language as an actor was like a foreign one to Marilyn, who didn't have his traditional training. If he talked her language, simply, directly, Pop felt it would make all the difference in their relationship. Marilyn responded to metaphors, examples, not orders. "He talks to me as if he's slumming," Marilyn complained.

After getting all this advice from people who had worked with MM and gotten positive results, he proceeded to ignore it. In fact, he bent over backward to do the exact opposite, like a willful child. I expected it from her, but not from him.

Actors who had worked with Olivier, even friends and admirers, acknowledged that he was totally competitive as a performer; he'd eat anyone up. So there he was, with a huge star, more important than he was, with her entourage and the head of the Actors Studio at her shoulders. Maybe it was predictable that they wouldn't be able to communicate. She had reason to be insecure. She was fighting for a career as a serious actress, and here she was, working with the man considered by many to be the greatest actor in the world. It was her project, but he tried to dominate her, and she reacted and then overreacted. MM could play the part with her eyes shut. Unfortunately Olivier asked her to play it as Vivien had when she'd done it on the London stage.

The first week he directed her to come into a room and "be sexy." Was sugar sweet?

"Lee . . ." She was hysterical. "How do you act sexy? What should I do?" My father was furious with Olivier.

"Maybe he was joking," I suggested timidly. The English had that sardonic, sarcastic humor, I'd noticed.

Whatever he'd meant, it was too late; Marilyn had taken it as a declaration of war.

He insisted on so many false pieces—nose, mustache, monocle, an exaggerated accent—he made his part near caricature. As if that weren't enough, he insisted on having his good side favored in one love scene with Marilyn; it was, of course, the same as her genuinely good side. She had a weakness or unevenness in the chin that she and Whitey, her makeup man over the years, worked on for hours. Mom was aghast, "Olivier has on a fake nose, for God's sake. What difference does it make where they shot him from? He's a great actor. How could he let himself sink to such spitefulness?" I commiserated with her. I remembered that he and I had the same birthday. I hoped Marilyn had forgotten.

She didn't forget much. No matter how many pills she took or how much champagne she downed, she had only temporary sanctuary from her memories. Afterward they returned with renewed power.

Olivier seemed to loathe my mother, who had been one of his biggest fans when the movie began. Her admiration fled in the face of his contempt for her. He thought she was unnecessary—my mother, who was nursemaid, surrogate mother, drama coach. Twenty-four hours a day she was on call; she was expected to coach Marilyn, dole out the pills, bolster her sagging ego, keep her sober enough to work. Arthur, too, seemed not to understand Mom's work with Marilyn and to resent her. Hedda Rosten was there to help as MM's secretary; Hedda felt the situation was too difficult and went home.

Olivier made fun of my mother because he overheard her tell Marilyn, "Think of Frank Sinatra and Coca-Cola," for one shot when Marilyn had to flirt with him. Given that Marilyn didn't trust him and thought he hated her, when she looked at him on camera she had to think of something she liked, which happened to be Sinatra and Coca-Cola.

Marilyn was drinking more now. Her sleeping pills were not working again. She was late, late, later. Mom shouldered the blame for this, too—my mother, who made me get to the theater hours early.

MM's body was loaded with time bombs. She got sick. What went off was her endometriosis. Tissue formed in her womb as a lining, but instead of growing where it was supposed to, it grew in other parts of her insides, causing great pain. She knew that every month when she menstruated, she would have this terrible pain that only drugs could ease. This condition would grow progressively worse unless she had a hysterectomy. She refused to because she wanted children. In the hassle of getting to England, she had run out of medication, so in the middle of the night Delos was sent out to get more, which was infinitely more complicated in England than at home. The pharmacy would dispense only two pills to get her through the night. After so many years, two pills wasn't even an hors d'oeuvre for her. It seemed so ironic that she, the love goddess, should have this horrendous attack from her own reproductive organs every month. My own bouts with menstrual cramps had eased in the last year. I no longer had to lie on the cold bathroom floor, naked, in pain, moaning like a stricken cow, praying, "Dear God, please, let me die." I couldn't imagine facing that every month of my life, and her condition was much worse.

"Susan, she's sick, the girl is really sick. Olivier thinks she's doing this on purpose, but if he saw her in the middle of the night in pain as I have . . . if he just wouldn't smile at her like he was the dentist . . ." This helplessness of my mother's was uncharacteristic. Usually the only thing she was helpless about was her own life.

Just to add more spice, Arthur and Milton were fighting about business aspects of the company. "He's a writer, he should write," Mom said. "Why is he getting pulled into all this?" Obviously Marilyn wanted him involved. She had suddenly decided Milton was not trustworthy. Arthur had to protect her; that's what knights were for.

While Mother faced the "enemy," my father and I went to museums and the theater and walked the streets of London. Elizabethan history was one of my passions, and it was also one of my dad's. Of course, he was interested in art, literature, and plays, and I was interested in the juicy stuff, the romances, intrigues, and beheadings.

As Marilyn got sicker, my father, who was engaged in helping Mother help Marilyn, had no time for me. When I complained, he said, "Darling, it's not that she's more important than you are, it's that she hasn't had the advantages you have. Therefore we have to help her. Mommy needs help. Marilyn has to work."

Mother, always making things right, arranged for other people to escort me around and found young people for me to be with. "Susan, don't be jealous. God knows you wouldn't want her problems, believe me."

I protested. "I'm not jealous, how can you say that?" Tears of indignation sprang to my eyes, and I would have sworn I was telling the truth.

Josh Logan showed up in London and came to see his star. She wouldn't let him into her dressing room and refused to open the door. "Why?" he pleaded.

"You cut my scene in *Bus Stop*. The scene where I cry. You promised me and you cut it." She shook with indignation.

"I didn't have the final cut, Marilyn. I wanted it in, but they wouldn't let me. I fought for it, dear, what could I do?" He adored her. He had championed her. It bewildered him that she could lose faith in him so illogically and unfairly. He apologized anyway. She remained intractable. She had been betrayed, and unless he'd gone with a sword and killed the head of 20th Century-Fox, I don't think she'd have relented. Life was so black and white, all or nothing, for her. Everything that happened was written in capital letters with exclamation points in nonerasable blood. Maybe because she'd come so close to death so many times, with her overdoses and her suicide attempts, life had become more intense for her than for the rest of us. I felt sorry for Josh. I imagined she would be a bad person to cross because you didn't have to do anything. If she decided you had, that was it. She'd get mad and even. She never forgot or forgave. What a strain that must have been, to carry around all those grudges in your memory. All those enemies, real or imagined, who lived rent free in your head.

The Strasbergs were invited to Notely Abbey, the Oliviers' country home. I had the impression it was a peace offering. No one talked about the film that afternoon. It was all flowers, a gleaming silver tea set, the scent of English roses, and the sweetness of Vivien Leigh's perfume wafting behind her as she moved catlike through the well-appointed rooms. The rooms were impeccable, all shine and glow and warmth, subdued, aged colors. Only the people were jarring.

Vivien Leigh was one of my favorite actresses. Olivier I'd wept over in *Wuthering Heights*, so I was totally in awe. The English accents helped. Why did inanities sound better with a British accent than with a Brooklyn one? Maybe I was a snob.

The intimate atmosphere of this impeccably served luncheon was strained, if civil. Vivien seemed nervous, a hummingbird on the wing; she quivered in midair. Olivier talked at us, if not to us. He was charming, with no warmth. My father was reserved; if he'd only had an English accent, I thought. Mother was overcompensating, as usual, pushing, laughing too loud— she had a deep, vibrating laugh—eating too much. Well, at least she was alive. I had the feeling the lunch had been arranged to facilitate some kind of reconciliation with Marilyn. As if my parents could tell her what to do and she'd obey. It was too little, too late. . . .

The next day it was announced in the newspapers that Lady Olivier had suffered a miscarriage. She had run around the house, with Olivier begging her to rest. At one point she'd run upstairs to see if Mom had left her charm necklace in the bathroom. My mother, of course, felt responsible.

"Another bad omen," intoned my mother, doing her Witches of Endor imitation. She was right again.

I wasn't surprised when Marilyn went into crisis again. As one of the world's great drama queens, she didn't need a crisis to be in one. The volcano that lay inside her was ready to erupt at the least provocation. This next one was just closer to home and her heart than the others.

It was dawning on me that maybe we were all perpetual crisis patients in the mental institution we called the world.

My parents had gone to Eggham to visit the Millers. Marilyn was distraught and nervous. As soon as she was alone with them, she broke down, weeping uncontrollably. "It's so terrible," she cried, "so terrible." Between her tears and her anger, it was hard for them to calm her enough to get an idea of what was troubling her. In an almost incoherent torrent, her voice shaking with indignation and hurt, she told them that she'd been looking for her script and found it next to Arthur's notebook diary. Seeing it was left open, she'd read it, and had been mortified to discover that "he was ashamed of me, ashamed to love me, how at first he thought I was an angel, and now he'd realized how he was wrong, I'd disappointed him." She went on about a reference to his first wife. Something about her problems with Olivier being her fault because she was a bitch. Whatever he had written it meant to her that he was taking Olivier's side against her, which she had already suspected. . . .

My parents, forced into the midst of this domestic feud, attempted to bring some sense into it. They encouraged Marilyn to work it out rather than run off. They suggested it might not be the ultimate betrayal. Perhaps she had misinterpreted.

"Marilyn, if you keep a diary, you write all the things you think, good and bad. You don't necessarily mean them," my mother said, searching frantically to dispel the despair. "They're only for him as a writer to see. Don't you think things you wouldn't want anyone else to know?"

"Yeah, but I wouldn't leave my head wide open for the person I was thinking about to see. That's a little too Freudian. He wanted me to see what he really thought about me."

My father calmed her, but he, too, was deeply disturbed that Arthur had just happened to leave his notebook open to something that private. Marilyn was obsessed with finding Freudian theories for everything. She made a mystery of life. She was a mystery. Then she tried to rationalize it away. Mother and I were attracted to Jungian and Reichian concepts. Pop was fascinated by Pavlov. So the family embraced a cross section of modern psychology.

"Even Freud said sometimes a cigar is just a cigar." Mother tried humor.

"This cigar was on purpose, it wasn't an accident," Marilyn insisted.

All her support staff worked to reassure her that this wasn't the ultimate betrayal she felt it was. Though it was painful, it wasn't the end. It was hard to tell if they made any impact. She listened but didn't hear, or she heard without listening. The louder they talked, the softer she listened.

Oscar Wilde wrote "each man kills the thing he loves, some with a bitter look, some with a flattering word. The coward does it with a kiss . . ." This was their honeymoon; Arthur and Marilyn kissed and made up but his hand had begun to write the end.

The crisis passed. Marilyn seemed to forgive and forget. Actually she had dropped the experience into some dark space in her unconscious, where it could sprout like a seed and fertilize future battlegrounds.

My mother dramatized everything. My mother, the drama junkie, longed for a life bigger, more glamorous, than life. She projected passions, intrigues, talent, beauty, a life of Shakespearean proportions. Mom had met her match in Marilyn, the adrenaline addict. Marilyn filled her own life that way. She lived like a legend. I'd thought legends happened after you died.

For me the difference between what I was and what I wanted to be seemed impossibly far apart. I felt like a heretic sometimes because the idea of being just life-size appealed to me.

My father looked as if he missed his books and records. He had acquired cases of new ones. He looked as if he wanted to go home and remove himself from all this *kinderspiel*.

A young Englishman invited me away for the weekend at his family's castle on the White Cliffs of Dover. I hesitated. "Go," Pop urged. "None of this is your problem." His voice implied, I wish it weren't mine, either.

It is a small world. These people knew the Oliviers. They wanted to know all about MM. I couldn't escape.

But I did. Drunk on champagne, laughing into the wind, I leaned over the cliffs as the wind held me in its arms. I forgot everything but that I was young, eager to have a good time, to laugh, to fall in love, to be free. I was sick of being the good little girl, worrying about other people. I was tired of dancing for love and approval.

That day I decided to go home early. I felt selfish because I didn't care what happened with Marilyn, how it turned out. The people in *Anne Frank* had life-and-death problems. I knew who were the heroes, who were the villains, whom to love, whom to hate. Whom to believe.

I returned to New York, clutching my newly acquired possessions under my arm: a Rembrandt etching of a bucolic country scene, and a first edition set of Andrew Lang's fairy-tale books. I still loved fairy tales.

I broke off my engagement. I wanted to risk my life hanging off more cliffs before I settled down. I didn't want to *get* married. It sounded like *get* sick, *get* the measles, *get* the flu. I didn't want anything you caught or that trapped you. Marilyn and Arthur were better off before they *got* married.

When I was little, I'd asked a friend, "What do you think my husbands will be like?" At eight I'd already been anticipating multiple marriages.

Philosophically, Mother commented, "Life goes in circles, my darling girl, and some princes just turn back into frogs." She laughed when she said it, but the dark circles under her eyes belied her smile. On second thought, I wasn't sure which prince Mother had meant, Olivier, Arthur, or my fiancé.

Mother had come home for a week. I never knew if she'd been sent home or had come voluntarily. There was something about a lapsed work permit whose renewal may have been put off by Olivier. Mom may have agreed to leave because she'd been told by the doctor that Marilyn was overly dependent on her. Dr. Kris flew to be with Marilyn that week in England. Mother finally returned when MM refused to work any longer without her. Amazingly, Marilyn looked more beautiful, seemingly untouched by the storms that had swirled around her. When she returned to America, she seemed almost rejuvenated by her survival.

Marilyn went back to work in the classes. She was really consistent about her studies. I was surprised, perhaps because I was mostly consistent about being inconsistent. She was also talking about becoming a mother and wanting to be a good wife. "I just think a woman should take care of a man." When she talked like that, it sounded like an ad for a woman's magazine—nice, but not her. Instead it was her idea of what she'd have to do to be "normal," accepted. Not crazy.

When Marilyn said she wanted children more than anything, I wondered if it was children or the *idea* of children she loved. She responded to young people, but babies were something else. She'd seemed frightened holding a friend's infant, as if the reality intruded on her fantasy. Having a child would validate her as a complete woman in her mind. I knew I would have children too one day; it was what you did unless you were a spinster or someone like Edith Sitwell or Helen Keller or Joan of Arc. Of course she was going to do all the things for her child that had not been done for her. She'd pay attention to it, never send it away, never lock it in a closet. It was strange to hear her talk about being a mother when she seemed such a child herself, but she swore fervently, "I'd love it to death."

She spoke as if a baby would make up for her past. She was always improving those memories. Improvement often meant making it worse, more dramatic. She seemed so free and open about intimate subjects, yet she avoided talking about certain things in her past, at least to me. She never mentioned her first husband, any early friends, or her mother.

DELOS

She avoided anything about her mother. She'd discuss her sister, her half sister, and I think the woman who'd raised her whom she liked, Aunt Ana. She talked about Joe. I told her I liked Joe for her. I thought he was loyal and the best man I'd seen around her. This was after Arthur, and I thought he was good for her, and she just said, "I know, but he was awfully jealous." She told me how he'd busted the door down in Los Angeles, and she was afraid of the jealous Italian bursting out again. She'd say really nasty things about people. She'd talk to one about the other and vice versa. She never said anything bad about you, but she was jealous of you and your bond with Paula since she'd made Paula her mother. And sometimes in an interview she'd say her mother was dead when she wasn't; she was still in that institution.

She got to practice being a mother when her cat was pregnant. The way Marilyn empathized with that cat, she was having the kittens. She made a special bed for her, played music for her.

The night Mitsou went into labor, MM called Norman Rosten at two in the morning to help. He sent love but went back to sleep. Marilyn was alone in the city apartment, calling the vet, who wouldn't come. Finally she reached Delos, who rushed over on an errand of mercy. Marilyn was on her hands and knees, cleaning the white carpet in between kittens. It was a mess. There was blood everywhere, and Hugo, the beagle Arthur had given her, sat up on a chair and howled. The cat delivered every twenty minutes, and she was going crazy and calling the vet, "Help, this is Marilyn."

The next day when he finally showed up and saw her, he said, "My God, if I'd known you were Marilyn Monroe, I'd have come right over."

She was resigned. "I told them, they wouldn't believe me."

She didn't believe who she was either half the time, or maybe she just hadn't decided who she wanted to be when she grew up, the way I had. I was going to be her.

THERE WERE PARATROOPERS IN LITTLE ROCK, Arkansas, and Jack Kerouac's *On the Road* came out, bringing with it beatniks and the beat generation. Sputnik went up. Fourteen-year-old Bobby Fischer became U.S. chess champion. Congress enacted the Civil Rights Act prohibiting discrimination. Toscanini and Bogart died and were mourned; Joseph McCarthy died also, although his death elicited more ambivalent reactions. *West Side Story* opened to unanimous acclaim. "Something's coming, something great, if I can wait . . ." I hummed. I believed every word; it became my mantra, my prayer for the new year.

If life was like wine, this was not forecast to be a vintage year, for Marilyn or me.

"Blanca says 1957 is going to be a difficult year," Mother announced mournfully. Blanca Holmes was the famous

Hollywood astrologer who had done astrology charts of Marilyn and me for the past few years and had this disconcerting habit, like my mother, of usually being right. "It is the stars, the stars above that do govern us," my mother quoted, clasping her bosom and emitting a dark sigh.

Disturbed by her fatalism, I jumped in: "The stars *impel*, Mom, they don't *compel!*" I contradicted her further by quoting back, "The fault, dear Brutus, is *not* in our stars, but in ourselves, that we are underlings." It was funny how Shakespeare, through his characters, argued both sides of any question.

Marilyn and I had the world on a string. What could go wrong?

The people I knew were always undergoing so much fluctuation in their lives—ups, downs, dramatic mood swings. Did everyone go through these kinds of upheavals? Were the butcher, the baker, and the candlestick maker as vulnerable to the tides of emotions and fortunes as my family and friends were? Were these the occupational hazards of being in "show" business? Or was it just the business of being human?

I was looking for some predictable order to things, like the tides, the phases of the moon. Not so predictable that it would be dull, of course. I wanted life to be exciting, like the arrival of spring, and mysterious, like the pull of gravity, only not dangerous, not painful. Marilyn joked, "Only gravity can get me down." Did she mean this literally, like "My breasts are falling"? She wore no bra but slept with one on when she was alone to "keep my muscles strong." Or did she mean "get me down," like depressed?

What I really craved was meaning. What did it all mean? And what could I do about it?

My mother, Marilyn, and I shared a weakness for word plays, puns, and double entendres. We'd get on a roll, trying to top one another. Me: "Mom, this is great sauce." Mom: "I've always been a good *sauce*ress." There's a pause; Marilyn was stymied, unable to keep the ball rolling. Just as I decided to jump in, she made this gleeful noise and said, "Witch kind?"

My father shook his head. He was a pundit, not a punster. We were too corny for him and his Talmudic jokes. But he indulged us the way he did when we gossiped. We loved to gossip. Curiosity killed the cat, but satisfaction revived it. While he read something I couldn't pronounce the name of, we dished the dirt to the strains of Beethoven. Life was actually normal; the question was, for how long?

Marilyn and Arthur rented a house on the ocean until construction on theirs was completed. She wasn't working. She was rested from the toll of her personal and professional life and waiting for a good script to come along. Whenever she was in town, she went to class. Her life seemed to be her main priority, not her career, for a change. She attacked it the way she did her work.

It was the reverse for me; my career was the only active area of my life. My parents and I, mostly my parents, had decided on a script they thought was right for me. *Stage Struck*, a remake of a Katharine Hepburn film, was the story of a young actress who comes to New York and winds up on Broadway and in love. This was my first grown-up part. Henry Fonda and Christopher Plummer had the male leads. I had director approval, so my parents picked young Sidney Lumet. Marilyn wasn't the only one with director approval, and Mom was going to coach me as she had Marilyn.

Marilyn and Arthur were getting ready to move into their new home. They'd bought a two-hundred-acre farm in Connecticut next door to Arthur's old home, which he'd sold while they were in England. The traumatic incident with his diary/notes seemed forgiven, if not forgotten. They appeared to be very happy. Marilyn was playing housewife, cooking, watching Arthur fish in the ocean near the Amagansett house they'd rented till theirs was ready. "The country is wonderful," she enthused. "So quiet . . . sometimes a little too quiet."

Marilyn saw the new friends she'd made since coming east, her "families": the Rostens and their daughter, Patricia; Eli Wallach, whom she'd met at the studio. He'd made her laugh and was a great dancer. Marilyn had been thrilled to receive a photo from one of her heroes, Albert Einstein, signed, "To my dear Marilyn, Love Albert." When she found out that Eli had signed and sent it as a joke, she admitted, "I was a little disappointed."

Mom said, "Relatively disappointed, you mean."

"But, hey, one photo is worth a thousand you-know-whats. But that Eli's a little tricky. I gotta watch out for him."

I thought it was a little sadistic of him. I was sure if Einstein had known about her admiration, he would have sent a photo with love, and would have wanted to meet her, too.

Nobody didn't want to meet Marilyn. Robert Frost, Aldous Huxley, Dame Edith Sitwell, all did. When the first contingent of Russian artists came to America with the thaw in the cold war, my parents gave a huge welcoming party for them. The artists they asked to meet included Joan Crawford, but Marilyn was their favorite. At the party in our home, she enchanted them. She quoted something in Russian that Natalie Wood had taught her when Khrushchev came to America and visited Hollywood. It was something about the workers of America greeting him. It could have been anything, the Russians loved her.

She had a great sense of humor about herself, except when she didn't, and then it was terrible. There was a line in *Anne Frank* Marilyn had identified with, a quote from Goethe she paraphrased with a sigh, "I'm either in the heights of elation or the depths of despair, boy, that guy's got my number."

"Mine too," I chimed in.

"It's the schizophrenic Gemini twins," Mom told us for the hundredth time.

"It feels more like quadruplets or quintuplets . . . whichever is more," Marilyn cracked. She was often deadly serious beneath her humor. "I figure if I laugh, too, people have to laugh with me, not at me."

She had bad days, like the little girl with the curl right in the middle of her forehead. . . .

Her face was puffy, her hair unkempt cotton candy, her blue eyes bloodshot. She was complaining, her voice on the verge of hysteria, rising like the wind. She could have been heard in a theater. "Shit, it's so shitty, life. Sometimes I wonder why I go on. I feel miserable, I hate it, it hurts too much. Death has got to be better than this shit."

"Darling, be grateful for all that shit. As an actress at least you can use it. It makes you a Rockefeller, a Getty. It's actor's gold."

Mom attempted to get the last word in like a slide ball. "Remember, manure fertilizes roses."

Marilyn was tenacious. "Yeah, but it's still shitty."

Mother was more tenacious.

"But at least we're alive to be miserable, that's something we can be grateful for."

Marilyn got more blues than anyone else I knew. When she was with someone, she had the "they don't really love me" blues. When she was alone, it was "the empty bed" blues. When she worked, it turned to "I'm not good enough" blues. "Why was I born? Why am I living?" . . . "Blue Moon," Sinatra's lament, "I've got a right to sing the blues," all those songs she'd listen to by the hour when she was alone. If she wasn't depressed to begin with, half those songs would have been enough to make her depressed. It was true, "Nothing is as potent as cheap music."

She lived half in color, half in black and white. And all that vacillating trying to make up her mind! "I can't help it," she explained. "I've got this Jacuzzi in my head."

"We all have a voice in our heads," Mother announced.

"What voice?" I asked.

"The one that just said 'What voice?' "

"What if you've got more than one?" Marilyn asked anxiously.

"Well, Jung says we have all these persona inside us, male, female, anima, and animus."

"It feels like I've got a committee up there...." Marilyn winced and hit herself on the head.

I was aware of one voice in my head. It kept whispering, "You're not good enough." It seemed there was this little man up there who loved to tell me that I was not good enough, not good enough, not good enough, like the wheels of a train. The little engine that couldn't.

Marilyn was concerned that she was gaining weight. "Somebody shoot me if I blow up anymore ... unless I'm pregnant, then it would be great. I could eat for two and not feel guilty. Wouldn't that be something."

As much as Marilyn wanted to become pregnant, I couldn't picture her with her own baby. She loved children and animals, but she had no patience for herself. She was so harshly self-critical. How would she have patience for a child twenty-four hours a day? Then there was her fear of the pain of childbirth and what it might do to her body. She'd insinuated that her inability to conceive now might be a punishment. I asked Mother what she meant, and she said, "Susan, she's had abortions, I don't know how many." I tried not to look shocked.

"I'm sure God forgives her"—Mom shook her head sadly—"but I'm not sure she forgives herself." Having an abortion seemed as inconceivable to me as having a baby.

She was so free around kids. They were no threat to her. They accepted her as she was, and the child in her came out to play. But that was children, not babies. To have a baby she would have to become a mother ... like her mother, whom she never mentioned. Her mother's presence was omnipotent. Her mother's blood flowed in her veins. She didn't want to be anything like her own tormented, mad mother. Ever. That was clear. She supported her mom in the institution she was in but rarely saw her. However, out of sight was never out of mind. It occurred to me that maybe Marilyn's roles would be her babies.

ANDREAS VOUTSINAS—A Greek director, actor, and student of my father's

Your father was like a child with Marilyn; it was strange for me to be with them. We went to see the Macbeth the Old Vic was doing, and Marilyn talked about how she had wanted to play the role ever since Michael Chekhov in the old days in Hollywood had suggested she do it. She wanted to play it using Lee's vision of Lady Macbeth, and we talked about how, as time goes by, there are roles you can't do anymore, but time also brings other roles. And I said, "You would be a fantastic Mrs. Alving in Ibsen's Ghosts. I wasn't thinking anything personal about her, I just thought of the part. It was a good one for her, that mother with the crazy child. She turned on me in a rage. I don't think she liked me anyway, and she hissed, "You play it. Why don't you play it. I'd never play that kind of part, never a crazy mother and son, you do it," and I realized that just under the surface she carried all that fear inside her.

When Marilyn remarked that she'd like to do Lady Macbeth, she was ridiculed. People said it was another example of how my father was encouraging her to think she was better than she was. This was partially my father's fault, because he never bothered to explain what he would do with her in the part. His vision of Lady Macbeth was of a sensitive, driven, compulsive woman, who used her sexuality and power to get her husband to do these terrible things. It was a side Marilyn possessed, but that she had never shown in her work. Other qualified and respected people had seen the same potential, starting with Michael Chekhov, her acting teacher in Hollywood, who'd played Lear to her Cordelia in his class.

In New York, Marilyn studied briefly with Constance Collier, the English drama coach and actress who'd worked with Katharine Hepburn and Garbo. My parents had sent me to her to prepare the role of Juliet when I was fourteen. She said about Marilyn, "She is a beautiful child . . . she has, this presence, this luminosity, this flickering intelligence . . . it's so fragile and subtle . . . but anyone who thinks this girl is simply another Harlow or harlot, or whatever, is mad. I hope, I really pray, she survives long enough to free the strange, lovely talent that wanders through her like a jailed ghost."

She and Garbo decided Marilyn would be a perfect Ophelia. Dame Edith Sitwell, after meeting her, also wrote about Marilyn's extreme intelligence and sensitivity. She remarked, "What willpower she must have needed in order to remain the human being she was, after the cruelty with which . . . she was treated." Dame Edith felt Marilyn was attacked by people who were "devoid of beauty; by those who could not believe that beauty and gaiety were a part of goodness," and by the "heartless stupidity of those who have never known a great and terrifying poverty."

Marilyn had homed in like a pigeon to my dad as the person with the key to free her from her cage. Marilyn and my father knew it wasn't enough just to free the volcanic subterranean energies that she'd suppressed for so long. She needed to use them. I watched her fight harder and harder to keep her anger sedated with pills, drinks, or sexual exploits. She talked about needing structure, rules, a technique to focus and ground her. She was trying to acknowledge her rebelliousness, resentment, frustration, guilt, self-hatred, instead of turning them against herself with erratic behavior or overdoses. Who could handle all that alone? This is what my father's life was about, the transformation and transmutation of primal energies. As Pop said to MM, "Yes, we want your feelings and sensitivity but we want you to be able to arouse them from the things you consciously give to your imagination, not to what is unconsciously elicited." Energies that were unacknowledged, uncontrolled, could make anyone a tyrant, a fanatic, or mad. If they could be controlled and expressed, they might make you a genius. Marilyn's therapy hadn't supplied the solutions. Love hadn't turned out to be a panacea. Drugs didn't even guarantee her a good night's sleep. Nothing had given her peace of mind or self-esteem. Her work might.

The greatest victory of Marilyn's life so far was her career. Just that she'd done it, that she hadn't been cannibalized by the families and schools and churches and orphanage, or by the studios for whom she was just product. She hadn't died like Jean Harlow or been destroyed like Clara Bow, who, with a nightmare history similar to Marilyn's, had been driven out of the business by her own studio when she was twenty-six years old. She'd married and had children, Marilyn's dream. Still, she'd been overcome by schizophrenia and become a recluse with a nurse, separated from her family, her peers, and the world.

My father believed that Marilyn's work as an actress held the greatest hope of integration for her. It seemed cruelly ironic that the image she'd created, that had brought her all this success, now had become the cocoon that was suffocating her metamorphosis.

Even her detractors would have been impressed to see Marilyn onstage in class. I didn't think that she could do it every night—great actors through the ages had trouble with that—but from what I'd observed, she was going to surprise a lot of people, including herself.

Then she'd have to deal with whether the public would accept the real her. I was sure they would, just as we all had.

She had a lucidity about her dark side. One night, when she'd fought with Arthur and was sleeping over, she sat in the kitchen, her head drooping like a dying swan. "Listen, if I expressed everything inside me, nobody would ever talk to me again. I'd explode like, you know, Hiroshima, and I'd probably kill someone . . . maybe myself. Didn't Shakespeare say . . ."

Her voice was becoming slurred, and I figured she'd taken something. "Your father says Willy said everything, sort of like the Bible. . . . Yeah, 'Hell is empty and all the devils are up here.' He got that right." She clasped her hands to her head in a gesture of such despair that I couldn't look.

She was a sponge; my father had been lecturing about Shakespeare just the day before. She'd soaked it up and taken it personally. She took everything so personally, the way children do. Of course I did, too.

What I couldn't understand was, if she was so smart, why was she so miserable? And why couldn't she do anything about it? I knew so many brilliant people whose lives were a mess.

Criticism of my father and the Method was escalating. Pop ignored it. Mom couldn't; she agonized over it. "Ever since the Group Theatre, they've blamed your father for everything except the Dark Ages. It's because he's such a father figure, and it's the transference, then they reject him." It seemed to me Pop helped his detractors by refusing to explain certain of his theories. If you didn't get it, that was your problem. He understood it.

Mom was in therapy now with a Freudian doctor like Marilyn, and they would name-drop psychological terms. Ego, id, Oedipal, penis envy, Freudian slips, repressed, suppressed, impressed. I used the same terms, not knowing what half of them meant. If Oedipus had a problem with his Mom and Electra had a problem with her dad, then Marilyn with her mother and father would have to be . . . Electrapus?

The few times Marilyn and I talked about therapy, we would end up trying to outdo each other in who was more suggestible and sensitive, who needed therapy more. With her background I knew she would win hands down. Stubbornly I refused to acknowledge defeat. "Well, it's not what happens to you, it's how it feels to you. I bruise more easily than most people because I've got thin skin inside and out."

"When my emotions kick me on the inside and the world kicks me on the outside, where do I go from there?" She had the last word. The image of her being kicked from the inside stayed with me. That's what babies did. Maybe the baby she needed to give birth to was herself.

I started attending the Actors Studio more regularly. I hadn't gone for a while because one morning when I rushed out of the house to go with Pop (he hated to be late), Mother had stopped me, grabbing my hand. "You're going like that with no makeup? You look mousy." It was one of those tossed-away remarks that stuck in my mind. What bothered me particularly was that Marilyn went with no makeup and my mother never criticized her. She was the big glamorous movie star. I was the theater actress. If Marilyn and Audrey Hepburn didn't need makeup, why did I? Obviously because they weren't mousy, and I was. I'd stopped going.

Now I was frantically worried about my performance. The pleasure had deteriorated as I strained to keep it fresh after nearly a year and a half. I hoped at the studio my father might reveal some trick, some secret, to help me, without my having actually to ask him, beg him, to come to my rescue. So I put on mascara and lipstick and went.

The studio was a magical place then. It was like going to a great church, an inspiring experience. The building the Actors Studio had purchased was an old church with a worn brick facade on the west side. At exactly eleven in the morning, twice a week, Tuesdays and Fridays, a hundred actors were in attendance, which was voluntary.

At a few minutes before eleven, actors were milling about downstairs, drinking awful coffee, smoking, and gossiping. Some of the faces might be familiar. In the early days a passerby might see Marlon Brando; Jimmy Dean pulling up on his bike, gunning it for attention; Geraldine Page, looking like an elegant bag lady; and Steve McQueen, another biker fiend. "So dangerous," my mother moaned. "Biker cowboys." Caroll Baker, Anne Bancroft, Shelley Winters ... No one wore makeup. Since most of the young actors couldn't afford anything but jeans, nobody dressed up. Jane Fonda, when she became a member, was an exception. She'd arrive, hair and makeup perfect.

Upstairs in the stage area of the Actors Studio, the set was empty. Behind the scenes you could hear the actors preparing for the scene, relaxing, making sounds, or running lines. Where the pulpit and pews once were was the stage.

Downstairs, the front door opened to admit a small, pale, delicately boned but solid man, dressed in understated, slightly baggy clothes; he was followed closely by a woman, his wife. The waiting actors greeted him; he barely acknowledged them, a nod, a half grunt, as he continued up the steps. If he looked at someone, they saw the intensity of his gaze behind his thick glasses. The man with the laser vision, he seemed to look inside them, through them. As he entered the room, the people already there fell silent, and the ones who had followed him up slipped quickly onto seats. It was the silence of a church when the priest entered.

The stage manager called, "Session," in a loud voice. The lights dimmed. The man walked to a director's chair in the front row. Before it was a small table with an ice-cream glass filled with hot tea and cradled in a silver holder and, next to it, two index cards containing the names of the two scenes to be done and the actors' names. He seated himself, pulled out a small gold travel watch, opened it, placed it in front of him, took the top card, held it to the light, and read the name of the scene in a flat, neutral voice. There was a moment of anticipation, like in a wedding before they say "I do"; everyone held their breath. The lights went out, the scene began. If you watched the man's face, it was difficult to know what he was thinking. He might look up at the ceiling, his lips might tighten, his fingers might play with the pen; otherwise he was still, contained. Scene over, lights on full, he took a sip of tea, cleared his throat. "So, darling, tell me . . . what did you work on? . . ."

That was Friday morning at the Actors Studio. My father was at work.

The actors answered, sometimes reluctantly, sometimes emotionally weeping; a few responded with confidence. Pop might or might not interrupt.

When he finally began to speak, the most amazing transfor-mation took place. That shy, aloof man began to come alive. His comments were a stream of consciousness. He could talk, and he often did, for over an hour in one sentence. But what a sentence. He spoke about the scene, the meaning of the play, the ideas of the author. He leaped up to demonstrate how a baseball pitcher adjusted his body before throwing, to relax himself—spit on his hands, wiggle his behind, he elicited a big laugh from the audience; he demonstrated how Toscanini conducted. His hands—short, stubby, almost child's hands, like mine—became eloquent. He used them to paint pictures, to make music. His dark eyes behind their thick lenses burned with a *feu dévorant*. He was gentle, then harsh, furious at moments when the actor didn't understand. If he yelled, I'd shrink on my seat. I hated it when he lost control like that, and I knew that afterward he would hate it, too. Control was so important to him. Once I asked him, "Why do you scream like that? Why are you so angry with them?"

"Please, darling, I wasn't angry. I was trying to awaken his will. It's asleep, and without it he'll never be a good actor."

He still seemed angry to me. And sometimes the actors were so upset by what he told them.

Shelley Winters said, "Susan, if you go to a doctor and he gives you the right medicine and you're cured, you don't have to like the doctor." All I knew was I would die if he ever screamed at me like that. How could he be so gentle with some people, so kind and generous, and then be so harsh with others? Was it because he perceived something about them, some resistance, some lack of respect for their own talent, some laziness that made him mad? I wasn't getting up there.

Whatever he said or did, he had the capacity to inspire the room, to take it beyond his personality. There were intimations of greatness, of transformation, of possibilities. The actor, the writer, the director, the artist as seer, light bearer, magician, alchemist. With his Lower East Side New York accent, and the funny click in his throat from his perpetual sinus congestion, and the rasp of emotion in his voice, he brought a vision into the room. We became supermen, senses alive, awake, living in the moment, spontaneous, disciplined. He embodied that poem of Kenneth Patchen's, "It's your life, put your soul in it."

He'd go from Greek mythology to Beethoven to Jackie Robinson, then he was on to how you make a fruit salad, preparing it, peeling it, cleaning the fruit, mixing it, step by step. It was the same with preparing a scene, he explained. Mike Nichols said he'd always think of fruit salad when he directed after listening to my dad.

Like all great teachers he told stories, about his family, actors, a man on the street. And he was perceptive. A new student, Ellen Burstyn, was doing an exercise re-creating a cup to train concentration. "Darling," he asked, "do you horseback ride?"

Surprised, she nodded. "How did you know?"

"Because, darling, you're riding that cup too hard."

He was blunt. To Paul Newman, who had repeated a scene he'd done before: "Why did you do this again?"

"Lee, I wanted to improve it."

"Well, darling, you improved it into a failure."

To Annie and Eli Wallach, who had done a scene improvising because they wanted to experiment as actors, he yelled,

"That kind of work is for people without your degree of experience and knowledge. The only reason you should do anything is to enhance the vision and the words of the author." To another actor he explained, "The exercise work is like aspirins, you only use it if you've got a headache."

Marilyn would often slip in late for the session, dressed in jeans, an oversize sweater, dark glasses, a scarf over her head, and a loose coat if it was cold. She could walk the streets of New York dressed like that without attracting attention.

One day after class, we were walking down Broadway. No one was paying attention to Marilyn. Maybe a few eagle-eyed spirits would take a second look—"Could that be . . . no!"—and then go on their way.

"Do you want to see me be her?" she asked casually. Of course we did, though I wasn't sure what she meant. As we watched, she switched on some inner light, the hips swung, and the body rhythm shifted. She whipped off the scarf, revealing her tousled blond hair. It was as if she'd sent out some invisible signal, the way birds fly or bees find honey. "Look! Oh, my God, it can't be! It *is*! Marilyn, Marilyn!"

She looked at us as if to say, See? As people started to close in, she was excited, in her element. She loved this display of her power, and we were properly impressed. They loved her so much, were so fascinated by her. They wanted to touch her, not just look, the way they did with Garbo or the other stars I'd seen accosted. Then they would want a piece of her. It was scary. People were very respectful to me; they asked for my autograph, they said wonderful things, but they didn't desire me that way, they didn't act as if they owned me that way.

A flicker of fear sparked in her eyes as the crowd pressed in. We ran for a taxi. Safe inside, the driver said, looking at Marilyn in the mirror, "You know, you're prettier than Jayne Mansfield. I bet you could be an actress if you wanted."

Secret smiles all around. "Gee, you really think so? Maybe I'll give it a try. Thanks."

Curious, I asked her later if she didn't mind people rushing at her like that. She was very thoughtful before saying, "I wouldn't be anywhere without people like them. The studio didn't do a thing for me until those people asked for me, and they've stuck with me more than most of the guys I've known. Although sometimes"—she was wistful—"it would be nice just to be able to go anywhere and not have to put on a show, you know, entertain. Korea was different. That was the best thing I ever did. But most of the time people expect so much, not just out there"—she waved at the passing streets of New York—"in private."

I'd found common ground. "I know, I hate it when people expect me to be their image of Anne Frank, saintly, perfect. And she wasn't at all, she was more human. She hated her mother sometimes and got mad and was funny with a great sense of humor. But people forget; they treat me as if I'm wrapped in cotton bunting. And if that isn't enough, people expect me to be serious, intellectual, like my dad. . . ."

"It's crazy, isn't it? With me, it's the opposite. Nobody ever thought I was a saint, they expect me to be—the men especially—the happy-go-lucky, anything goes, sexy girl . . . *her*. They go to bed with *her*, and they wake up with *me*, and they feel cheated. I feel for these guys. They expected the rockets red glare, fireworks, and bombs bursting, you know, all that stuff, only I feel sorry for me, too. What can I do? I've got the same anatomy as anyone else, only not even in such great shape. . . ."

It occurred to me that MM's *her* was her Frankenstein. She loved/hated it, but it was her own creation and she was stuck with it, unless Pop or her doctor or her husband could help her get unstuck.

Writers say that sometimes their imaginary characters take over and they can't control them. It was the same for Marilyn—worse. She couldn't crumple the page and throw it away; it was her.

ANDREAS VOUTSINAS

Most of the time I was with her she didn't care if she was recognized. But this time we were in a taxi and the driver freaked out with excitement because he saw Marlene Dietrich. He went on and on, and Marilyn started talking about her contract with Fox, but he wasn't listening, and when we got out he said, "What about that! We actually saw Dietrich!" And I saw Marilyn was annoyed, so I said, "Look right behind you; you've got Marilyn Monroe in your cab." He looked, and then he started to laugh. He didn't recognize her, and she became enraged, as if, if he didn't recognize her, she was nobody.

One cold morning I arrived late at the studio, unnoticed by my mother, who'd saved me a seat up front. I sat next to Marilyn, who'd just arrived too, in the back.

The second scene that morning, performed by a young actress, was the potion scene from *Romeo and Juliet*. She was not as young as me, though. It was important to me that I was still the youngest there; it served as an excuse in my mind for anything I might do wrong. My father had coached, yelled, and encouraged her throughout the scene. She was having trouble expressing her emotions freely, and he wanted her not just to cry, but to jump around and dance, whatever the physical actions were, and to continue the emotion at the same time.

After the scene she tried to explain that she had these impulses in life to throw things and get violent, but that she couldn't do it. He advised her, "You go buy something soft and keep it in your pocket, and whenever you get this impulse to throw something, take it out and throw that."

She started laughing, and he cut in, "This is serious. I know this intelligent, sensitive girl who's very sensible, too, and she keeps things in her closet just for this purpose, things she doesn't want that are old or finished, so she puts them away in her closet, and when she gets frustrated, she goes into the closet and shuts the door and rips these things to pieces. She's like you are in that she has this same overabundance of feelings and emotions, and so this is the way she deals with it very sensibly." As he was explaining this, it dawned on me that he was speaking about me. I felt this hot flush suffuse my body, and then I broke out in a prickling sweat all over. My heart started going kaboom so hard that I was sure everyone would hear and turn to look at me. They all had to know whom he was talking about.

Marilyn was doodling in her notebook and writing barely legible notes, fragments of what my dad had said, half-completed rough sketches of faces, notes to herself: "Don't be nervous . . . stop being afraid . . . shit, what's the matter with me?"

"Can you imagine locking yourself in a closet?" I whispered, pretending it wasn't me in case she suspected.

"I like my bedroom better," she whispered back. "Closets are scary. I was locked in a closet when I was a little girl."

I sent her a look of sympathy, then I wondered if it was true or if she was making it up. If she was lying, I knew Pop's response: "There's a little bit of truth in everything."

I couldn't imagine anyone being so cruel as to lock a child in a closet, a child they loved.

"For some people, love can only be painful," Mom had once told me in a tone of voice that was almost a lament, a complaint addressed to the universe.

I was livid. My father had betrayed me. It wasn't that he'd used me as an example; he'd done that before. It wasn't that he'd said I was overemotional; it was probably true. What enraged me was that he had called me *sensible*. Sensible was the kiss of death. Marilyn, Monty Clift, Kim Stanley, Gerry Page, Marlon, Jimmy Dean, were they sensible? No one we knew who was really talented was sensible. They were closer to *crazy* than to *sensible*. All the people I admired as artists were at the least "closet" revolutionaries, or outsiders, or out-right rebels. None of them had a nodding acquaintance with sensible. My worst fears were confirmed. He didn't think I was a good actress. He didn't think I measured up to the others. He thought I was sensible. The little voice in my head was right; I wasn't good enough. I'd never be.

At home I crept into my closet, shut the door, and cried silently until I became afraid there would be no tears left for that night's performance. Sensible.

Not long after that, I overheard someone congratulating my father on my success, and he acknowledged proudly, "Yes, yes, it shows we did the right thing with her. We always let her express herself."

I was bewildered. How could he consider my shutting myself in a closet expressing myself? I couldn't even cry in front of him without feeling there was something wrong with me. Once not long before this, I'd stood in the hallway outside the study and ripped a towel with my teeth, then torn it with my hands while weeping profusely. He'd gone on reading his book. "What do I have to do for him to take me seriously?" I complained to a friend. "No matter what I do, he ignores me."

One day I'd come out of that closet. I'd talk up and out and back. I might even tell the truth, but not abruptly. My desire to tell the truth was tempered by my need to be liked.

SUSAN'S OFFICIAL BIO—Written by Paula, Delos, and the press agents

The home which produced outstanding teenagers Susan and John Strasberg is interesting to other young people. The dynamic Paula and the philosophic Lee Strasberg have been the foremost American exponents of the Stanislavsky Method of acting. Surrounded by thousands of books and records, their children were automatically brought up on these same principles . . . to bring out the Reality and Truth of the individual. All their impulses were allowed expression, and long before adolescence, the Strasberg children were mature, poised, and considerate. They had never been repressed or frustrated in their formative years and escaped the strange parallel behavior which young people often manifest as their idea of what adults expect of them. Susan and John express any opinion or discuss any subject freely with their parents and are treated as adults.

Each Strasberg respects the other's personality: Susan is poetic, artistic, sympathetic, gay, and amusing; Paula is warm, eager, full-emotioned, and intensely loyal; John is athletic, serious, organizes his studies, and has the future doctor's respect for convention; Lee, tender and paternal with his family, is a past master of drama, literature, art, music, and baseball and apt to be relaxed and miles away in the midst of the most spirited discussion.

Paula and Lee Strasberg take turns awakening John at 6:30 A.M. for breakfast and preparing a lunch to take to the Bronx High School of Science and feeding Susan her late supper at 11:30 P.M. after the theatre and listening to her unwind or check her newly discovered theories of acting with the family's well-thought-out system. Susan was never formally trained and is free to experiment, test her creative impulses, and stretch herself artistically.

As much as I loved doing *Anne Frank*, it now overwhelmed me. After a year and a half the high emotional pitch of the performance had taken a toll on my energy and psyche. I was getting every germ that floated into Manhattan. I was losing weight, unable to eat. The year before, Marilyn had brought Laurence Olivier to see the play. Afterward he'd been very complimentary. As we were taking publicity photos, all smiling our best airline stewardess smiles, I'd pleaded, "Please, Sir Laurence . . ."

"Larry," he'd insisted.

"Please . . . Sir . . . Larry, tell me what you really thought."

He cleared his throat. "Well, dear child," he'd said precisely, "half the effort would have had twice the effect."

I was devastated. My smile evaporated, as did his. The flash popped, and the moment was stamped indelibly on film, and on my ego. Marilyn came to my defense. "She does that because she cares. She wants the people who came to see her to get their money's worth." I was grateful to her.

It was true I'd asked, but he didn't have to tell me. He was supposed to be an English gentleman. I knew how the actress felt who had screamed at my father backstage after her opening night, "How dare you come back here and tell me the truth?"

What had been true then was more true now. I was really pushing. It seemed to me there was something unnatural in doing the same play over and over. In the old days actors at least had rotated plays in repertory. That was one purpose of the work my father was doing, to train you so you could repeat at will on cue whenever you had to, like a dancer or musician or athlete (except the actor doesn't just represent life, he embodies it, so sometimes it's even harder). My parents and I decided it was time for me to leave the play. It felt like leaving home, because that small theater had become my second home, as real to me as my offstage home. And I was aware that in some way I didn't fully understand that I'd been blessed to do this, and leaving a blessing was sad.

As my sense of inadequacy increased as an actress, Marilyn's work in class was improving. She was continuing to surprise the small group of actors who saw her work and to surpass even her own expectations. My father's perception of her innermost self had freed her, whereas his expectations for me were having the reverse effect. After I'd opened in *Anne Frank*, we were sitting one night in the kitchen. He'd just made me one of his famous pineapple ice-cream sodas. On a sugar high, he turned to me and blurted out, "You know, when you're up there, I feel that through you I touch the world." It was too much of a responsibility. What if I let him down? What if, what if . . . My mind was filled with what if's, none of them good.

MM was even on time for class . . . almost. Not always, but a lot of the time. For the past two years Delos had been assigned the unenviable task of getting her there. And we didn't know what magic he worked, but he did it.

DELOS

When I'd first get there she'd be taking one of those long baths because she said she'd had to bathe in the dirty water from her foster families. Well, I realized that after she'd finished bathing, she'd come out and automatically get into bed to lie down, and after that it was impossible to get her moving, good luck. So when she was in there bathing, I'd climb into her bed with my shoes on and be lying there when she came out, so when she'd start to get in, she'd see me and not say anything, she just got dressed and we'd go.

In class she'd pinch me hard if any of the kids from class came what she felt was too close. She'd retreat. She didn't feel comfortable around a lot of people. She sensed things about people she couldn't put into words. She was always nice to me, I think because I didn't take money, she wasn't paying me. With Paula, Ralph, she felt if she paid someone, they were hers. She didn't allow them their independence, and she was suspicious of a lot of people. She was like a crippled child or animal, and at home, she lost all that star glamour. Her clothes were unkempt, I don't know what that maid was doing all the time. She'd give me these strange gifts, the label out of her Maximilian black mink coat, a thirty-five-cent makeup mirror. Once she stuck a pair of those bootie socks you get on a plane in my pocket. In the class she always made noise getting in. I'd go first, and Lee would turn around and look. He'd just throw a tolerant look, indulgent of her; he took us as we were. She was very shy till she got on that stage.

Some of the scenes she did she prepared like MGM screen tests for Cecil B. De Mille. She made elaborate preparations, she wasn't taking any chances. She staged the scene, got the props designed, the set for this one we did, all bookshelves. She was nervous and knocked them over, but we went right on with the scene while we picked up the books. Your mama helped with the acting, and MM brought in a makeup man to do her hair and face. She did the same with the scene from Breakfast at Tiffany's *she did with* Michael Pollard. *Capote wanted her to play that part; she was perfect for it.*

When we did this French scene in class, she picked it— Damaged Goods, *a French boulevard play from the twenties or thirties by Brieux. She played a French prostitute with syphilis who's being hounded by a bureaucrat. Your mother told me, "Delos, you have to hold your own because they're going to be looking at her, so do anything you feel like, improvise, it helps the scene. You're not taking anything away from her, it's just survival." She wore this white Jax silk sheath with nothing on underneath, nipples, smiles, and dimples beaming through at the public, and pearls, not the good pearls from Japan that I took on a student's motorcycle to restring, that she later gave to your mama that you have now, but long costume pearls. And during the scene, as she relaxed, she began to just twirl those pearls, swinging them around, and I unconsciously began to swing my stethoscope. She didn't get mad, but I was getting a lot of laughs. We just went on with the scene; though she was startled at first,* she adjusted. Lee liked the scene, but your mother said, "You looked like two goddamned pinwheels up there going round."

With certain women your father was more permissive, he couldn't say no. He was very warm with Marilyn, and she'd just as easily have kicked one hundred children out of the nest to make room for herself. He was a complicated person, he loved his own world. You were his first baby, he'd have stirrings of fatherhood, but I didn't see him cradling you like Marilyn. Marilyn's life was like the road map of Asia, all those homes, all those neurotic tendencies. In your case, he didn't want any of those neuroses to start, so he'd step on them before it got into temperament. He was actually even more indulgent of Johnny in a way, though they'd fight, he was gentler some ways with Johnny. He expected more from you than from anyone, in acting and in other ways. You didn't see much of your paychecks, they went into the books and records, the house on Fire Island. You took care of him, too, and Paula threw everything she earned into the kitty; you never complained, and they took your money whenever they needed it as their due. Your mama, she could be quite a prima donna. You weren't a prima donna, you had a mother who was one, a stage mama and prima donna, and she had to stage-mother Marilyn, too.

She'd made Paula her mother, but I think she loved Lee more. Poor Paula, she'd work day and night for three hundred dollars a week at first and then have to pick up all her own expenses and Marilyn's entourage's lunch bills and those nightly phone calls to Daddy. Later she earned more but she deserved it. She had no life and Marilyn got Lee for free. You were so sweet and demure then, well, you were sweet later, also, too much so, but much later you became more like your dad than any of the other kids, inscrutable, and you thought like him, too. Both parents loved you very

*much, yet they reminded me of guppies. They'd transferred
you from the uterus to the stomach, and they would eat you
up. It was just the cycle, it wasn't anything against the
babies. They just had their goals, and anybody who got in
the way got utilized for food.*

*Your mother was always giving presents, too, from Seren-
dipity in New York. We'd go there and she'd ooh and ahh
over all these things she wanted to get you, but you were
complaining you didn't want her to do that, so instead she'd
buy things for Marilyn. You'd get jealous, so sometimes
she'd buy you and Marilyn the same thing.*

Spring was in the air, and I was longing for everything spring
makes you long for. Feeling unusually daring, I attended the
opera in a sky-blue-and-gold silk sari Santha Rama Rau, a
friend, had brought me from India. With my hair pulled back
and a red dot in the middle of my forehead, I felt like an Indian
princess in a past life. It was a relief to be someone else.

The consummate disguise artist remained MM. She'd go out
"incognito," a baggy sweater, slacks, three-inch high heels, a
Venetian gondolier's hat, a full-length mink, and huge dark
glasses . . . and act surprised if anyone recognized her. Her
serious nonstar getup was a babushka and skirt and sweater, no
makeup. Then there were those dresses in which she undulated
because they were too tight to just walk in. Or what she called
her black leopard suit, almost like Danskin's, and her schoolgirl
look, pedal pushers, a shirt tied under her bosom, hat perched
on her head. She had an outfit to reflect every mood.

Stage Struck was filmed in New York, and my mother began
to coach me more intensely with readings and bits of business
the way she had Marilyn. I resented it but at the same time I
was afraid to be without her. When I got my first real screen
kiss from Hank Fonda she left me alone. I improvised.

Filming the last scene in the movie, I couldn't stop crying.

The producer, played by Hank, and my character, who'd been in love, were parting. The director said, "She's supposed to be contained, self-controlled." I desperately wanted them to be together. "I can't bear the thought of them alone," I sobbed. Finally he convinced me that we might get back together after the picture was over, and I was able to do the scene.

In class I was working up my courage to do a scene. Marilyn had waited a year before doing her first one. Finally my parents told her, "It's time." I had a month in class before they said, "It's time." When I'd started acting I told my friends, "You have to want to act so hard it hurts. And you have to love every minute of it." There was no way to love it anymore. I was too terrified of failing.

On "the day" I awakened with diarrhea, like an animal in danger; shit and run, only where was I going to run—home? To Mother and Father? And they'd love me whatever I decided to do. Wouldn't they?

ANDREAS

Your father—oh, my God, he loved you. When we did "The Last Tea," the Dorothy Parker short story, before the scene he was perspiring and running around fixing the lights, and then he jumped up again to fix them again. He'd asked me to do this scene with you. Actually he'd come to me and said, "It's time for Susan to do a scene." In those days you were caught in the middle between your mother and father, and if you weren't jealous of someone, she was jealous for you. She pushed you all the time.

The scene I had chosen was an encounter between a young woman and her date at a sidewalk café. I wore my hair long and loose, Veronica Lake-style over one eye, hoping that if I was terrible, I could throw my hair over my face and hide. I had no impression of the scene except that I got my laughs while wanting to throw up. And afterward I was happy my heart was still beating as my father objectively tore the scene and me apart. It was a far cry from his response to Marilyn's first efforts. It felt awful. I was being operated on by my father the doctor, without anesthetic. I didn't want him to be objective, I wanted him to be my daddy. After Pop finished his criticism, the class spontaneously began to offer comments. They loved the scene. They thought I had done a terrific job. They defended me against my dad's critique. He was as flabbergasted as I was.

RODDY MCDOWALL—Actor, friend

I was furious with your father for the way he treated you. He was unnecessarily unkind, a martinet. He was unkind to the person he should have been most kind to. It was awful. Anyway, when one is in that position one has the responsibility of kindness. He had this gloriously original talented person . . . you were, at your age, one of the most talented young people I ever saw, a spirit aglow, a native talent that needed nurturing support. Instead he was bitchy, critical, mean-minded. He tried you in front of people. Also, he was in a position of opulent attention. He could have made an entirely different atmosphere for you. You were so genuinely original, you had a presence that filled the stage, true innocence. I was angry at him, too, furious, because he was very disdainful of me. In those days I was in the company of too many actors, artists, who were at a loss because they needed Lee. They were too dependent on him.

I first met Marilyn when I was doing this final movie at Columbia about Jack Donahue and Marilyn Miller. I was a terrible dancer. They had this procedure, like racehorses.

They brought in a pacer, a young girl with a terrific body, very pretty. She'd stand off to the side and pace me, but she only looked at the floor. We danced together for weeks and never said a word. I asked someone what was the matter with her. They said, "Marilyn doesn't like men. Everybody tries to lay her. . . ." I didn't see her again until Chicago. We were both on tour doing publicity for different movies. I was maybe nineteen or twenty. I was lonely. We met. She was lonely. Those tours were horrendous. We played strip poker that night. She was so sweet and so lonely. When I met her again in New York, I didn't befriend her, I had too many friends like her, I couldn't handle it. Monty [Clift] and she were birds of a feather. They had that despairing neurosis. I admired her, though, personally and professionally.

My mother had been seeing a psychotherapist. I knew my father didn't exactly approve of that. Actually he didn't disapprove, he just didn't want to be involved. She was always trying to include him. Yet it was my father who'd encouraged Marilyn to see a therapist regularly. She'd found Dr. Kris, who happened to live in the same building we did. Three mornings a week MM came by after her sessions and hung out in the kitchen. Since I had developed the habit of sleeping late during the run of the play, we'd pass in the hall as I staggered in for brunch. I'd get mail and phone messages from the secretary, whose office bordered on the kitchen. Everything in our house bordered on the kitchen, even if it was six rooms away. If we were depressed we ate, if we were happy we ate, if we were sick, psychotic, hysterical, we ate more. Feed me, feed me; love me, love me.

The tides turned, bringing me good news. Jerry Wald called from California with an offer to star in his next movie, which began filming in two months. I saw the light at the end of my emotional tunnel. It signaled escape. The film was the adaptation of a best-selling book that had swept the country two years before, *Peyton Place*, a steamy novel about small-town America. Mom adored Jerry. Marilyn spoke well of him, he'd produced *Clash By Night*, one of her early films. Lana Turner was the mother, and they offered me Allison, the daughter, a wonderful part, different from anything I'd done so far, and it was in California. I'd be getting away, and they offered me more money than I'd dreamed of making. I was thrilled and so was Mom. Then we talked to Pop. We had to explain, or rather Mother did, that it was a novel that had been very popular, not *War and Peace* . . . well, not even *Gone With the Wind*. He listened, was silent, and then just looked at us.

"What do you think, Lee?" Mother prodded. He shrugged and went to clean his record with a cloth. "They really want her." They did. Jerry had been calling personally for two days, bypassing my agent, with assurances that my mother was welcome with me, the part would be improved, I'd have everything I needed.

"I don't think so, darling," my father finally responded.

"*Why?*" I was determined not to cry. I was nineteen, getting too old to cry like a baby; it was boring and too predictable. I was like Pavlov's dog—I heard my father say no, and I started to weep.

My mother was not giving up. "This is a lovely part for her. I know after *Anne Frank* and *Stage Struck* it's not the star part in the same way, but she has the time. . . ."

"Ask for more money. It's not enough money for this kind of a project, Twentieth can afford it."

I spoke up. "But it's more money than Marilyn ever made there and—"

He cut me off. "She was under contract, and this is entirely different, darling. If they want you, they'll pay more." He picked up his book; the discussion was closed. Jerry Wald tried his best, but they would not come up with any more than the considerable one hundred and fifty thousand dollars they had offered me.

"Do it anyway," a blasphemous friend suggested.

"How could I? My father said no."

"You're almost twenty years old, you're supporting yourself and the family, just go do it."

"On my own, I couldn't. What if I was terrible?"

"So you've got another movie coming out, you'll go on to the play. Take the chance." He was preaching anarchy!

I went to see Mom's therapist. "Make up your own mind," he said. If I had been able to do that, I wouldn't have come to him. I agonized over my decision. Earlier I had turned down *Until They Sail* and *Gidget*. A young actress called Sandra Dee had gotten her start doing them. This was a better project. I decided to do it and be damned, like Marilyn. I undecided; maybe I'd better not. How could I go against my father? But it was my father who was telling me to be more responsible. I turned the movie down, too scared to make the decision on my own. It was a huge success. The girl who played my part became a star. Nobody ever remembered or cared that I'd said no, except me. I was furious at myself. Why hadn't I been able just once to take the responsibility and do something I wanted to do? Whose life was I living? Whose dreams was I dreaming?

From something my mother had inferred, I'd gathered that as 20th Century-Fox was the studio that had once fired my father, he hadn't been as objective as he might have been when negotiating. Furthermore, he'd been angry at them for the way they'd treated Marilyn. That assuaged my regret. I hadn't passed up this movie because I was a coward. I had sacrificed myself to avenge my father's honor.

MARTY FRIED

At that time you weren't made to use your own instincts. You had normal ones, but you weren't animalistic in the sense that an animal leaves its mother and father and goes on its own and says "Fuck it." You were his daughter and very proud of it, and there were certain rights that come with being a child, automatic rights that were just not present, and you tried to get them. From his point of view, he was mainly interested in you as an instrument, and he felt you weren't doing the training, the work, on a daily consistent basis. As to that film, Peyton Place, he didn't care, he didn't give a damn, it was unimportant to him, it didn't exist. He didn't read those books, that wasn't what he wanted you to do, and he didn't think about whether it might have been good for you personally.

I loved him and he taught me everything, so if what I say sounds terrible, it's said with awareness and love. . . . He was a creature of the theater, a separate breed in a literal sense. You were too young to accept that as an animal that was his nature. Lee was an alien, he was a genius of the theater. Your father walked like a human being, he talked like a human being, but he was a rare case, he was like few others. It's hard to accept that what guided him was this alien brilliant way of looking at a situation. It sounds very small to say he had common sense—who hasn't got it?—but when you have it to the degree that he did, it led to perceptions about the brain and about human behavior, but always applied to acting, not just loving or ordinary life, although outside the family he could do that. You always fought to make him human, maudlin, sentimental, when he was a creature of his own mind, attached to the theater and practical, like Shaw's Saint Joan was practical, where she saw things that no one else did and that was her genius.

I was nineteen and making a living, but a living wasn't a life. Who was going to write my life?

I began rehearsals for my next play, a French romantic comedy by Jean Anouilh. Helen Hayes and Richard Burton were the costars. My role was that of a simple milliner who impersonates an exotic, glamorous woman and falls in love with a prince, Burton. Finally glamour.

Richard Burton had temperament, fire, the face of a slightly depraved angel, and the silver tongue of a poet. His words spun a lovely, dazzling mist inside my brain. It felt wonderful. First he snake-charmed my mind, my body followed soon after.

Helen Hayes was very protective of me. She treated me like her own daughter. I learned later that Pop had gone to her and asked her to help me with the part.

Richard and Helen engaged in a battle for control of the stage, the production, and my body. I was twenty and falling in love with Richard. Where could my loyalties lie? I had prayed for passion. Richard was my answer.

We opened in New York. His wife and children arrived, too late to give me guilt. I was upside down and inside out. I'd lost my mind and come to my senses, all of them, tingling, alive, shooting sparks.

It dawned on me that Richard drank a lot. He loved to drink. He was an alcoholic. Even that seemed romantic. Mother was right, I'd emulate Isadora Duncan and have affairs with the great talents of the century and be a free spirit and express myself.

I waited for protest from my parents about Richard. Mother empathized and enjoyed it. My father ignored it.

Opening night I got a note from Mom, "Have faith," and one from Pop, "For you my darling, *Time Remembered* is the future—not the past." I panicked. Could I live up to *Anne Frank*? I performed constricted with fear, feeling like an automobile whose bolts were too tight, praying no one noticed. When I ran to embrace Mother backstage, she pushed me away, crying, "You were terrible, how could you do this to me?" Pop allowed me to hug him as Mom fled. Marty told me that Dad turned on Mother furiously just before I'd seen her, saying, "How could you let her give that performance?" I was so ashamed of my performance I barely made it to the opening night party.

Stage Struck opened to mixed reviews. I had no reservations, I hated myself. My voice sounded like Donald Duck to me, some of my best scenes were cut, and I loathed the way I looked. I was afraid that if Helen and Richard read my bad reviews, they wouldn't want to appear on the same stage with me. Helen told me she'd been crucified after she did *Caesar and Cleopatra,* and Richard said his early reviews said he was "a no talent flash-in-the-pan." I knew Pop didn't like my performance so none of that helped.

Rebelliously I immersed myself in my affair with Richard. I double-dared anyone to criticize me for that.

Adopting Marilyn's motto, "Life is short, so what the hell," I hoped my actions spoke louder than words.

We made love anywhere we could be alone, at my house and especially in my dressing room. A few months after we had opened I went into Helen Hayes's dressing room, which was next to mine. She wasn't there, but I heard people talking in my dressing room and realized that there was a connecting transom between the two rooms and that you could hear everything going on in mine. I was horrified and bewildered. Why hadn't she said anything, banged on the wall, told my dresser, Kathy, done something? She had lain in her dressing room in the dark, upside down on that slant board she used to relax before and in between shows, and listened to everything that had gone on in my room. She'd heard the fights, seductions, lovemaking, poems, the most private and intimate rituals of my love life. I was humiliated and shocked, for myself and her.

Richard laughed when he found out. "Hypocrite," he sneered. That night he came to my room and made more noise than before, if that was possible. It felt terrible and thrilling. I prayed that Helen would turn up her radio and that God would forgive me.

The next day I got Marty to help me and found an apartment where Richard and I could go to have privacy.

Rich gave me a bracelet inscribed "Forever and a day." I gave him a watch, not engraved with anything because of his wife. Arthur's ring had only said "Forever" to Marilyn. "Forever and a day" was better.

Marilyn showed up at the house in the midst of all this Sturm und Drang, and I poured out the whole story about Helen and Richard and our affair. She said thoughtfully, "Maybe Helen's going through menopause. When women go through that they go crazy, if they aren't already." She had to explain all the technical and medical ramifications. I'd never heard of it, but the way Marilyn said the word *menopause* I knew it was something she was afraid of.

She wanted to know if Burton's reputation as a lover was justified. "I'm not sure," I confessed, "I don't have much to compare him with. But I think he's wonderful." Then I confessed that he exhausted me at times, staying up all night making love, and she explained that if he was drinking, he probably couldn't climax. I was relieved that there was someone I could ask about these things who wouldn't condemn me as wild or a bad girl. When I talked about it to her, sex seemed natural.

Leaning close, she asked, "Have you ever done any of those positions from the *Kama Sutra*?"

"Have you?" I asked.

"Men don't have much imagination," she said, not answering. "I think we women are much freer."

I was thrilled. She'd included me as "we women."

Marilyn and my dad had worked privately on the role of Grushenka. She'd been considered for the part when *The Brothers Karamazov* was being cast. She'd had a brief affair

with Yul Brynner, who was playing the lead. Because of con-
tractual problems, she had no chance of doing it, really. A
European actress got the part.

"Well, what the heck, I'd rather have a baby, right?" Marilyn said. She was pregnant at last! She made plans, thrilled,
euphoric. "I hope my kid's as happy about getting me as I am
about getting him." She wanted a boy, she confessed. "Unless
it's a her, sorry." She patted her flat stomach.

The euphoria was short-lived. She suffered a miscarriage
and was rushed to a New York hospital, where her condition
was diagnosed as a tubular pregnancy. The baby was surgically
terminated.

Soon after that she took an overdose of pills. Arthur found
her comatose. He barely managed to get her to the hospital in
time to save her life. Whenever Marilyn's pain turned into
depression and then into hopelessness, her way of coping was
to escape—any way she could. After all she'd been through,
to lose that baby, I could understand why she'd try to numb
herself. What made no sense to me were all the other times
she'd tried to jailbreak from her body. Life was so mysterious.
Could I ever really know anyone—including myself?

As time passed MM's adopted families rarely met or were
together. She kept the people in her life segregated in cells, the
way revolutionaries do. She was so secretive about certain
things. She loved mystery and drama. Her life was a spy story.
For a number of years she had a room she rented in New York
that no one knew about except my parents and one or two
other people. She would rehearse there, take long baths. It was
barely furnished, someplace where no one could find her, a
lair.

Our home was where she came when she was really down
and out. With most people she tried to hide parts of herself.
She was afraid she'd lose them if they ever saw her demons. We
didn't expect her to be anything, especially normal, because as
Mom reiterated, "After all, normal is not necessarily good, it's

just a numerical statistic that describes what most people are."
We didn't expect her to be sweet or entertaining or witty or
happy. She could listen to music with my father, eat or not
eat, cry, and not have to make up an explanation of why. She
often didn't know. She would just be overtaken with a sudden
darkening of her spirit.

Something began to happen to me whenever I was in a room
with Marilyn. I could have sworn she was getting bigger, taller,
whiter, more expanses of pale flesh, and louder. It felt as if she
were inhaling more air, leaving less for me to breathe. If she
kept expanding like that, there wouldn't be any space left for
me.

Whom could I share such absurd notions with? Not my just-
found analyst; I was busy convincing him of my sanity. Once
I would have shared these fears with Johnny, but the three
years' difference between us was like the Grand Canyon now
that I was out in the world working and traveling. We lived
in the same house in two separate worlds. My career and the
fact that I was worrying about Marilyn, Richard, that my
girlfriends were getting married and having babies. It made me
feel so old. He was in orbit in his own universe. He was angry
and combative, hiding in his room, the music blasting, or "out
doing God knows what"—Mother, the consummate worrier,
wrung her hands—"getting into gang wars."

Physically he slept in our house, but it was as if he'd run
away from home in his head.

JOHNNY

*I was mad. Mother was constantly martyring herself at the
feet of our father's fame, so we absolutely had to revere this
greatness she was sacrificing herself for. You were always
giving everything away to get love, you always felt wrong
taking any credit for yourself, you had to give all the credit*

to our father. You used to run from reality, you ran fast even when you were sitting still.

I kind of said good-bye to the family, literally. I used to dream this recurring dream where Mom and Pop and you died in an airplane crash. Sometimes you lived. I was in my own world, rejecting the theater and angry, trying to defend myself. I missed a lot of Marilyn, although it seemed to me she was trying to defend herself too, and the only way she had of defending herself was in the drugs or drink. She tried to find love a lot, too, and she was willing to do anything for it. I thought the thing that would help her was if she found a doctor capable of treating her. If you need help and you go to a doctor and the doctor can't help you, there's nothing you can do. You have the disease.

Marilyn had my room when she slept over. I didn't volunteer my bed, it was more like "We need your room." That's when you were still at home; after you went away, of course, she got your bed.

In the middle of one of those nights she came into where I was sleeping, and I think she woke me or maybe I was still awake, and she said, "I'm afraid to wake them. I know how hard your daddy works, he needs his sleep." She was out of it, her eyes glazed; she was groggy. She came over to the couch where I was sleeping and we sat there on the couch together. She had on a bathrobe with nothing underneath, and I was thinking, Would I, should I, could I? I was a virgin still, and I sensed she would have done anything for comfort, but she was like a member of the family, and I also sensed there was something precious about her, not something you could touch. We were close, but there was no way it could come from me. We sat there talking for a long time; her speech was slurred, but there was a sense of sensuality because she was drugged, very loose. Maybe if I'd been different . . . She had this look of longing, but there was something else, not attractive, the smell of drugs, her breath was off, whatever, there was this smell coming out of her pores, her skin. She was barely conscious by then; she tried to stand, but she could hardly walk. "I can't sleep," she said. "I can't wake them, can I sit with you?" she repeated. Well, we were, she seemed to be fighting the pills. So we just sat there leaning on one another.

She'd come and sleep over whenever she had problems with Arthur. I always thought maybe Arthur's hatred of Paula was because Marilyn had us, Mom and Pop, as her family to come to. He was such an emotionally dishonest man, I thought. I was just a kid, but I felt that his love for her was the kind an intellectual like him has. He falls in love with this sex symbol and inside him is this contempt of any kind of real sexuality or sensuality, and because she was so sensitive, she sensed it without being able to get hold of it. . . .

Here she's already had the epitome of one kind of world in Hollywood and with DiMaggio, which bored her, and now she comes to New York to educate herself and falls in love with this intellectual, like falling in love with a part of herself she doesn't know. This gives it all to him; he doesn't have a chance. Maybe if they'd both been in therapy, found out who they really were on the deepest level, maybe it could have lasted. She was aggressively angry at him, yet she wasn't direct.

It was crazy. Here you'd achieved all those things at that early age on your own, and she was your image of what you had to be to get love. And because of that, you stopped, you lost trust in yourself.

I wanted Mom's and Pop's approval, too. It was a hard time for me. I was so angry and I also wanted my freedom. I was trying to be my own person, and this kept me outside when I wanted to be inside.

Of all the people who were around, she was special, she was the only one they let live in the house. No one else had *that relationship with Lee. She got all the attention because she was sick; he could give to someone who was sick because there was no threat to his control, and she needed him. Here she was, this big star, sensitive, more than most people realized, and she came to him to learn how to act. You had already done it on your own, for yourself, not him or the family. It was almost as if he were jealous of you, though I know people say parents aren't supposed to be jealous of their children. You had the fame on your own, his fame came through other people. For a giant, a genius, he was also a little man. He was a great teacher, but very insecure as a man; he put the best of himself into his work. He was fascinated by sickness, too, so if he held her, she was sick, so unhappy. At that point I don't think he cared what we did if it didn't reflect on him. People fantasized about her so much that they didn't want to demystify her, as if they owned her. He didn't do that, and she appreciated it. Marilyn was crazy and fucked up, but she was more in contact with reality than most of the people we knew.*

By the end of the year, our home was the Heartbreak Hotel and the honeymooners' haven.

If Marilyn wasn't sleeping in Johnny's bed, Richard was sleeping in mine. We'd fall asleep, intertwined until he'd stagger off to go home. It was ecstasy when we were together, agony when he left. When I'd dreamed of love, I'd had no idea it would feel like that. It surpassed all my expectations. It was so real—realer than real. I'd fallen in love and into the fast lane, and I loved it. Most important, my pain was proof that I was finally an "artist."

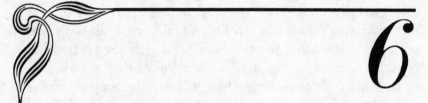

IT WAS 1958. THE COMMON MARKET HAD BEEN FORMED. Civil rights tensions mounted as the Supreme Court ordered states not to delay school desegregation. ·The United States launched *Explorer I*, its first satellite.

The U.S. Marines were sent to Lebanon to restore order. Nelson A. Rockefeller was elected governor of New York. Egypt and Syria formed the United Arab Republic. The Van Allen belts of radiation were discovered to surround the Earth. The Nobel Prize was awarded to the scientists who proved that genes are the units of heredity. We cha-cha-cha'd and sang "Volare, Chanson d'Amour," "That Certain Smile," and "Catch a Falling Star." The smile was Richard's. The falling star was me, falling more and more hopelessly in love with him.

The beatnik movement spread from California to

Europe. I thought Marilyn would have made a great beatnik if she hadn't been who she already was.

For Marilyn and Arthur, the honeymoon seemed to be over. One cold night in midwinter, they came over before the theater. Arthur seemed uncomfortable with my parents, a discomfort bordering on hostility. Marilyn was very upset with him. In front of the other people there, strangers, she treated him terribly—contradicting him with a combative manner, insulting him. He took it, seething silently the way my father might have. They were arguing about something, and finally she screamed at him, "Where's my mink coat? Get me my mink!" As if he were her slave. Arthur fled from the room to get her coat.

Andreas, whom Marilyn didn't particularly like, was very disturbed at the way she had treated her husband. He knew it wasn't his business, but he burst out, "Marilyn, how can you talk to that man that way, like he's shit? It's degrading, it's terrible."

Instantly her mood changed and she looked at him, totally calm. "You think I shouldn't have talked to him like that? Then why didn't he slap me? He should have slapped me." She said this with complete ingenuousness, like a child.

Marilyn was intuitive, and she knew the weaknesses of others. She knew how to find the soft spots. When she felt vulnerable, she could fight dirty, like a street fighter. Probably it was what had helped her survive. It was still painful to watch her get so raw.

Time had been cruel to their love. The mutual adoration of a few years ago had evaporated. Arthur may have taught her about politics, but he didn't seem very well versed in the politics of love. Perhaps she was getting bigger for Arthur, taking up more space in his life, the way she was in mine.

My mother observed all this helplessly. "She's preprogrammed for betrayal and rejection. If anyone looks at her crooked or makes one wrong move or she hears a certain tone in the voice, it reminds her of something that happened before in her childhood. She's off. . . . I try to help her discriminate, but she doesn't listen. She doesn't believe me. If I can get her to laugh, that's the key. Otherwise . . . you don't want to know."

I wanted to pour out *my* troubles. Compassion oozed out of my mother, inspiring friends to call her Mother Courage, Mother Earth. I wanted some of that. In earlier years we'd sit together, my feet in her lap while Mom massaged them after a long day on the set. We'd laugh, sharing confidences and stories. Those days were past.

Somehow Marilyn was business that had become personal and I was personal that had become business. That's the way it felt. I was contributing to the finances of the family. I was younger. I was an actress, too. I was their daughter! Why couldn't I get equal time? Ashamed of my longing, I told no one.

The work came first, like a Chekhov play—"We must work so as not to be fools, to get on with it, to go to Moscow . . ." or Paris or Hollywood or wherever. Calvinist Jews to the core.

In her efforts to bolster Marilyn's confidence, to cut through her self-castigating moods, Mother would exaggerate her own positive viewpoints. They never quite found the balance point. In England, when they'd been filming, Mom's metaphors had grown more and more grandiose as MM's insecurity ballooned. They'd been driving with Olivier to the theater. Marilyn had been worrying that she was losing popularity, that her performance wasn't good enough. She felt that the English press hated her. Finally Mother told Marilyn she was imagining this, that she was more popular than ever. MM wasn't buying it. In desperation Mom said, "Why, you, you're more popular than . . . than . . . Christ even." That had stopped both of them dead. In the front seat, Olivier had gone into shock.

My affair with Richard was becoming masochistic. He was drinking more and sleeping less . . . not necessarily with me.

He'd promise to call and not show up. I'd take a sleeping pill, just like Marilyn. That way I didn't listen for the phone. We fought and made up and fought again: "The sleepless nights, the endless fights . . ." My great romance was deteriorating into a popular song.

The few friends who knew what was taking place urged me to end it while I was still intact. "When the pain is greater than the pleasure, it's time to get out," a male friend advised. They didn't comprehend that as painful as the relationship might be, I was feeling more than I had since my childhood except onstage. In my mind the pleasure and freedom justified the pain.

Richard asked me to marry him. I wondered if he meant it. Everyone said he'd never leave his wife. He only asked when he was drunk. When he was sober he was another person. The transformation was astounding, like the one Marilyn could go through. He became much quieter, much less flamboyant, but nicer. More human.

Sobriety revealed another side of him. He was a scholar, a teacher, like my father. And they were both Scorpios. Rich felt he was boring and ordinary when sober. He and Marilyn had a lot in common. They had giant images to sustain.

I wanted to be with Richard forever, but getting married wasn't part of the scenario I'd envisioned. I didn't know which idea was more terrifying, losing him because he would go home with his family at the end of the play's run or marrying him. I looked at my parents' marriage, I looked at Rich and his wife, at Arthur and Marilyn, Vivien Leigh and Olivier. The message I received from my brain circuits was marriage . . . help . . . trapped.

"This too shall pass," was one of Mom's favorite quotes. "If it's good, it passes, and if it's bad . . ." I refused to believe that, so I paid no attention to her.

Richard announced he was going home to Switzerland, *en*

famille. I wept even in my sleep; pills didn't help. I lost my appetite, fifteen pounds, and I felt I was losing my mind. I railed against God for doing this to me. It was his fault, my parents' fault, his wife's fault. Finally I blamed myself.

Whoever's fault it was, it wasn't fair. I was in misery and he wasn't. He was abandoning me. The more he swore we would be together, the more I wept, because although he protested eternal devotion, he never said how or where or when. He was going home. I'd just been a vacation for him.

I had never even imagined I could feel this bereft, this alone, this nonexistent. When he said good-bye, he had erased me.

Sleepless, I sobbed into the long, slow, quietly cruel hours before dawn. Finally one morning my father heard me. He came into my room and sat down on the bed. I couldn't bear to look at him because I was too ashamed, as if I had betrayed him and the family, not just myself. I knew I had not been good enough again; my lover testified to that with his desertion.

I lay there, distraught, with Pop sitting by my side, not touching or speaking to me. Curled into the fetal position, I protested, "Why, why does it hurt like this? It hurts too much, Daddy. I don't want to hurt like this, I want it to stop, I want to die. . . . Please help me, oh, God . . ."

As the sun rose violet and gold, light reflected in the mirrors in my room. Pop's body made a half-involuntary movement toward me. Unable to stop myself, I fell into his arms. Oh, God, it felt good, dark and safe, to be held by my father. It didn't assuage the sense of dying, but as he began slowly to rock me, as he cradled me in his arms the way he would a baby, I felt real again, validated. His hand was warm against my icy skin, and he consoled me, his voice low, fervent with feeling. "Snookie . . ." It was his childhood name for me. "Snookie"—I laughed through my sobs—"some people need to *be* loved. I'm like that, but others need *to* love; they have this great capacity to love others, to experience passion and the height of human emotions. It's a gift, no one can take it away from you. Be grateful that you can experience this. Some of us can't, and you will have other loves, I promise you."

And he held me with my head nestled into his shoulder until the sun came up, the way he had held Marilyn. At last.

My mother, preparing to join Marilyn in Los Angeles for *Some Like It Hot*, was torn about leaving me in the pitiful state I was in. "You'll laugh at this in ten years, Susan, you'll laugh. Oh, my darling girl, I know it's hard now, but believe me, you will laugh. You think you're going to die, but you'll survive and go on to better things." She was trying to convince herself as well as me. "And he'll be old and drunk, and your life is ahead of you, you're young, just beginning." Her voice was fierce as she embraced me so hard I could barely breathe.

But I felt so old at twenty. I realized that never again would I be that eternally young girl whom age couldn't touch and for whom the years didn't count. No matter what anyone said I knew this was true, just as I knew I would never get over this and that my life was ruined.

My parents had rented a house on the beach in California for the summer. Mother insisted I drive out to the coast with my brother and Marty as baby-sitters.

Most of the trip I spent flat on my back, dazed, in the backseat. Like Sweet Betsy from Pike, I reached California with tears instead of sand in my eyes.

Johnny met Peter Fonda soon after we arrived and disappeared for the rest of the summer. Peter's sister, Jane, was around a lot, long-legged, blond, serious, searching. We urged her to become an actress. She was undecided. Peter and Jane had this strange ambivalent relationship with their father, Henry. They both seemed so rebellious. Her father had treated me more warmly than he did her now. Of course, my father seemed more responsive to Jane than he was to me. There seemed to be some curse that afflicted these fathers; they could respond emotionally to any girl except their own daughter.

Marilyn the day I met her on the set of *There's No Business Like Show Business* with Sidney Skolsky. (From the collection of Steffi Skolsky)

The very young Dennis Hopper, me and Steffi Skolsky at the Chateau Marmont. (From the collection of Steffi Skolsky)

Michael Wager, Pop and me, Ben Gazzara and Frank Corsaro after an Actors Studio session. (Leonard McCombe, *Life* magazine © Time Warner Inc.)

Mom and me in front of a few of Pop's beloved books. Mother is wearing Marilyn's pearls she had received as a surprise gift.

Marilyn radiant in her pearls from Japan. (From the collection of
George Zeno)

Two Geminis at the Actors Studio. (Roy Schatt)

Marilyn looking elegant. She's posing with Warren Fischer, a secret friend she often met on Fridays for drinks at the St. Regis Hotel. (From the collection of Jeanne Avery)

Backstage opening night of *Anne Frank*.
(Leonard McCombe, *Life* magazine © 1955 Time Warner Inc.)

Delos, my friend Annabella and "La Strasberg" (me) in Venice for the film festival.

Tanya and me sweating it out in Montecatini Terme.

Marty and me—cross-country. I'm dressed all in black, mourning for the end of my romance with Richard Burton.

Pop and some students, Susan, Shelley Winters, Andreas Voutsinas and Jane Fonda. (Author's collection)

Opening night. Marilyn looks on as my godfather Anderson Lawler presents me with his mother's sapphire ring. (Leonard McCombe, *Life* magazine © Time Warner Inc.)

Glamour in Hollywood.
(Author's collection)

Me, trying in New York.
(Author's collection)

Mom, Marilyn and Pop. Family night out. (From the collection of George Zeno)

Me and Marilyn listening intently to Pop while Leonard Lyons looks on and Jayne Mansfield moves in to get a picture with Marilyn. (From the collection of George Zeno)

Pop, Johnny, Mom and me at the kitchen table. (© Dennis Stock, Magnum Photos, Inc.)

Richard Burton and me at the kitchen table. (© Dennis Stock, Magnum Photos, Inc.)

Happy times, Laurence Olivier, MM and SS (before the filming of *The Prince and the Showgirl*). (From the collection of George Zeno)

My birthday at Sardi's. Marilyn gave me a Chagall. (From the collection of George Zeno)

Johnny and I read the reviews after *Time Remembered*. (© Dennis Stock, Magnum Photos, Inc.)

Some Like It Hot—Mom and Marilyn cool off between takes. (From the collection of George Zeno)

Whitey, Marilyn's rarely photographed left side (she didn't like it) and Ralph during *The Misfits*. (From the collection of Ralph Roberts)

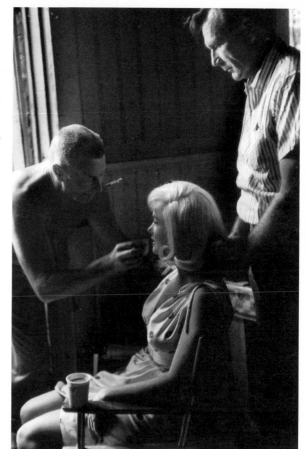

Inspired by Marilyn, me in my Roman décolleté with Pop and the Golden Girl at a benefit. (Bob Gomel, *Life* Magazine © Time Warner Inc.)

Private smile on *The Misfits*. When Marilyn saw this picture she told Ralph, "It's the only real smile I've had on this whole film." (From the collection of Ralph Roberts)

Desert, *The Misfits*, 1961.
(Magnum Photos, Inc.)

Actress and coach break-
ing down a script. (John
Bryson)

My father and Marilyn in the light from "a ribbon of dreams." (From the collection of James Haspiel)

Our house was a constant flow of people seeking advice, as they had in New York. Most of the actors from the Actors Studio who were working in the West came rushing to sit at my father's feet.

Marilyn had Ralph to massage her, a makeup woman, hair-dresser, press representative, secretary, Rudy (her chauffeur), her stand-in, and an attentive Arthur standing guard. She still needed my mother and father on twenty-four-hour call. My arrival went not unnoticed, but was sloughed off, except for my mother's usual all-embracing concern and affection. Enveloping me in her arms, my head sinking onto her full, cloudlike bosom, I felt the constricting cold spell around my heart begin to dissolve. As the pain began to lift, the anger began to flood me. I was still a mess, but I was now a mad mess instead of a martyred mess.

As my ego staggered to its feet, I determined that Richard, who hadn't answered my barrage of letters, would get in touch with me. I plotted with Marty how to get his immediate response. We decided on a letter announcing that if I didn't hear from him in a week, I'd call him at home. I mailed it air mail special delivery and waited.

Mother would come back to the beach at night wiped out. There were horrible problems on the set. Marilyn was showing up hours late. Director Billy Wilder and the other actors were upset because she was requiring up to thirty takes for a simple scene. Her concentration was off.

"Why can't they handle this the way Josh Logan did?" Mom was resigned. "He respected her, and Marilyn sensed it. She's wonderful in this part; we're really giving it some character, some humanity, so it's not just another blonde. It's written as a supporting part, but she'll make it a star one. They treat her like a star on the surface, but underneath there's this contempt, as if 'Who does she think she is?' With her antennas, she feels it, and my God, it's hard work and she's been sick. . . .

Just between us I think she may be pregnant." When I visited on the set, the antagonisms were not apparent to me.

Costar Tony Curtis, in a dark screening room watching the rushes, cracked, "Kissing her was like kissing Hitler."

Mother burst into tears. "Tony, how could you, how could you say a thing like that?"

He replied, "You work with her as an actor, see how you feel, Paula."

"He doesn't understand." She was inconsolable. "He doesn't understand." My mother had identified with Marilyn the way she did with me. She tried to keep her objectivity, to be like my father. It was a losing battle. "Just do the work, darling," my father ordered, sending her back to the front lines while he sat in the sun, looking out at the ocean, reading and listening to one of his favorite records he'd brought with him.

The paradox of human nature was incomprehensible to me. I was dying of a broken heart, how could I also be dying to go to Will Wright's for a milk shake? How could Marilyn be on top of the world one minute and down in the dumps the next? How could she long for a baby and continue to abuse her body? Where did this come from—this ability to feel two things at once, to crave life and long for extinction? How could life sound and smell and feel and taste so sweet when I knew it was over?

Were there two personalities inside all of us, two selves at war with one another—one the affirmer, the other the denier? And what about the other part of me that just observed, objective, dispassionate, the watcher. Which one was the real me?

Marilyn and Arthur came to visit, to play on the beach. Watching them, I was torn between jealousy and admiration for the love they shared. The chill of months before seemed to have passed. Now it was again, "Art, Arturo, Papa, Popsie."

Marilyn had nicknames for everyone: Mom was "Black Bart" in her pointed black sun hats and black muumuu; my father was "the great white father"; a press representative was

"Sybil" for sibling rivalry; Marlon Brando was "Carlo"; her friend Norman Rosten was "Claude" because he looked like Claude Rains. Marilyn's nom de plume for herself was "Zelda Zonk."

Her life was an espionage novel. She'd talk to one group of friends about another. She had secret friends no one knew about unless you ran into them accidentally. Then there were the secrets locked in her head. She said she dreamed what Brueghel and Bosch painted, depraved demons, orgies, the underworld. So many secrets to remember; what if she forgot?

She always called me "Susie." I would have liked a nickname, too.

Marilyn, Arthur, and I watched the grunions run that summer. These tiny phosphorescent fish come up on land to lay eggs in the sand. They turn the ocean into a shimmering mirage of light and foam, illuminating the waves as they surf-ride them in. It's legal to catch them while they're on shore, and we had bucketsful. Marilyn and I insisted everyone throw them back in the ocean. We ran into the water, letting the fish play over our feet, kicking luminous sprays of water into the air. She was as glowing as the fish, painted in invisible star ink that glowed in the dark.

Champagne, sun, and laughter, Marilyn was pregnant and thrilled. Richard had finally called me. I decided to live . . . just to spite him.

MARTY

I drove her around a lot that summer. Marilyn to me was just not sexy. When I saw her in the movies, I watched her like any other guy, but because I knew her and had been around her . . . I never said, Gee, I'd love to . . . you know. . . . Most men if she ever said yes, they'd have a heart attack!

She couldn't just know somebody. She didn't want to be accepted on terms that she was Marilyn Monroe or have you be attracted to her or have a friendship with her because she was a star. So no matter how much someone liked her, she always put something else into it.

I'd been on the set a lot with Paula, and she asked me to drive Marilyn to the airport in that little red Thunderbird. I think Paula had told her that I was an orphan too and had been in foster homes. I knew her well enough to have a conversation with her, but not to initiate it. I felt that, and she sensed that and didn't like it, and she started this conversation, saying, "I know you've been fostered out, just like I was."

And we talked about foster parents and what they're in it for, a lot of them, the money. We talked about the good ones and the bad people, and every time I thought the conversation was finished, she wouldn't let it go, it was like we were bonding here. I didn't mind talking about it but wished she'd stop because it turned out my situation was a lot worse than hers. I had nothing but negative things to say about the whole system. I was in New York and I thought it was all a racket, but she kept pointing out positive things she'd learned.

She bought me a record the next time I drove her. She was so fucking sweet. I took her to a record shop, and she bought me a classical record, two records, one was Respighi Overtures, the other an Albinoni, and I thought, What does she know about classical music? Lee had taught me, you know, so I said, "Oh, that's very nice." I didn't know the pieces, but I mean, a record of overtures? And I'd never heard of Albinoni, but she really liked it, she played it all the time, music you heard in the movies. It was very moving. Later I used it in a play I directed.

One day I picked her up at the hotel she was staying at

with Arthur. I was waiting for her. It was then I realized things weren't right. He was making this effort to talk to me, and I'd met him and knew he didn't care about me. I thought, Why is he making friends with me out of the blue? I could feel he was trying to connect to me. Suddenly I realized he didn't want to make enemies of any more friends of hers.

She used to tell me little things that were so revealing, sexual things. She liked to talk indirectly about sex. She told me, "I have to initiate relationships. With men it's hands off. They don't know what the hell to do with me." She was so open about this. She told me she almost had to say "Do you want to fuck?" to get it out of the way. "After they get me, they don't know what to do, either."

She told me, "Arthur is so vulnerable, and he hates being in a vulnerable position." She indicated she would manipulate him. She said, "Arthur hates being vulnerable because he hates being out of control," and it was clear to me she meant sexually because the most vulnerable moment for a man is when he can't stop anymore. When he's crazy. Marilyn knew how to do that.

Of course, Marilyn never felt guilty about sex. She used it. It's not pornographic or dirty. She knew men, she knew how to deal with them. She'd started early, she wasn't passive, and she was a doer. The power she had gave her great pleasure. She enjoyed it like a game. She was not what everyone thought. I think Lee knew that because she shared an awful lot with him, more than with her doctor. He said no to her, but she played and flirted with him, too.

With her there were lots of half-truths, sad stories. Her stories were not as sad as she said. The early days in Hollywood hadn't been that sad, how she was taken advantage of. She wasn't a virgin. She knew by the time of the nude calendar how to feel good with the lights on.

I was brought up on the streets, too, and whenever anyone would give me sympathy, I'd say, "No, it's okay," but I liked it because they were giving all this attention to me and it's hard not to play up to that. When you're out there as a kid you enjoy a lot of it; it's afterward you look and say, "Boy, how did I survive that?" Marilyn always had protection, she always had the wing of someone who really cared for her. It wasn't that she took advantage of what she looked like—she couldn't help that—but most people automatically did things for her because of her looks and encouraged her to take advantage of that. Her friends, even her doctor, told her she should only do light comedies. Lee was the only person who encouraged her to be true to her sensitivity, to her real self. . . .

Later Lee wanted her to be Natasha in Three Sisters. *Chekhov had written that there were four heroines and the fourth was Natasha. Lee said everyone played her as the villainess, and Chekhov said she wasn't the villain, she was the only survivor. She was the only one who went on, had children. She was pragmatic and terribly sexy. That's why André can't go to Moscow. He can't not go to bed with her. She touches him and it's all over. But when it came down to casting her, Lee said, "I can't get Marilyn because Kim [Stanley, who was playing the lead] will walk," and she was more important for the play. Your father loved raw jewels like Julie, John Garfield, like Marilyn.*

Can you imagine knowing that you could do more than people thought you could, but people are always telling you you're just a funny, sexy kid, and then the world's greatest authority on acting tells you that you can do Rain and other things you hadn't dared imagine? It had to be like double jeopardy, breaking one mold while trying to form another, and all the time you're this huge money

*commodity to people who don't want you to change, even
if it's to get better.*

Johnny, Dad, and I headed home. This was Johnny's last
year at the Bronx High School of Science. Classes were starting
for the fall sessions of the Actors Studio and my dad's private
classes. I got an offer to do a play for the City Centre, which
was to represent America in the U.S. pavilion of the World's
Fair that winter in Brussels.

The play was William Saroyan's *Time of Your Life*. Franchot
Tone and I were working together again; we'd done *Caesar
and Cleopatra* many summers before. I was playing Kitty, the
young prostitute. Most important, I'd be one hour's plane ride
from London, where Richard would be filming *Look Back in
Anger*. It was *bershert*! Unless, he whom God wants to punish,
he answers his prayers.

Some Like It Hot was complete, and everyone was burned
out by the effort. Mother was home for the holidays. Marilyn
lost the child she had conceived shortly before the completion
of filming. This was her second miscarriage in as many years.

For Marilyn the miscarriage was a personal failure, a sign
that she was unloved, cursed by the universe.

That New Year's Eve we had our celebrated party. It had
become such an event that people like Salvador Dalí called to
be invited. My mother's "salon" had fulfilled her earlier
dreams, surpassed them, even. The thing that made it so special
was the mixture of people—starving actors and writers and
directors, the famous, the infamous, the young, from my brother and his friends to the elder statesmen. Mom asked the pretti-
est girls at the Actors Studio and classes to come and help out.
The food was not fancy, but it was plentiful. Our old dining
room table moaned and groaned, and the champagne and drinks
were abundant.

RADIE HARRIS—In her "Broadway Ballyhoo" column

I caught a fleeing glimpse of Susie, in a white sari, as I struggled past Bill Inge, Pat Neal, Huntington Hartford, Marjorie Steele, Geoff Horne, Peter Ustinov, and Caroll Baker (who takes up room for two now, and there was just enough space to breathe where she and her heir apparent were squeezed in the entrance hall), and suddenly I found myself in a roomful of male teenagers! Seems that 15-year-old Johnny Strasberg had invited his 38 classmates to his parents' New Year's Eve party (without apprising them of this magnanimous gesture), but they were holding their own exclusive soiree in Johnny's bedroom, being entertained by two femme "crashers" named Judy Holliday and Siobhan McKenna! . . .

But there had been a pall over this year. I was in mourning for my lost love. Marilyn was in mourning for her lost child.

7

FIDEL CASTRO BECAME PREMIER OF CUBA. Alaska and Hawaii became the forty-ninth and fiftieth states. The Dalai Lama, driven out by the Red Chinese, sought asylum in India. Lorraine Hansberry's play *Raisin in the Sun* was the first drama by a black woman on Broadway. Scientists began listening for radio signals from intelligent life in outer space. Pierre Teilhard de Chardin's book, *The Phenomenon of Man*, was published. In it he said, "Some day . . . we will harness for God the energies of love; and then for the second time in the history of the world, man will have discovered fire." I wept. Mahalia Jackson sang "He's Got the Whole World in His Hands." I cried again. *The Miracle Worker* came out; Marilyn and I both cried and agreed that if Helen Keller, deaf, dumb, and blind, could affirm that "life is a daring adventure or nothing," who were we to say less? "High Hopes" was high on

"Your Hit Parade" and in our hearts: Marilyn's with her dreams of fulfillment in domestic bliss, mine with dreams of reunion with the love of my life and being healed in his arms. D. H. Lawrence's *Lady Chatterley's Lover*, released for publication after a thirty-year ban for obscenity, was banned from the mail. "They'd probably ban me from the males too if they could," Marilyn joked.

Time flies even when you're not having fun.

When I flew in from Brussels, London was shrouded in fog, just like in an espionage novel. Richard and I were reunited at Shepperton Studios.

He had "no time" for me. He was afraid that "someone might tell his wife," and "God," he was sorry, but he couldn't even take me into the hotel or have a drink. He had to get home. It was incomprehensible to me. Why had he encouraged me to come? He was polite to me, as if I were a stranger. Yet he swore his undying love for me while saying good-bye again. I felt humiliated, degraded. I watched his car drive off into the gray swirls of smoke surrounding us. He had abandoned me for the second time.

I walked aimlessly, mindlessly, through the streets. The fog lifted for a moment, and I saw I was on Waterloo Bridge. As I looked into the murky waters, for the first time I understood how Marilyn could have wanted to kill herself. So did I. Death seemed to offer peace and an absence of pain. As I leaned farther over the side of the bridge, willing myself to surrender to the dark river, to slip, to let go, I thought wildly, I'm going to die. I'm going to drown. I won't have to feel anything, thank God. And then another thought flashed: My coat, my new mink coat I just bought myself, all that money. It's going to get ruined; I have to take it off. As I stood up to slip off my coat, a rush of cold air shot through my body. My head cleared. Frightened, but glad to be alive, I fled, back to the warmth of the hotel.

I knew my parents would tell me that one day I'd be able

to use this suffering, that it wasn't a total loss, but I was too disheartened and wallowing in self-pity even to talk to them about it. I wasn't sure anymore that all people were really good at heart. People's hearts were so hidden, such mysteries, and as Marilyn had said, even if I could use this in my work, it was still "shit."

Mother had flown to Europe to be with me to help out on the show. She wrote home now: "Susan marvelous! Wonderful audience reaction. Franchot better than I've ever seen him. Production—? Paula." It was signed, as always, with a drawing of a heart with an arrow through it. Then she added, "I worked hard and got results." Not a word about Richard and me. It didn't fit her image of me as a femme fatale for me to be unceremoniously dumped.

Back in New York, I rushed to my psychiatrist to tell him my latest dream:

I was lying on my bed in an all-white, pristine bedroom, white walls, carpet, bedspread, furniture. In back of the bed was a large window covered with sheer lace curtains. The window was open, and a breeze stirred the drapes. I heard heavy footsteps outside the window. They shook the walls. I looked up. An enormous gray elephant was backing up into my window until his behind filled the frame.

I was flabbergasted. Without warning the pachyderm broke wind. Its huge gust of hot air filled the room with an awful stink. It will go away soon, I thought. It's just air.

Suddenly this animal dumped an enormous load of shit on my beautiful white bedspread. "That's it!" I said, jumping up. "When an elephant shits on your bed, it's time to get out."

My analyst smiled and commented, "You're more in contact when you're sleeping than when you're awake."

Marty drove Mom and Pop and me to visit Arthur and Marilyn—actually Marilyn, since there was a widening split between Arthur and my parents. Their farm was much simpler than I'd imagined it, no white or mirrors to reflect Marilyn. It was beautiful in the country, quiet, clean, healing. I felt I could breathe freely. Marilyn didn't seem to appreciate the surroundings, although in the past she'd raved about the virtues and advantages of country living. "There's a lot of time to think, and you know it's all in the head, they say." Now she was less enchanted with it. I think empty hours weighed on her mind. How many more times could she move the furniture around?

After a two-and-one-half-hour drive, Arthur barely greeted us. Marilyn finally drifted downstairs an hour after we'd arrived. When she joined us, she still wasn't "there." She'd told me that most of her life "men weren't all there." Now it was her turn. She cheered up enough to have champagne, and we laughed, but both seemed slightly flat.

We got the "grand tour," during which she excitedly showed us the improvements she'd made in the house. I got the impression these meant more to her than Arthur. This was the first home she'd ever owned with anyone (she'd never had one of her own, either). Like an animal, with every change she made she was leaving her spore, marking "MM was here!"

Pop and Arthur were certainly alike. Arthur was as silent as my father, as antisocial, as withdrawn; maybe Arthur didn't like him because he saw himself.

Marilyn's idea of playing hostess was a little lacking. In a movie the prop department prepares the meal for you, sets the table. You just come in and act. She needed a prop man for her life. I didn't think Arthur liked that part so much. I didn't blame him. He was supposed to be the costar.

She wasn't gazing in adoration at him anymore. She was giving him a much more guarded look. He didn't seem very happy, either; his overt displays of affection were missing. Mother was trying too hard, it was exhausting, and neither Marilyn nor Arthur fed us. Finally she went to the freezer and pulled out a hunk of meat to defrost, and Marty and I looked at one another. The steak would take hours to thaw. We excused ourselves and drove to get food at a nearby county fair we'd passed. Friend or foe, good times or bad, the one thing you could count on at the Strasbergs' was being fed, emotionally, intellectually, or literally. It was unimaginable to me that they didn't feed us. If my mother was dying, she'd make sure you got a good meal.

I knew Arthur didn't like Mom and Pop, but I hadn't realized till then the extent of his antagonism. I had nothing to do with all that, yet he'd treated me as coldly as he had them. Guilt by association? It surprised me because he was reputed to be such a liberal and I'd thought they were supposed to be compassionate. I guessed maybe it was easier to have compassion for the masses of people you didn't have to know and talk to. When we left Marilyn begged us, "Come back soon." But once had been enough and we never did. Marilyn had seemed so restless because she wasn't working that I thanked God I had a job.

The Actors Studio had begun producing plays with the idea of building a national theater with a floating company of actors. *The Shadow of a Gunman*, the Sean O'Casey play I'd performed in at the studio a few years before, was the next production. I was reprising the young Irish girl I'd played before. It should have been easy.

More nervous than ever, I was frightened that I'd be unable to produce whatever I'd done the last time. I also felt obligated to make up for my last performance, which I knew Pop had considered a failure.

A week before we opened, the studio board saw the play and decided to replace the director. The new director was my father.

Pop was working with me without Mother running interference. As my self-esteem plummeted as I anticipated failing him,

I regretted not jumping off Waterloo Bridge when I'd had the chance. In my hysteria I became so tense that I totally lost my voice—the voice everyone had loved. It seemed to be the first part of me to break down whenever I was in trouble.

"What's the matter with me?" I wrote my mother on the pad I carried around to communicate on so I'd rest my vocal cords. I doodled on the yellow pages, "Who's the matter with me? . . ." I knew Marilyn would say it was "very Freudian."

Was this the primal panic that Marilyn experienced when she froze before the camera? If it was, I could sympathize with her trying to obliterate this bottomless grinding anticipation with whatever she could get her hands on.

She'd said in the midst of one of her crises, "I'd almost rather be crazy than feel this anxiety churning inside me; I'd rather be dead."

I'd thought she was exaggerating. She hadn't been. I wasn't terrified just of what was happening, but of what might happen and what *had* happened.

All I knew was I wanted my parents to love me even if I gave a rotten performance, and I didn't think that was possible.

My voice returned, with professional help from a friend who did bioenergetics work. The play got decent reviews, but . . . I was starting to hate acting.

Marilyn had collapsed in tears during *Bus Stop* at the end of a long day. "I can't handle this, I can't take it anymore, I hate it so much. Why do I do this? I want some man to take me away from this. [She was waiting for Arthur to be divorced then.] I want to lead a normal life."

I'd heard Maestro Arturo Toscanini scream at his orchestra, "I hate to conduct, I hate it because I suffer too much, you look at me like I am crazy. No. I hate it!"

How could we all hate something we loved so much?

I was invited to Jane Fonda and Andreas Voutsinas's house. They had met in class. He became her mentor and coach, and she was deeply influenced by him, to the chagrin of her father and other friends. But Jane had a mind of her own, a strong one I admired. Jane was in her early perfection period. She was one of the few people besides me who came to the Actors Studio dressed and in full makeup. She took ballet classes every day, even if she'd been up all night. I knew my parents admired this iron will and discipline. Mother used to try and arouse my competitive spirit by extolling Jane's fortitude and commitment.

That night, when I arrived, I was surprised to see my father there. I hadn't known he was invited. Also present was an actress from the Actors Studio whom I didn't know very well. As the minutes passed I realized she and my father were "together." She was so familiar with Pop that she seemed almost proprietary.

After dinner we all sat in the living room. I watched my father, who was seated across from me on a couch. Next to him was Annie, the blond actress. She began to inch closer and closer to him. When she was practically on top of him, she began to kiss and fondle him. He sat there passively. He didn't get up. He didn't move away. There was no indication of what was going through his mind, but he just sat there and allowed her to do whatever she wanted. The walls began to close in on me until I thought I was going to pass out.

She was practically raping him there in the living room. Panicked, I had no idea what to do. I wanted desperately to do the right thing. Committing murder at a dinner party wasn't the right thing. Inside I was like a cyclone, outside I was as quiet as the eye of that cyclone. Everything was inside out. I tried to be nice, but it's hard to be nice when you want to kill someone.

Finally I burst into tears and ran out of the apartment. I was furious with everyone, Pop, her, and with Andreas for inviting me.

How could he have done this? My father, who had such purity of intent in his work; my father, whom I tried so desperately to please; my father, who barely kissed or touched me . . . The idol I'd made of him was crumbling. Maybe this was what Marilyn felt with Arthur, this sense of betrayal. It was different from what I'd felt with a lover: worse. Men were one thing, my father was another. I didn't understand anything. The higher I climbed, in terms of money, success, and fame, the more my life was falling apart, just like Marilyn's.

I began to remember how Dad had talked about women and sensual things, food, the texture of things, silk, velvet, skin, and how in class he used erotic imagery when he directed a love scene. Of course he enjoyed all those women and girls wanting to make love to him, or at least to whom and what he represented to them. I realized my father was still in some way the little boy from the Bronx; he was seduced by the glitter and the lights and the high living just like I was.

The worst part was not the anger or the pain or even the deep disappointment and disillusionment I felt. Something had been lost, something irretrievable I couldn't name; but I felt the dark, empty space it left inside me. I couldn't separate Pop's work from his life. He had been the purest in morals, the clearest in beliefs about standards and behavior. He'd seemed so self-abnegating, I couldn't accept his being needy or this human. He'd lied somehow, and everything he'd ever taught me became suspect. And because I had been a witness, I felt I bore the responsibility along with him.

I wanted my mother to have revenge for all her years of sacrifice. I wanted her to have some pleasure instead of the backseat life she had. I wanted her to have love affairs with all the beautiful young actors she adopted who adored her. It was a pipe dream, I knew. With her excess weight, her low self-esteem as a woman, and the way she felt about my father and herself, it would never happen. She'd never have an affair, but I could. I began deliberately to flirt with my father's favorite male protégés in front of him. I necked and petted, kissing passionately, shamelessly, in front of my father. Daring him to what? Of course I should have known he would never react. Whatever he felt was hidden from me. I didn't go to bed with these students; most of them I didn't even like particularly. So on top of everything I hated myself for behaving like that.

For the next year, I thought about confronting my father, but I didn't. I was an emotional coward, one more reason to despise myself. But so was he. And he never said one word about what had happened, and I never told anyone, not even my best friend. Maybe Marilyn had so many secrets because some things were better hidden.

DELOS

You can truthfully say Lee was a matrimonial bed husband; later, too. He would coach Paula till early morning on how to launch trial balloons; she would talk like the southern wife of Kuwaiti is now doing to the press. When the Group Theatre and other actors would dump on Paula, Lee would be quiet and let her take the flak; he never came out to defend her. The same thing happened later; and Lee would avoid discussion and act uninvolved, as if the whole thing weren't important.

Paula's request from the West Coast with Marilyn was, She wanted me beside him at the studio, to keep pretty ladies at a distance. I quit lunching with them on Eighth Avenue after sessions, as I could have gotten cancers from gals elbowing me out of their way. He was Ado Annie, who "cain't say 'No.'"

I knew which nubile maidens would interest Lee, but he

never voiced it and he whispered exactly nothing to them. He was like Leslie Howard; he submitted gracefully and once involved he played the scene with gusto, but attack and seduction came from the lady. I always suspected minimal foreplay and even less postproduction.

Lee could be very seductive and attentive when hooking you, and once you were securely in his corner, he relaxed and went back to being self-involved. When I came from Kansas you were in Boston with Diary, and I can remember him twinkling and being charming as Paula was away. He didn't alienate but moved in to get equal billing and make Paula and Susie a troika with himself. He had a risqué side and he could leer faintly, but he didn't voice it in one-liners. I told you how he'd laugh out loud when I used "stumpsucker" or some such western term (horse that chewed the manger). I always thought of him as a guru, wise in nearly every area, but I also protected him.

JOHNNY

I was not consciously aware, but I knew or sensed he was having an affair. We, he and I, went to her house on a Saturday, book day, and it was something I felt, the energy between them. But he never acknowledged anything. Lee always knew when it was convenient to him to know something and when it wasn't. He wasn't always a nice man. So later, years later, when you got into trouble, how could you face that you were angry with any man when you hadn't dealt with him?

It was around this time that he came into my room and said, "Johnny, if you ever need to talk, I'm here," and that was unusual for him, unheard of, and I said, "Okay." He seemed softer, more vulnerable, and I was sure it was because of the affair he was having.

Life seemed like a movie or play to me. It was all show business magic, done with mirrors. Now you see it, now you don't. I didn't know anymore what was real or true. There was a story about a man, a great teacher who had sought the truth all his life. When he was dying, he made a pilgrimage to the top of the highest peak in the Himalayas. He'd heard that truth lived on that mountain. His native guides deserted him, but he fought through blizzards and avalanches and lack of oxygen to finally reach the top. It was deserted. As he lay there freezing, heart close to expiring, he looked up to see a wrinkled, ugly old hag standing over him. "Please," he begged. "Help me. I've heard the truth lives here. I must speak to the truth."

She cackled and said, "My son, I am the truth."

In horror he stared at the hideous-looking crone. "How can I go back to the world, to my students, and tell them that the truth is an ugly old woman? They'll all be suicidal."

"Simple," she replied. "Tell them I'm young and beautiful."

Was that what we were all doing? Pop said you could tell the truth in your work. Why? Was it too painful in life? Maybe that's what Marilyn knew, why she lied so much.

Johnny went off to college, very reluctantly. My life continued in suspended animation—eating, sleeping, classes, shopping. Marilyn and I went dress hunting together. I thought I was over my shyness about physical things. I had hidden my body behind a towel in the dressing room after gym when I'd been in high school. When Marilyn slipped off her dress in the fitting room and was naked, I still got embarrassed. I thought the saleslady was going to faint. I imagined the *Variety* headline: MM BOFFO BOX OFFICE IN BUFF AT BLOOMINGDALE'S. I took off my glasses and pretended to clean them. I blushed, but she was as free as a child, examining her breasts, asking my opinion of them, looking at her rear view—"Well, I still don't have to back out of a room yet." Next to her I felt inhibited, self-conscious. Next to her I was.

Ralph had told me that when he massaged her, there was more life or electromagnetic energy to her flesh than to most people's, more bounce, more resiliency. She and I tried pressing our skin to see how fast it popped up again. Mine was slower. I should have known.

When I turned twenty-one, Marilyn gave me a Chagall etching to add to my growing collection. It was a sketch of a woman in a window with a flowerpot, whimsical and happy. She said she'd picked it because "it looked like you."

Marilyn's expansive mood continued through Christmas. She had rung the doorbell of our apartment and disappeared, leaving a paper bag marked "Paula" outside the front door. Inside the sack were the beautiful lustrous pearls my mother had admired. MM had been given them on her Japanese honeymoon with Joe and worn them up through her divorce. The material possession that meant the most to her was her body, despite the way she treated it. Furs, jewels, clothes were unimportant to her. She was not a material girl.

Although I prayed for fulfillment in the new year, I wasn't quite so sure that it was going to be as easy to attain as I'd thought. My philosophy was "You've got to do it till you do it right." Marilyn took a deep breath and added, "It just takes so long." What if I never did it right, I thought?

Twenty-one was almost an anticlimax. I was afraid I wasn't going to be doing anything I hadn't already done. I'd been in love and lost. I'd drunk champagne and eaten caviar. I'd dated a real prince, Aly Khan. I'd danced all night. I'd starred on Broadway, in movies. I'd been flown to Paris just for dinner. I'd spoken at the UN with Mrs. Roosevelt. I'd been to the White House. I'd almost died for love, though I hadn't been married or had a baby or changed the world. I really thought I had lived. Yet I was worried. I mean, the minutes went slowly but the days and months were going by too quickly. I wasn't getting any younger and I wasn't sure I was getting better.

Marilyn was feeling the same dissatisfactions. Without work to distract her, her life problems loomed larger. "It's the ups and downs. I don't mind them so much, if they just weren't so far up and so far down. Arthur can write all day; he's happy, he doesn't need anything else. I don't think I'm meant to be a housewife. I kind of need my own work to have something to look forward to." She sounded apologetic.

Marilyn turned thirty-three the next week. She confessed, "I know I have to die, Susie, but I hope I don't have to get old and sick to do it." Thirty-three, I thought; she was getting close to middle age. Mom was somewhere around forty-five; she never told her age. Forty-five was . . . old.

Johnny, who was eighteen, had not fared so well at college. He'd shed his baby fat and turned into a five-foot-ten (the tallest in our family) solid young man with wavy, thick, light brown hair and intense hazel eyes. He'd acknowledged that he didn't want to be the family doctor, and he was unable to tolerate the sudden freedom he'd so longed and fought for. His marks were awful, he was cutting classes, and the only operation he wanted to perform was to remove himself from school.

So he came home again, dropped out, kicked out. I never knew and didn't want to ask. Some friend of his, braver than I, did. "What did you do at school, Johnny?"

He replied with his customary bluntness, "Well, I was in misery. I didn't go to class. Basically you could say I drank." I envied his directness and honesty and wished I could emulate it.

At home he followed pretty much the same pattern. Mother was wild. "What have I done wrong, have I been such a terrible mother? He's my baby, he ruined my stomach when he was born." She clasped the loose skin that had accumulated in her middle, as if that were proof that she had sacrificed for him. "I worry about him, so I don't worry about you, Susan, you're a survivor." She meant it as a compliment, but I took it as an insult. What did I have to do to get worried about? Get a terminal illness, become a drug addict, hang myself?

She and Pop put Johnny into therapy, hoping, I think, that the therapist would deal with him and they wouldn't have to. Instead he was feistier than ever and now when he said "Fuck you," it was therapeutic.

Marilyn was in better spirits, but her moods were as fragile as her health.

She was continuing to work in class. Her plans for the future included female surgery to help her get pregnant again. With luck this would also clear up some of her chronic health problems in the reproductive area. She'd won a best actress Crystal Star award for *The Prince and the Showgirl*. The Crystal Star was the equivalent of the French Oscar, and she'd won, not Olivier. Vindication!

Some Like It Hot was opening, and we all looked forward to it. Marilyn saw a preview and went wild. She hated herself. She seemed to have forgotten that she'd been pregnant. All she saw on that screen was fat.

On screen, every flaw is exaggerated, larger than life. It can be overwhelming to your ego. On top of that, seeing the film triggered all MM's memories of the fights and traumas she'd experienced making it. *Some Like It Hot* was a huge hit, and much of the credit was hers. Critics acknowledged that no other actress could have done this part with the color, verve, and innocence she had. They celebrated her uniqueness as a great comedienne. She was not satisfied. "Yeah, but they don't think I can be a serious actress," she complained, with justification. "I want them to see what else I can do. They don't think I can, Lee. I know they don't."

"You will, darling, we can't rush, but you will," he promised. They began to make plans for doing something together that he would direct, some part that would allow Marilyn to show the world the range and depth only hinted at in her roles so far. "If I were a car, they'd be driving me in low gear. That's bad for the engine and it's depressing for the car, you know what I mean?"

In private class Marilyn did a scene from *Ulysses* by James Joyce, the Molly Bloom soliloquy. It's the sensual stream of consciousness of a woman who awakens, alone and in the middle of the night, restless, filled with desire. With its rich language and sexual images, it was one of the most difficult scenes she'd attempted. In a black velvet dress that seemed painted on her body, she surpassed everyone else who'd done it. She was completely sensual, real sexuality, not the whispery Hollywood mask, but an earthy, longing, resilient woman. I doubted if any lover had ever seen her like this. I wondered whether they'd be able to tolerate her this way. Marilyn in bloom. This was no waif. She was strong, very strong, like one of those D. H. Lawrence heroines who throbs with life.

Marilyn was very sympathetic to Johnny's plight. She seemed to empathize with him the way she had with me when I'd been younger and had problems. Moreover, he was the baby and the one who got left out, the way she'd felt left out as a child. Like my father, she always seemed more responsive to people who were in trouble, crippled in some way. At those times her concern and generosity of spirit were unbounded.

She sat and held his hand. "Listen, Johnny, just growing up in this house you've got a better education than most people get in their whole lives. And you're a lot smarter than some people I know who run certain corporations." A few days later, in a moment of generosity, she gave him her black Thunderbird for his eighteenth birthday present.

JOHNNY

I think I was talking about cars to Mother and Father. You know how I loved cars. I'd just come home and it was going to be my eighteenth birthday; I'd wanted to come for that.

Mother and Father hadn't wanted me to come. "Why don't you wait till the end of the year?" Well, I'd already been kicked out of college. They didn't know yet.

When I'd gone off at the airport, I'd turned to Mother and said, "For two cents, I won't go." Nobody gave me the two cents, but I'd meant it. What I'd wanted to do was work. I'd wanted to work from the time I was fifteen, and they were always against any effort on my part to be strong or independent. I remember how much I resented it. "You don't have to work, we'll take care of everything," undermining me.

So I was talking about cars, no one was listening, and Marilyn was there and out of the blue said, "Why don't you take my car, Johnny?"

I thought I hadn't heard her right, and I said, "What?" She had remembered the summer before, in California, I'd had that Chevy I'd rented. God, I loved that car, a '57 Bel Air silver Chevy, and she had the Thunderbird.

She continued, "I've got the Ford Mustang the corporation gave me, so Arthur and I have a car. That one's just sitting in the garage, we don't use it."

I was stunned. I couldn't believe she meant it.

Mother and Father were horrified; they didn't like it at all. I don't know if it felt like too much to give me or if they were worried about my driving in my state of mind, but they objected strenuously. "He's too young. Maybe later, Marilyn. You don't have to. It's impossible, he can't afford it, it could be dangerous."

Marilyn just said, "Well, don't worry about any of that,

*it's in the corporation's name, so I'll take care of the insur-
ance."*

*I'll never forget that. . . . There were so few, so very few
people who were generous like that. Especially to me, who
couldn't do anything for her.*

I think that car saved my life.

Johnny and Marilyn were working on changing their lives.
I felt helpless about mine, out of control. If something didn't
happen, I felt I might explode.

Marilyn and I reminisced about our childhoods. We agreed
that there had been a part of us when we were young that
believed anything was possible, that we were invincible.
"What happened?" Marilyn asked. "What happened to her,
me? What happened?" I had no answer.

I received an offer to go to Europe and do a film. Freedom
beckoned me, if I just had the guts to follow.

"Go, my darling girl, it's best, perhaps. You'll be away from
Daddy, you'll have a chance to test your wings. I'm just a plane
ride away. Oh, God, why do I have to be with Marilyn? I
should be with you. Anything you need, you call me, promise?
It's time for you to be away from your father, begin to please
yourself." Tears choked my mother's voice.

I went and asked Pop. "Go, it's time, it's the best. You
should get away from Mommy; she means well, but you have
to start to take responsibility for yourself, and you can always
come home, it's not forever. You're too dependent on Mommy.
It's natural under the circumstances, but this is for the best."

Both oracles had given me their blessing. There was no
excuse not to go.

So instead of exploding, I ran away from home for the second
time in twenty-one years. Ideally this time I'd get farther than
across the street.

Wearing my new wardrobe and my new independent attitude, I prepared to fly to Italy. I hoped they'd hide my real feelings. Inside I felt like Jell-O, wobbly, shaky, and very nervous.

That fall Marilyn got another award for *The Prince and the Showgirl*, this time Italy's Oscar; she was being recognized everywhere but in Hollywood. "To them I'm just another pretty girl who made it." She wasn't bitter, just realistic.

She raved about a French singer she'd seen in a one-man show, Yves Montand. "He looks a little like Joe, but he's more ooh-la-la and all that French jazz."

She and Mother were beginning to work on *Let's Make Love*, which was being cast and rewritten. Marilyn had agreed to do the film she knew was "lousy," a step backward, even, only to work off her remaining commitments to 20th Century-Fox. She also needed the money.

"It's a crime, the material they submit to her. By the way, you don't mind if she uses your bedroom sometimes, do you, Susie?" Mother asked casually.

What could I say? "Of course not." I felt guilty about doing it so begrudgingly when Marilyn thanked me profusely.

"I really appreciate it, Suz." She flung her arms around me and kissed me.

"Don't let her mess up my things," I instructed Mom. When I left the room looked like a hurricane had struck. There wasn't much more to mess. I was leaving, but I hadn't expected Marilyn to take my place.

Johnny now worked up the courage to ask Pop if he could be in the classes, and apprehensively he said yes. However, he confessed his doubts to Mom. "What if he doesn't have any talent?"

Mother, taken by surprise, assured him, "He's your son, he will."

My father had taken a number of young people into his class on the strength of their parents' reputation in the business. He responded to the beautiful, needy young girls. I didn't blame him; I just wanted to be included. Brooke Hayward, Margaret Sullavan's daughter, was one. He'd told her that he would take her into the class without waiting for a place to open up; the classes were jammed in those days. He said he was doing it not because of "favoritism," but because "since both your parents are talented, the odds of your having inherited that talent are high." Jane Fonda was another girl he'd accepted partially for the same reason, but also because "her eyes held such panic, there was a lot more going on than she let you see."

If Johnny was panicked, he hid it well. He made up his mind to take his time. In class he observed first, taking in everything my father was doing, what he wanted, very, as he put it, "methodically." One of the first scenes he did was with Marilyn. They chose Tennessee Williams' *A Streetcar Named Desire*. He played the young messenger who comes to the door, whom Blanche attempts pathetically to seduce. MM was Blanche.

Blanche is one of the great female parts. A lonely, desperate woman seeking a man, protection, she is a misfit, a fantasist, a liar, a woman driven by her inner demons. Vulnerable, tender, loving, needy, charming ... she runs the gamut of human emotions. It was a part Marilyn could create wonderfully, if she was willing to expose the elements of herself she had taken such great pains to hide.

JOHNNY

When we worked on our scene together, she asked me, "What should I work on?" I wasn't very aware then, I lived in my own world a great deal. She kept asking me, "What?"

I told her, "How can I tell you what to work on, what do you want to work on?" She was afraid to take responsi-

bility, just like you. We talked a couple of days about the characters, the place, the situation, Blanche. It's funny, everyone plans how they're going to be spontaneous; I wouldn't do that. I liked to dream about the characters, make a world for them. So I think that kind of freed her. When we did the scene, she really made the place, the room, real. She brought in all this stuff and props and makeup. She'd done a lot of homework alone.

She was one of the best listeners I knew. When she relaxed, she changed. She became this soft, lovely person with a sweet smile and a good, full laugh. She was even shyer than me, she had those wide, frightened eyes.

Pop believed there was a rational explanation for everything, logical, rational. No mysteries were permitted in our house, but he loved the mysteries of the unconscious. He felt at home there, exploring the deep inner depths. For Pop, his knowledge was a defense against the fear and insecurity of the unknown.

But he had shared a deep love of and for knowledge and was in this sense a spiritual leader.

Anyway, Marilyn and I were incredibly shy with one another. I was terrified to be alone with her. The only other person I'd met who trembled with life the way she did was Monty Clift.

Doing the scene, we sat anxiously looking, searching for something, hungry, longing. She had all this bizarre makeup on, too much, but perfect for the character. I didn't know if she was acting. Sometimes acting is falling into being, like falling in love, a loss of personal identity, ego.

When I looked at her onstage and saw her desperation, I couldn't wait to get off the stage, which of course was perfect for the part, that's what that young boy felt.

Dad loved her, of course, and she was fantastic. The other scenes I'd done, Pop had been very supportive and complimentary to me. But for the first time he was very

critical of me. I felt it had to do with my working with her,
but I didn't know what.

Something bothered me. I couldn't get it out of my mind.
Strangers were accepted in class, yet Pop had doubts about his
own son. Perhaps he didn't really know him. Maybe until
Johnny decided to become an actor, he just hadn't interested
Pop that much.

Johnny confessed to me, "The reason I decided to become
an actor is because it's the only way I can belong to the family."

Then why some days did I feel I'd been adopted?

IN 1960, JOHN F. KENNEDY, AT FORTY-THREE YEARS OLD, became the youngest, and first Roman Catholic, president of the United States. Sylvia Pankhurst, author of *The Suffragette Movement* and daughter of suffragette pioneer Emmeline Goulden Pankhurst, died, as did Emily Post. Gary Powers's U-2 was shot down over Russia. The French cinema invented the New Wave. Jane Goodall was studying African chimpanzees while we danced the twist.

Mother, Marilyn, and Yves Montand were doing the "lousy movie" together in California. "I hope it's not as bad as I know it is," Marilyn had said of *Let's Make Love*. Marilyn had fought to get Yves, over my parents' objections.

After arriving in Rome, I'd found out the film I was doing was being shot in Yugoslavia. Mother shipped me care packages and phoned as often as possible. Over the crack-ling transatlantic wires, Hollywood seemed like another plan-et. I was freezing in Belgrade, shooting a powerful film, *Kapo*, about a concentration camp. Mom was burning up in Los Angeles, obsessed with Marilyn and her problems and her oth-er great fear that my father was seeing other women. "The ones that are aggressive, he can't resist, I know it. None of my friends will tell me the truth, but I can feel it in my bones."

How could I tell her that right now I didn't care? She would know how selfish I was. What mattered to me was that I was expanding the boundaries of my life with new friends who didn't know how I was supposed to be because I was a Stras-berg. Here, Strasbourg was a city in France or a pâté. This was my chance to live a great adventure.

There was an actors' strike in America, and shooting on *Let's Make Love* shut down; Mother decided to "drop in" eight thousand miles away and see how I was faring.

After she arrived, one part of me wanted to cling to her and thank her for coming; the other part couldn't wait till she left. And she talked so much about Marilyn, I wanted to shout, "*Basta!*"

"Let's face it, to say this movie is lousy would be a compli-ment, and Montand is weak on camera, but Marilyn wanted him and no one else we thought was right was available. . . . She and Arthur are having problems. . . ." She sighed, a weary Mother Earth, bewildered by her children's shenanigans. "Marilyn is taking *Let's Make Love* literally and having an affair with Yves. Simone, a wonderful actress, charming but very bitchy, found out and went back to Paris because she didn't want to be humiliated. Arthur's left for New York to see his children, then to Ireland to see John Huston about directing the script he's writing for Marilyn. She's won the Golden Globe for *Some Like It Hot*, but she's still demoralized because she's not up for the Oscar, which she should have been. She's got this new psychiatrist in L.A. she likes, and I only hope he can do something for her. I don't know what will make her happy. Maybe your father's right and we're not supposed to be happy. But then what's the point of it all? It would be nice to have a little peace and quiet in my life. I'm in terrible pain, terrible. . . . I just hope Marilyn doesn't get hurt anymore, she's so vulnerable. I think Montand is like Burton; those men are tied to their wives, who are really their mothers. Can you believe when I told Marilyn I was coming to see you, she got upset and said I was neglecting her for you, my own child. . . ."

My mother was crying for help, an SOS behind every sigh, but I was too busy to pay attention; Marilyn's needs, Lee's demands, and all her own unrequited dreams, "I thought my life would be different," she admitted. Mom talked about producing, "when Marilyn doesn't need me so much. . . ." She was a born producer. Look at all our lives. She threatened to write her book again. "They'll all be sorry. I'm going to tell the truth for once, what a relief. I'm keeping notes," and she waved a notebook threateningly.

She was doubly concerned with Marilyn's behavior and misbehavior. It reflected on both of them. "The girl is so sick, we're all crazy, let's face it. But we function. . . . She needs my help, yet she treats me so badly sometimes, it's as if she's confused me with her real mother and she distrusts me, no matter what I do. It's making me sick. I should be with you, with my husband, with my baby, and no matter what I do, it's never enough; if she didn't need me, I'd leave. Life is too short for all this."

I listened sympathetically. For the first time in years I wasn't burning with envy. Instead I felt relief that all these problems, hers, Pop's, Marilyn's, weren't mine.

Mother went back to Marilyn and all the attendant *tsouris* that was killing her but that she couldn't live without. I wondered if tragedy could be an addiction.

I went to Rome to finish the film and thought about moving

there permanently and making a life alone for myself. I fell in love with Italy. The Italians were so passionate. It was the first place I'd ever been where I wasn't considered too emotional. I was even controlled, by their standards. As "la Strasberg," I was entitled to temperamental fits; it was expected. When Marilyn heard about this later, she was ready to get on the next plane to Rome with me. "It's hard to keep my spirits up in Hollywood," she confessed. "Sometimes I gotta really hit the bottle for my spirits."

So I followed Marilyn's trail of sorrows with Yves Montand through my mother's letters and what I read in the Italian rags, which was plentiful.

When I wasn't envying Marilyn, I felt such compassion for her. She was so proud, so insecure. All this public exposure she was getting over her affair with Yves had to be so humiliating to her. Montand went home to his wife after announcing to the press that MM was such a "sweet child," he hadn't known she was so serious or he would never have gotten involved. He didn't say anything about Simone's calling Marilyn, begging her not to see him, or about his own reputation as a womanizer. He acted as if he'd just been doing her a favor. His lack of discretion was matched by his lack of taste. If anyone had missed the affair, they couldn't now.

Maybe tragedy was catching, like a virus.

Like everything in my life, the move to Rome had been precipitous, unexpected. I was overwhelmed. Between buying furniture, there was the rush of my first Italian affair, which ended quickly. It had three stages: first, I was a madonna to him, then when I gave in I was a whore, and when the honeymoon period was over he wanted me to be "Mama." Since I still wanted mine, I wasn't about to be his. I had a brief romance with Warren Beatty, who was, or was not, engaged to Joan Collins. I couldn't get it straight. He was fun and seductive, and my wounded ego was soothed somewhat by all the attention. Most actors I knew were compulsive—eaters, talkers, drinkers, buyers—but not Warren. His drug seemed to be women, which, relatively, seemed pretty healthy.

When that ended, I met another Italian. I was determined not to get too involved. I was going too fast. My life was taking my breath away. I felt lonely, homesick, confused. In the middle of the night, I awoke from unremembered nightmares. The responsibility. Who would I blame if things went wrong? If I failed to make a real life for myself?

Months passed. I began to have fainting spells. I felt like a lamp wired for two hundred watts that had been run on one hundred. Suddenly I'd turned up the switch and I was getting three hundred watts. Alone at night I couldn't sleep. I buzzed around the clock. I couldn't stop weeping. I felt I was short-circuiting. The doctor gave me calcium shots for my nerves, and he also gave me urgent advice: "Go home, see the mama and the papa, not for good, just for a while."

"But what's wrong with me?" I pleaded.

"Go home," he was insistent, "go home."

I never gave another thought to my Italian beau. He was easier to give up than chocolate. Depressed, I booked a ticket to New York. I'd just cut the umbilical cord, why did I have to have a nervous breakdown?

The mama was in Reno, Nevada, with Marilyn, and the papa was getting ready to join her during *The Misfits*, a horribly ironic title. Marilyn had pointed out, "Arthur wanted to give me a present, and this is it. The men's parts are better than mine, as usual. If this is what he thinks of me, I don't know."

"You'll join Daddy in New York and then come be with us in Reno," Mother directed.

We arrived at high noon. It was one hundred and ten degrees. Pop and I went and bought cowboy boots, hats, and shirts. The two Jewish greenhorns were determined to fit in. My father was like a little kid showing off those boots. I saw a glimpse of the little boy who'd arrived in America on a cattle boat from Eastern Europe, terrified but excited. Pop had been one of the "tired and poor," and now he had hand-tooled, genuine-leather cowboy boots and wasn't too sophisticated or jaded to brag about them.

If only I had known, Reno was the worst time and place for me to have a nervous breakdown or recover from one. Marilyn was having a much bigger breakdown than mine, and Mom was not too far behind.

Marilyn and Arthur were still living together, but barely. When my mother had moved out of the hotel they were all at, trying to get some peace, Marilyn had packed and followed with Arthur. The script had problems, which Marilyn complained about vociferously. It was ostensibly Arthur's valentine to Marilyn, but just as in *Some Like It Hot*, the men's roles were more fully developed. Her character was drunk through much of the film. He'd used things she'd told him, personal things about her life, out of context. Her instincts were right, even when she was on the razor's edge, but it was too late. If she hadn't been Marilyn and all that that entailed, and if she had been able to present her feelings less emotionally, perhaps someone might have been able to really listen to her. As it was, neither John Huston, who'd directed her in *The Asphalt Jungle* when she'd first started, nor Arthur, with all the personal complications, could hear her.

She'd begged, "Please, I'm exhausted. I'm supposed to work six days a week here. I'm thirty-four years old, and I've been dancing and singing for five months on that lousy picture. I need time to rest and get my spirits up, I'm so tired, and hey, I'm not so young. It takes me longer to get my motor running if I even do." There was no film without her. They had to shoot now. It meant money. She didn't get the time.

When MM agonized over keeping everyone waiting, Mother tried to calm her, "You can't worry about production costs." Here she was surrounded by her "family": makeup man, masseur, coach, body makeup women, secretary, hairdresser, stand-in, wardrobe women, driver, a husband on the sidelines, my father in the wings, and she felt alone and lonely just like me in Rome, worse.

So did Mom. Both of them with good cause. It turned out that the men, Huston, Miller, etc., decided to be polite to Mom but to freeze her out. On top of all this, Marilyn had become even more addicted to the barbiturates she'd been taking, with few pauses, for more than ten years. It amazed me that she functioned as well as she did. She'd told me, "I know more about pills than any doctor, so I'm always in control." I'd believed her because I figured otherwise she'd be dead by now. She'd had close calls, accidental and deliberate. I'd seen her out of control with alcohol, too, but always life had seemed to entice her back or someone would catch her just as she was about to bail out of her life.

My mother, too, was really sick with some unspecified malady. I suspected she was a hypochondriac. She was always in pain these past years, her feet, her head, her back. She refused an invitation to go to an intimate dinner party for Marilyn because "I'm going to have a headache by six o'clock." She wasn't being rude. Twelve hours in the desert heat, dressed in her black cone-shaped hat and flowing dress, her useless palm leaf fan fluttering futilely against the heat and rage of the desert and the situation, did her in. She, who loathed the sun on her white, white skin, would come back to the air-conditioned hotel and have a headache, almost a migraine. The pills she took didn't seem to make a dent in her pain.

Occasionally she managed to pull herself together for Pop and me, and we dined lavishly. In the long hours when she was on the set, waiting with the rest of the crew for Marilyn to show up for work, my dad and I and Ralph would drive into the desert. Ralph had a part in the movie and was massaging MM during the day and in the middle of the night to help her sleep. We all three gazed in wonderment at the glory of Pyramid Lake in the desert. I felt so small and strangely peaceful in this golden dreamscape desert. My life before and my life after dissolved in the blinding noon light. For one moment I forgot my name, who I was. What a relief.

The set had divided into two "camps," Marilyn's and Arthur's. Arthur's side included Huston and Eli Wallach, whom Marilyn felt had criticized her. Marilyn's side was Mom, Ralph, May, whose legs Marilyn coveted because she said they were better than Dietrich's (May actually tried to remain neutral as she'd originally worked for Arthur), and the rest of her entourage. Gable was the oasis in the middle. Marilyn had adored Clark since she was a child and imagined he was her real father. Now she said, "He's the only gentleman on the set. He always gets a chair for me." She sounded pathetically grateful. He never complained, and she felt he understood her.

Mr. Gable and I talked about Marilyn's troubles. "You gals are different," he told me. "You have problems, female things we don't have, it's a lot harder. She's got to look good, too. . . . I'm glad I'm not a woman."

Eli Wallach, who had been friends with Marilyn and knew my mother well, seemed to resent Marilyn's dependence on my mom. He castigated her for it. "What the hell is she telling you, you don't know," he complained in the middle of a scene. The only one who understood was Monty Clift, because he and Marilyn's nightmares were peopled by the same demons. He kept to himself, got to work on time, knew his lines, and he and Marilyn adored each other. "He's the only person I know who's in worse shape than me," she said. She called him her "brother."

Soggy with medication, marriage disintegrating, knowing that "her" script was still the men's story, Marilyn continued to film, appearing unexpectedly, shimmering like a pale ghost mirage in the desert heat. The shoot had become the St. Valentine's Day Massacre. Arthur was going to get his movie and lose his wife.

Tempers sizzled. Marilyn was sometimes absent. The hours

drained away like the sands in an hourglass. At one point a fire broke out, causing a blackout of Reno. Even the city seemed under siege.

In the momentary freedom offered by this natural disaster, Marilyn relaxed. In the middle of the night she sat on a wardrobe trunk, having a drink in the dark with dear friends. Grabbing a wig, she did a razor-sharp imitation of Mitzi Gaynor, who'd snubbed her on some movie long ago. Singing and dancing in the dark, faceless, anonymous, she gave off blue sparks of lifelight.

Day after day Mom struggled valiantly to keep her own head above water while pulling Marilyn to a shore that kept receding. Mother had never taken a lifesaving course and the tides of this deep lake were treacherous. The trick was to get everybody out alive.

She lectured a desperate Marilyn and me, "You can't worry about being unhappy, there's no such thing as a happy artist, they experience too much to ever be happy." That seemed to console Marilyn but it made me more depressed.

Attempts at humor fell flat. Marilyn was late, hours late. Finally she arrived. As Mother followed her into the dressing room, she said, "Marilyn, you can afford to be late until you get to be a big star like Sandra Dee . . . then you'll have to be on time." Even groggy with medication, Marilyn got it and laughed. Nobody else did.

Another time Marilyn and Whitey were laughing and Whitey said, "This is like the old days," and Marilyn wilted and replied, "Yeah, but then we had hope."

MM had affectionately nicknamed Mom "Black Bart." Other people used this in a derogatory way.

My mother had become the whipping boy of the production. They couldn't take out their anger and frustration on MM. She was the star and had to perform. They had to go with the money. Mother was another case. They vilified Mom, who was Marilyn's representative. Even drugged and sick, MM knew that she was being insulted through Mom. They refused to speak to Mother, treating her as if she were a rank amateur (she'd done more than twenty-four films before this). On the other films she'd done, including the one a few years before, coaching Jennifer Jones, everyone had enjoyed and respected Mom.

I felt the charged atmosphere and wanted to do something to help Mom but had no idea what. It put me even more on the defensive than I already was. Besides all that, Mother still had the ability to embarrass me by extolling my virtues or singing out loud to herself or laughing too noisily, so I was ashamed to be thinking critically about her myself. This drove me to withdraw more.

Huston, tall, lanky, impeccably outfitted in an African safari suit, was patronizing, though not openly antagonistic. He got a kick out of putting Mother on with that smiling cobra grin of his. He was a wonderful director, but notorious for being sadistic to some actors. Because Marilyn was so sick, he had to treat her with some consideration. He was a real "macho" man. He needed a ten-gallon hat just to hold his ego. With Marilyn, his sadism took a more insidious form.

Mother was so distraught that she typed up a defense of herself to give the press; she never did:

> It's much more difficult to play yourself than someone you've never met. This is the most difficult part Marilyn has played, with the exception of one scene in The Prince and the Showgirl and Some Like It Hot. I believe it has been essential for me to be with her on this picture. It was essential because so much of it was close to her. Also, she is a creative actress, not just a personality. Almost every fine actor, including Walter Huston, always had someone to help them when they were working. Even Clark, in his first movies, had Josephine Dillon. I feel that I have contributed to every frame of The Misfits. If it doesn't work out, that's

something I must share with her. My work is not a mystery. This is my twenty-fourth picture. My work is evident on the screen.

ARNOLD SCHULMAN—Screenwriter, playwright, friend of the family

I saw your mother at the Bel-Air Hotel during The Misfits. *She'd had to get away from the set for a few days, she couldn't stand it. She asked me, "Please come, come back with me, talk to Marilyn, see what you can do."*

I went to Reno and it was just awful. The tension. And Miller sulking around like a two-year-old, glowering at everybody, particularly at her. If he'd looked at me like that, I would have withered and died on the spot. I don't know how they ever got through the days—your mother especially, because it was all dumped on her.

Everybody hated her. They were blaming her for everything. Your mother was constantly nurturing Marilyn, constantly doing for her. She really got a bum rap on this whole thing, she was really trying to hold this thing together, and everybody kept saying, "What a pain in the ass," and making jokes about her.

She wanted me to cheer Marilyn up because it was all so gloomy. Actually, I think Paula wanted me to cheer her up. She was so sad when I saw her. Arthur was still totally pissed off at that time, still because of Yves Montand. That was the whole thing, that's all there was, he was acting like a two-year-old. So she'd fucked Montand. As your father would say, What do you want her to do, what did you marry her for? She's going to do that with people, that's what she does. Marilyn was Marilyn, that was part of the package.

Your mother was a lover. You're supposed to love if you

can on this trip we're on, what else is there? Your father missed the whole point of love as great, more pleasure in loving. He had this built-in defense mechanism to prevent him from understanding that he was presenting himself as a Zen master. He wanted to be one, but he was a fake Zen master. He convinced others but not himself. He wasn't a fake. Basically he understood the concept of no ego, but his ego stood in the way of making it completely real.

Arthur, tall and lean and angular like Huston, tight-jawed, reserved, knew little about the process of actors, yet he was condescending to Mom, denigrating whatever she did because he didn't understand it. There was a special language Mom and Marilyn used because it worked. In one scene Huston couldn't get Marilyn to turn away from Eli slowly enough. Mom simply said to MM, "Think garlic; he's eaten garlic." Marilyn instantly got it and on the next take turned her head slowly disdainfully away from Eli.

The Misfits was an interesting script, but it wasn't Shakespeare, Chekhov, or the finely crafted comedy script of *Some Like It Hot*. MM was having enormous trouble retaining lines, a problem she'd had before. My father had trained me to honor the author's words, but Marilyn was far too sick to manage. She was improvising, and Huston and Arthur as writers were up in arms. They wouldn't permit it.

"Rosalie, Rosalie, Rosalie," Gable called.

"I'm here," Marilyn answered.

"No, dear," Huston said, "you say 'I'm here' after the fourth 'Rosalie.' "

"I'm sorry," she said, trembling.

"Rosalie," Gable yelled four times.

"Here I am." She waved.

"No dear, 'I'm here' is the line. . . ."

And so on and so forth. It was cruel. Marilyn could barely

remember her own name. What difference did it make, unless it was crucial to the story? It was as if the men needed to show they were in control. They were determined to win the battle, even if they lost the war.

Arthur backed John in this, while claiming sympathy for MM. I wondered if Arthur was recovered from the humiliation of having his wife's infidelity trumpeted in the world press. I wondered if he'd been angry or hurt. To me it would have been devastating, but he was an intellectual and I didn't know if they permitted themselves that kind of feeling or rationalized it away.

I had thought all creative, artistic men were more sensitive, different, until I'd once heard Clifford Odets say, "I loved Fay Wray, but God forgive me, I left her because she had no tits." And Clifford was supposed to be a genius.

Marilyn said, "Men, they're all the same. . . . They can't help it." If she was right, did that mean we women could help it, whatever "it" was?

They balked at making any changes Marilyn felt necessary for her role; she was only an actress and not a respected one at that. Yet she had an impeccable sense of herself on screen. She'd asked Billy Wilder to reshoot her entrance in *Some Like It Hot*, which had led to that classic shot of her walking through smoke puffs in her high heels. When my mother made some suggestions about silent shots to enhance the role, with Marilyn doing interesting behavior showing another side of Rosalie, she was ignored. They also ignored the fact that my father, when he'd been at 20th Century-Fox during World War II, had done dozens of screen tests and 95 percent of the actors he'd worked with had been signed. His suggestions, too, were sloughed off.

They had refused to give her the brief rest period she'd pleaded for before starting this film. The excuse was money, yet they'd lost far more money trying to push ahead when she was exhausted and getting sicker. It was so senseless.

Marilyn also felt that Arthur had done this project feeling he'd sacrificed himself, gone slumming to do a movie for her and that to him films were a lower art form than theater. She feared he might be using her. It had been difficult with her earning most of the money since the marriage.

He hadn't saved her from herself as she had dreamed; he had not been the safe harbor she'd sought. What had Arthur dreamed she'd save him from? They'd fallen in love with mirages, and here in the desert heat the mirages were evaporating.

Nobody wanted the responsibility. Huston begged Arthur, "Get her off the damn pills, they'll kill her." Arthur couldn't. He'd become too inexorably linked in her business, in areas of her life that disenfranchised his purity in her eyes.

Huston approached Paula, demanding, "Do something." Arthur told Paula, "You must stop Marilyn."

Mother was more despondent than I'd ever seen her. "It's a nightmare, I can't take it. They can't do it but they expect me to."

"Buddha said life is suffering, you always tell me that, Mom." I tried to cheer her up.

"Buddha didn't know the half of it," she cried out as if reproaching the avatar.

The day after we arrived, Arthur came to see Pop. He stood glowering down at him. Mother had dressed and perfumed herself, and instead of her black muumuu she wore a brightly colored silk Oriental robe. She told Dad, "I'll let you handle it, I can't anymore."

I listened to the tone of their voices—Arthur's condescending and angry, Pop's insistent, angry . . . Mother was mute. "What are you going to do about Marilyn?" Arthur demanded. We knew he thought Lee was a charlatan, so how could he expect him to save her.

"I'll talk to her later," my father said, "this comes first. I can't tolerate this behavior toward Paula. She's an artist. She's worked with many stars and never been treated like this. If something doesn't change, I'm afraid I'll have to pull her off the picture. She has to be shown some respect." To Dad, showing Mom respect meant that Marilyn might sense a change in attitude and atmosphere on the set and perhaps regain some of her lost confidence. Pop felt there was little he could do about the more serious problem of Marilyn's sinking, waterlogged with drugs, in the middle of a picture. He didn't think Arthur would be willing to stop shooting and hospitalize his wife. That was costly and could jeopardize the production. But that was what he felt should be done, and he was helpless to make it happen.

What Arthur and Huston didn't comprehend was that Marilyn was like an aeolian harp, a fine-tuned, responsive, delicate musical instrument so sensitive that the ancient Greeks could place them on hilltops and they would play music at the slightest breeze blowing through them. That was why the atmosphere was so important to Marilyn. With her supersensitivity, she had an instrument that could pick up thoughts, whispers, lies.

Marilyn was at the edge of a chasm that had destroyed some wonderful talents: Clara Bow, the "It girl," whose childhood and problems closely paralleled Marilyn's; Marie Falconetti, who had been the stunning Saint Joan in Dreyer's film.

And just because she was drugged and paranoid didn't mean they weren't after her. The laws of nature were being followed. Healthy fish will attack a wounded fish. Marilyn was wounded. Mother repeated like a mantra, "It doesn't have to be fatal, it doesn't have to be terminal."

With Marilyn nearing total collapse, Huston behaved in Mom's words, "like a mensh," and had her flown to Los Angeles wrapped in a wet sheet. She was admitted to a private hospital to detoxify. By then I was forgetting why I'd come to California.

Ralph drove Pop and me to Los Angeles while Mother flew ahead to be with Marilyn. Something snapped inside me while driving through those endless desert dunes. I couldn't stop talking, and something must have moved Pop too because he talked back. Finally we'd talked. Afterward, I couldn't remember one word of what was said.

We went to see MM in the hospital. I was shocked. She was a ghost of herself. She lay, white on white, helpless, like an overgrown child, as if some vampire had drained her life force. How could I complain about my life, seeing her like this?

"When some insects are ready to go to the next stage of evolution, they shed their hard outer protective shell. In that moment, when it goes, they're totally vulnerable to nature, to their enemies. But if it's going to evolve, it has no choice." My mother knew all these wonderful things. "Marilyn is like that now, no protection. But I know that if she can survive this, she'll take the next step. She's got a strong will, if she can only use it for herself instead of against herself." Mother's hands fluttered nervously to her face. "Maybe it only works for insects?"

JOHNNY

I think Marilyn was a sick woman, a classic schizophrenic. She was dedicated to love. It's a thing schizophrenics talk about, love. They'll do anything for love and, additionally, they are totally infantile; they have no ego, no boundaries, as the rest of us have. When they feel the walls moving, literally what's happening is when they pulse with life, they see the walls move, but they are actually the ones moving. They've projected it outward. Van Gogh, Nijinsky, Dostoyevski, Nietzsche, they all talk about God and love and changing the world.

The amazing thing about her is that she survived as long as she did. There was enough capacity for life that had she been lucky enough to find a therapist who could treat her problems, she might have . . . That's the tragedy. People loved her. But nobody could say no to her. No one would or could take responsibility for her. They had to cut off or abandon her, which is the thing she expected. With Marilyn, you're dealing with an abandoned infant who's not an infant anymore.

Marilyn returned to Reno rejuvenated, and I flew back to Europe. She finished the movie and her marriage.

Arthur, tall, stern-faced, with his dry wit and intellectual word fences of defense against his own feelings, was gone from Marilyn's life. For almost five years he had been the maypole around which she had danced and played. When he'd lost his center, bent too much in the prevailing wind, Marilyn had begun to panic and lash out. She needed a steady mooring. She was anchorless once again.

I fled back to Rome, counting my blessings.

When the film ended, Huston gallantly admitted that "perhaps Paula Strasberg was the only thing holding this movie together," and Marilyn made a toast: "Remember now, cheers, no tears."

Within the next year Arthur was engaged to be married again to a photographer he'd met on the set of *The Misfits*.

IT WAS 1961 . . . PRESIDENT KENNEDY ESTABLISHED the Peace Corps. Men and women, blacks and whites together, became freedom riders for integration. The Berlin Wall went up, and the Bay of Pigs went down. Nureyev defected from the USSR to dance in the free world. Alan Shepard was the first American man in space. Wilma Rudolph ran the twenty-two-yard-dash in twenty-five seconds, setting a world record. The *Orient Express* made its last train journey. We were singing "Moon River," "Love Makes the World Go Ground," and "Where Have All the Flowers Gone?" Roger Maris hit sixty-one home runs in one season, setting a record. Clark Gable had died of a heart attack at the end of the last year. His widow was pregnant with his child, whom he'd never see or know.

Marilyn was reescalating her heartbreak diet, pills and liquor, still reeling from her separation and Gable's death.

I was home when my father convinced her to stay with us for a few days. He was worried about her being alone. She was devastated, again.

She had tremendous guilt that unconsciously she may have kept Clark waiting in all that heat on the set of *The Misfits* because he had represented a father figure to her, and through him, she was getting revenge on her real father. We all tried to convince her that she'd been sick and that Gable had insist- ed on doing his own strenuous stunts. All her friends tried to assure her that his death hadn't been her fault. It didn't matter whether it was true or not. She'd gotten this idea in her head, and she was obsessed with it. And if that weren't enough, in the long dark days of winter her divorce from Arthur became final. Arthur got Hugo, the sad-faced basset hound he'd given Marilyn—Hugo, whom she'd tended and fretted over, giving him sips of whiskey, per her vet's instruc- tions, to cheer him up when he was depressed. "Wouldn't you know I'd have a dog who'd get depressions? If he starts to look like me, he's really in trouble. Or vice versa. Well, one of us is definitely in trouble." She'd worried that because he was so close to the ground, his penis would get hurt when he ran over the bumpy country terrain. "Be careful, Hugo," she would cry maternally.

Mother was deeply concerned about her, as were all her friends. "Susan, she's lost two men in one year, Montand and Arthur, and she had no confidence to begin with. I can't understand it. She has no sense of her own beauty or power or talent, she doesn't believe even Daddy and me; it's easier for her to believe the negative things, those she's used to."

Back in New York, Marilyn was withdrawing like a sick animal into a kind of semihibernation. Once she would have come over to our house before taking pills to escape her pain or hopelessness. Now she stayed locked in her bedroom in the dark. The apartment was unkempt, despite her housekeeper.

She'd play all those sad love songs over and over again. She had a reason to sing the blues, but it seemed irrational masochism to me for her to continue to torture herself like that. "Why was I born, why am I living, what am I getting? What am I giving? . . . I'm down in the dumps on the ninetieth floor."

The Misfits opened, which didn't help. By now she hated not only the film, but herself in it. She felt it represented Arthur's real feelings for her and the whole sad end of their story. She'd remember the good times in their marriage, but only when she wasn't harping on the bad times, which wasn't often.

Dr. Kris, her psychiatrist, felt Marilyn was at a point of no return and that she had to go into the hospital to detoxify from all that substance abuse. She finally convinced MM she needed medical care, and on a gloomy winter day, Marilyn checked herself into the hospital. Her friends, who had rallied around her in these difficult times, were relieved. Everyone close to her seemed aware by now that it was too late for friends or sympathy; she was engaged in some darker, more dangerous battle, not with the world, her husband, or Hollywood, but with her own demons. None of her friends had been able to say no to her because they would have had to take full responsibility for her, and she was a big responsibility. She needed twenty-four-hour supervision. Even when they offered to take part of the burden of the decisions, Marilyn wouldn't let them. Her stubbornness, her vacillation and indecisiveness about what to do ("I want to do the right thing"), combined with the buildup of the drugs she was taking, had put her in a marginally functional state.

"Daddy doesn't know what to do anymore, I've never seen him so helpless," Mother confided in me, and I remembered his tears when Jimmy Dean had died and his hopelessness about why these talented, sensitive people were so self-destructive.

On February 7, Marilyn checked into Payne Whitney Hospital in New York City. I heard so many versions of what happened next, it was like *Rashomon*.

Marilyn had expected to be in the same ward she'd been in during her other hospital stays, private room, star treatment, even though this had provided only temporary relief in the past. Instead she was held in the ward for the mentally ill. Her worst fears came true—she was locked up in a psychiatric ward. This was the terror she'd lived with continually for years; her fear of her genetic inheritance overtaking her so that she'd become like all her insane ancestors, her grandmother, grandfather, mother, and her uncle. During her last movies, she'd kept a limousine waiting outside wherever she was shooting so she could make a fast getaway any time the walls seemed to be closing in on her. She hated to feel closed in.

Understandably, she'd become violent when they'd first locked her in. They'd stared at her as if she were an animal in a zoo. One doctor had asked what was the matter with her. "How the hell do I know?" she'd responded desperately angry. "That's what you get paid for."

She'd managed to phone Joe DiMaggio, and her knight in white armor came to the rescue. He proved to be a better friend than a husband. "He threatened to pull the place apart brick by brick," she bragged about him later with admiration in her voice—but not so much admiration that she'd listen to him when he warned her against some of the people she socialized with, who he felt were a bad influence on her, particularly in Hollywood.

She had always claimed that sex was a lot more available than friendship—real friendship, the kind where she didn't have to worry that someone was using her, even if she was using them.

Four days later, with the press baying like bloodhounds after having run her to ground, she left Payne Whitney and entered Columbia Presbyterian, where she remained for a number of weeks, until once again the drugs that had accumulated in her system had been temporarily cleaned out.

"It's crazy, isn't it? I can't even have a nervous breakdown in private; everybody wants to be there, like it's a show. I ought to charge. God, next thing war'll be entertainment, like the Christians and the lions to the Romans. Your father says it's a career that develops in public, but that your talent has to develop in private, only it's impossible to get private." What she didn't say was that if she was private or quiet for too long, she got stir crazy, that on top of being addicted to pills, she was addicted to that energy she got from other people, friends, crowds, fans. She drank it up, all that energy, all those thoughts, all that attention being directed at her.

In some ways, I had gotten hooked on it, too. It's like eating something you know will make you sick, but in that one minute when it hits your taste buds, it's so good, and there's such a rush, that you can't help yourself; then, like a child, you are satisfied, and you feel loved . . . until the next minute, it's gone and you need another fix.

As usual, Marilyn told different people different things about that experience, tailoring her stories to fit the expectations of the person she was talking to. She was Maya, illusion, all things to all people. Whatever she said, the experience shocked her. That and her terror had done something positive, awakened her will sufficiently that she got mad enough to mobilize her anger and pull herself together.

RALPH

After Marilyn got out of Payne Whitney, she and Dr. Kris had a huge confrontation. Marilyn was screaming at the doctor as only she could. She was like a hurricane unleashed. I don't think Dr. Kris had ever seen her like that, and she was frightened and very shaken by the violence of Marilyn's response at their meeting. I wound up driving the doctor home. There was a lot of traffic, so we inched down the West Side Highway overlooking the river, and Dr. Kris was trembling and kept repeating over and over, "I did a terrible thing, a terrible, terrible thing. Oh, God I didn't mean to, but I did."

Later, Marilyn told me that one of the things that had really set her off was that the room they'd locked her in had no knobs on the drawers or doors, this room with no way out. She told me, "Rafe, the only thing that saved me in there was that I kept thinking, What would Marlon do if he was put in my position? That kept my sanity because I knew he'd do a lot more and worse than me."

She had a meeting with her lawyer, Aaron Frosch, to see about drawing up some kind of paper so that this could never happen to her again. Lee, Joe, Aaron, and May— who, although she'd originally been Arthur's secretary, had stayed with Marilyn—would all have to be notified before she could be locked up again.

Months later, when I was home on a visit, she brought it up. I wouldn't have, for fear of upsetting her. It surprised me how nonchalantly she spoke. "I was always afraid I was crazy like my mother or that I'd get that crazy with age. You know women sometimes do go nuts then, but when I got in there with really crazy people, I realized I had problems, but I saw I wasn't as bad as they were." She made it sound as if it hadn't been that bad. Yet I had heard that it had been worse. Was she trying to protect me from how horrible life was, or didn't she trust me? Whom was she lying to? Me or herself? Why?

My parents felt that Marilyn had to recapture the sense of responsibility and purpose for her life she'd had when she'd come east. They believed that if she could work in material where she could release her anger and frustrations within the structure of a part, she'd have a chance to transform the one whole aspect of herself she was denying, trying to annihilate. Therapy might take years to heal her, if at all. Acting might bring immediate relief, by transmuting her sublimated antisocial urges, energies, and rages into creativity. She'd become like a rage rat, stockpiling her anger until she was close to imploding. If she could use all this, it might earn her recognition instead of censorship. "While she's asking 'Why?' in the past, let her do something positive in the present." Pop's thinking made sense as usual. Doing it was the hard part.

They revived the idea to do *Rain*, with Marilyn playing the prostitute who falls in love with a preacher and undergoes a spiritual conversion. Plans moved ahead, until ABC refused to accept my father as the director because he had no television experience. MM was determined to find a network or sponsor who would allow her the freedom to do it her way. After Olivier and Fox, she wasn't about to give up control again.

Joe was going to Florida, and Marilyn joined him to get some rest. Her half sister, Bernice, lived there, and she was also going to reunite with her. After the hospital fiasco, she needed to find some part of her family that wasn't crazy, someone normal who carried the same genetic imprints and blood she did. In any case, nature had assuaged her in the past. Maybe she hoped the Florida sun would burn out all the shadows, all the ghosts. Her sister and she got on. Marilyn was pleased.

Spring arrived, and Marilyn returned to California to take care of business. She planned to be back in New York by June to have gall bladder surgery, another entry in her catalog of chronic illnesses. She'd take care of one, and another would appear.

Ralph was with her in California, lending his calming presence once again. He was tall, muscular, ruddy-complexioned and had clear, slightly slanted eyes. Physically imposing, he had an inner sense of being grounded that I thought might come from his American Indian blood. He was someone you could lean on physically and emotionally. And he was a true friend, someone you could be yourself with and who never judged you.

RALPH

She really looked around New York for a doctor she liked. She had realized she couldn't go back to Dr. Kris, but she couldn't find one, so she felt she might as well go back to California. "Oh, the hell with it, I'll go back and see Greenson in Los Angeles." He had treated her before when she'd been hospitalized during Misfits. So she asked me if I'd drive my car back cross-country so I could give her massages and drive her around out there. I was with her for months, from early morning until late evening. We had dinner most nights; I'd cook steaks on the barbecue. She was taking it easy. Greenson was taking over a lot of her life. She told me that he wanted her to drop all her old friends—he felt that we were all bad influences—and put herself in his hands. He brought Eunice Murray into the picture as a kind of a guardian. Marilyn said it felt like she had a keeper, but she was very taken by him at first.

Marilyn now attempted to put the pieces of her life together and prepare for her next movie. In Italy, Franco Zeffirelli asked me to play *Camille* on Broadway. I was thrilled, my parents were thrilled; this was the kind of project they'd envisioned for me. Perhaps I'd be the next first lady of the theater after all. "Better late than never."

Marilyn, six thousand miles away, in Los Angeles, was undergoing barbiturate withdrawal again, the second time that year. There had been more invasions and raids on her body than in Korea, chemical and human warfare. She had to call a truce with herself before it was too late. What was wrong with her? "Character is destiny," Mother declared. "Change your character and you can change your destiny. Marilyn has to accept that she is what she is. She wants to change the world. First she has to change herself . . . Don't we all?" she said in a weary tone.

U.S. TROOPS IN VIETNAM WERE ORDERED TO FIRE if fired upon by the enemy. Rachel Carson wrote *Silent Spring* about chemical pesticides ruining the environment and was accused of being an alarmist. James Meredith became the first black student to enroll in the University of Mississippi after three thousand troops put down riots there. Johnny Carson began a new nighttime TV program. Thalidomide damaged thousands of newborn babies. Nineteen sixty-two was the year of *A Clockwork Orange, Days of Wine and Roses,* and *One Flew Over the Cuckoo's Nest. Cleopatra* was ruining 20th Century-Fox with its escalating costs and Elizabeth Taylor's illnesses. Eleanor Roosevelt died, and Bob Dylan sang "Blowin' in the Wind." Sixty-six percent of the world's 1.6 billion adults were illiterate. Mother's astrologer did a yearly upgrade for Marilyn and me. This cosmic navigational system was a weather forecast of trends for the coming year. Marilyn's was so stormy and difficult my mother said, "I can't give it to her, she'll get too depressed, she's so suggestive, maybe later." When I asked exactly what the astrologer had predicted, Mother, with unaccustomed restraint, refused to tell me anything specific. "It's not fatal, it doesn't have to be fatal," she said more to herself than to me.

My mother took her metaphysics seriously.

DREAM—1991

I am on a film set, in my dressing room, being covered with thick pancake. They are making up my face, my body, my legs and breasts, and I am furious because I keep thinking that I'm too old for this. The people working on me are doing a good job, but I feel like an object, as if I don't matter, like a piece of meat being prepared for market. My anger builds until it bursts out of my skin and my face starts to erupt in red hives. Then I go to a mirror and look at myself. I hate the way I look. I say, "It's not me," and I wipe off all the makeup and tell them, "I'll redo it better myself." I can feel that everyone thinks I'm impossible because my anger is flying at everyone around me. I have this sense of helplessness because they're all acting as if they own this body, my body, and are entitled to do anything they want with it. When I try to take it back I alienate everyone with my rage, but I don't mean for them to be angry, I just can't control it anymore. I hurt too much, no one understands that it isn't personal.

Still asleep, I realize the body I'm inside isn't mine, it's Marilyn's. . . .

Since *Hemingway's Adventures of a Young Man* was being screened in Hollywood, Jerry Wald flew me out for last-minute dubbing. I decided to stay for a month.

Marilyn wasn't shooting yet, so Mother was still in New York. "Call Marilyn," she insisted. When I did, she invited me to see her new home. The house was simple, unpretentious, almost modest—not a movie star house, a person's. There were no mirrored ceilings or white-on-white carpets. It wasn't decorated yet and was mostly empty. MM was thrilled about her Mexican pottery and tiles done in that Mexican blue, deep like delphiniums. There was a plaster angel she'd bought because it was "good for a child's room, don't you think?" I thought its painted face would scare me if I was a child. She was so enthusiastic. She wasn't really asking, she was telling me.

The house was on the end of a tree-lined cul-de-sac, very private and quiet, almost too quiet. It didn't feel as if she lived there yet, but she was like that. No place she had inhabited seemed to totally belong to her. The New York apartment was her idea of a star's apartment, with Joan Crawford's white wall-to-walls. The country house was more like Arthur.

"Do you like it?" she asked over and over. I reassured her that I thought it was beautiful. "It's like my doctor's house. You gotta see it. Of course his is bigger." Was she ever going to do a house the way *she* wanted her home to be? It occurred to me that maybe she had no picture of home in her head, just all the fragmented nonhomes from her childhood.

Maf, the little white poodle Sinatra had given her, was bouncing around. "Maf is for Mafia, get it?" Another nickname.

The one thing that was the same was her bedroom. Like the one in New York, it was the messiest room in the house and the least done. She spent more time in her bedroom than in any other room of her house. But it was always the room that was incomplete. Maybe she didn't notice, since most of the time she was alone in her bed, talking on the phone or knocked out by pills.

Excited as she was about decorating the house, it seemed to be taking so much energy out of her. I thought she seemed awfully anxious about it, the way she was about her dress or her makeup, as if it were another obligation, another burden she was taking on to fulfill the expectations of other people.

Sitting in the kitchen, she showed me her newest scar from her gall bladder operation. I couldn't resist cracking, "They can't say you have too much gall, can they?"

She didn't smile.

"Look at my breasts," she insisted, pulling her loose shirt up above them and thrusting them in front of me.

"They look fantastic." I tried to hide my embarrassment at her baring herself to me. I hated being like this. How could I still be so prudish after Richard Burton and Warren Beatty?

"I'm in better shape than I was when you met me," she bragged. She was thinner now, and she looked pale but beautiful to me. She seemed proud of her scar, like a soldier exhibiting a medal for some war wound. Heroine of life, I thought.

This was the first time I'd been with her that she didn't ask me what I was doing. I was bursting to crow about *Camille* and Zeffirelli, talk Italian to her and show off about what a wonderful life I was going to make for myself. It didn't feel right so I kept silent.

"You gotta come back and swim and have dinner, maybe when Rafe's here, you promise? Nobody swims in my pool."

I promised. I meant to go back, but it was a short trip. There were other priorities. If she were in New York, and if she came early again like at *Anne Frank*, I'd invite her to the opening night of *Camille*.

She stood in the doorway of her home, her face lost in the shadows, waving good-bye. She looked like that self-portrait she'd given me years before, on Fire Island, the little girl she'd named "Lonely."

On that trip Cary Grant and I reconnected at Clifford Odets's house. We'd met before with my parents and danced together at the Berlin Film Festival. I'd never had a real conversation with him because he was so much older. Now that I was older, he was more interesting, or maybe I was smarter. We listened to Beethoven and Mozart, and Clifford expounded on art, philosophy, sex, and anything else that came into his mind.

Cary asked me out, and I thought, Does he mean for a "date" date? He did and I said yes. He was very nice and very different from his screen image, like Marilyn and most of the actors I knew.

We'd go to La Scala's, where he'd slip in the back door so no one ever knew he was there. Other nights we ate at his home in front of the television in his bedroom, a rather austere room with not much personality, as neat as Marilyn's was messy. At first I was very nervous that he might seduce me. When he made no move toward me I was very nervous that he might not. He almost seemed to be waiting for me to make the first gesture but I'd seen all his movies and was waiting for him. He was the man, he was older. What we did was, we sat there on his bed, eating TV dinners served by his butler on TV trays. Two things puzzled me: that we were so platonic and that a man as rich and successful as Cary would serve TV dinners.

We'd drive to the top of Mulholland Drive and park on the pullovers where all the young kids went to neck. We only talked. It was the best view in Los Angeles, and on clear evenings you could see to the ocean, and if there was a concert at the Hollywood Bowl, the music would waft up to the road, sweetening the night air.

We talked for hours. He felt incomplete without children, just like Marilyn. We held hands. He didn't want to be alone, he wanted to be happy. We cuddled. What bewildered me was that he had everything—he was a man, mature, with money, fame, acceptance, and experience. He still wasn't happy. We kissed, only it wasn't what I'd expected. I was waiting for the man I'd seen on screen to sweep me off my feet.

He confided that he was taking LSD, this new experimental drug that someone at Harvard had discovered. When I asked him why he'd take a chance on something like that, he said that he'd been trying to figure out what was missing from his life for years, and if he couldn't go deeper, his life was meaningless. "If I don't find out who I really am, I'm just another bunch of atoms and molecules." I wondered if when he found out who he really was, he'd also serve better dinners.

Marriage and children seemed to be his priority, and I felt he was looking me over, checking out my potential as a possible mate. Clifford informed me that Cary was looking for a Jewish woman because he was part Jewish, that he wanted someone who'd be a good mother, someone intelligent. I thought I qualified so far. But what about love?

He reminded me of my father. It made me uncomfortable. He didn't look like him or sound like him, but all the same there was something. He needed to be taken care of—was that it? Another insecure actor. Was there any other kind? Somehow I was winding up feeling like . . . like his mother, when I was the one looking for a father.

The thing was, if Marilyn Monroe and Cary Grant weren't happy, what chance did I have?

Just before I went back to Italy, I attended the Golden Globe Awards, where the foreign press give their "Oscars" for the year.

Marilyn was receiving the World Film Favorite Award. When she made her entrance, something happened that knocked me out. There was a room full of the biggest stars in the world, and when Marilyn walked in and made her way slowly to the table, her dress was so tight she could hardly move; some people in the room stood on chairs, just to get a look at her, like kids. I'd never seen stars react to another star like that.

Marilyn seemed oblivious of them all; she was in one of her armored vapor clouds. She had arrived already four sheets to the wind and proceeded to go for five; she was *arrivato*, as the Italians say.

She was with a Mexican writer. It wasn't his fault he looked like the gigolos I'd met in Rome, except not as good-looking. He may have possessed a great mind, but his pants were so tight that he had to ease himself onto his seat at a slant. Between her dress and his pants, there wasn't an inch to spare. And still I envied her. Even drunk, barely in control, overly made-up, she still exuded innocence and a vibrant life force that surrounded her like an aura.

She barely made it up on the stage to accept her award, and when she did her voice was slurred. Watching her weave in front of the microphone like a hypnotized cobra, I tried to reconcile that befogged woman with the clear-eyed, agile-witted, sensitive person I knew was hovering just beneath the surface. She was almost a parody of the girl I'd met ten years before, wearing the Carmen Miranda costume and shining through its ludicrousness. She mimicked her old Hollywood whispery voice in her thank-you speech. Didn't she know she was better than this? Worth more than this? How could she not know? After working so hard for awards like this, it didn't seem to be giving her genuine pleasure. I felt almost sorry for her, as if I should take care of her. I, who was barely able to take care of myself.

And the craziness of it. She mentioned that Mom had told her about my doing *Camille* and complained, "You get all the good parts, I get the shit." It sounded as if she were jealous of me, when I had coveted *her* life. I started to tell her how scared

I was about daring to follow in Garbo's footsteps and how beautiful she looked and that she could sleep in my room any time she wanted. But with the noise of the crowd, the music, the press, and the people pulling on her, it was impossible. I'd tell her next time I saw her.

I'd read that time doesn't really exist, but it was a convincing illusion, and it was moving fast.

Mother and I crossed in midair. As she flew to be with Marilyn, I flew home to New York, to look for an apartment and celebrate my twenty-fourth birthday there. Almost a quarter of a century. "My darling, I'm heartbroken that I can't stay to help. Marty and Delos will do it. Take care of your father, go out with him and make him help you with *Camille*."

Oh, Mother, I thought. As if I could make him do anything.

She continued, "Marilyn needs me, and it's awful here. The studio is out to get her." I thought my mother was starting to sound as paranoid as Marilyn. They'd been together too long.

ARNOLD SCHULMAN

I'd worked with Cukor, with whom I'd done my first picture. He called me. I, of course, wanted to work with Marilyn because I'd known her in New York when your father called me and asked me to take a friend to a poetry reading at the YMCA. He gave me the address and didn't tell me who it was. I rang the bell, and there she was. I adored her. So I was asked to write this script.

There was a new guy, called Jack Robinson something, an advertising guy, I think. Skouras had been kicked out. He, Jack, wanted to be a big hero with the board of directors. She had this bad rep from the last movie.

They were asking me to write the script, but they wouldn't let me talk to Marilyn. I would be in the room when she would call, and she'd say, "What do you mean I can't have my hairdresser?" They were really deliberately rude to her. And the point was, it became obvious. I began to suspect that maybe they wanted to make her quit and maybe they even wanted to sue her.

I just got crazy, I really got crazy. Who can understand what they were doing? All I knew was she was in a vulnerable place at the time and they were going to kill her. Maybe not deliberately kill her; they just wanted to break her arms and legs, you know. And I called her and I talked to her and I said, "I'm leaving, there's nothing I can do." I told her, "You've got to do something, they're trying to make you quit, they want to sue you. Talk to your lawyer. Talk to your agent."

And she said, "Please don't leave, you've got to write this for me."

And I said, "Don't you understand? No matter what I write, they're gonna fuck it up. They don't care, they don't want to make this picture. They want you to quit."

So I went back to New York, and she called me there three or four times a day, and I said, "Jeez, if I could do anything to help, I'd be there in a minute. But there's nothing anybody can do. You've got to work this out with your agent, your lawyer, and get them to stop doing what they're trying to do." Cukor was aware; it wasn't his plan, but he was going along with it.

The next thing I knew, I was on Fire Island and I saw the paper. She was dead. I just . . . I've regretted it. I know that had I stayed, I couldn't have done anything, but you wonder . . . if I'd stayed, could I have in some way done something, changed the karma, the direction? They got her into it, knowing they were going to get her out. Whatever happened to Robinson? He was going to be the hero, but a vulnerable creature was destroyed.

So I was in on the beginning of the plan, the inception, to destroy her. This was a definite plan. "We're not going to let any stars push us around." It was clearly stated.

Walking around New York in my new three-inch heels . . . I felt tall, sophisticated in my Chanels, and I was sure Marilyn wouldn't look good in Chanels, she was too tall, too curvy. Although she'd latched on to the Pucci silk dress I'd brought home last time. She'd run out and bought some for herself.

I was wearing a new hand-knit Italian sweater one winter. Marilyn and Pat Newcomb and I were sitting in the kitchen. Marilyn had been going on about this pale beige sweater— "It's my color, it's the style I love"—if she lived in Rome she would buy herself two. "Can I try it on?" she asked.

"Well, it might not fit, you could stretch it."

Pat interjected, "I think it will fit." They were railroading me.

"If it fits, I'll give it to you, but it won't."

Of course it did, perfectly, and I couldn't look at her wearing my sweater, which smelled of my perfume. I said, "It's too tight, otherwise you could have it." No one said anything. Later that night I found a note under my door. "Dear Susie," she had written. "Thanks for your first impulse. Maybe you could buy me one in Rome, I'd pay you back. Love, MM."

I felt so small and mean-spirited. I didn't wear that sweater again for a long time.

I was still smarting from what I considered a betrayal over a year ago. When Steffi had gotten married, I'd told MM I was sending her a silver Tiffany cigarette box with a message engraved in my handwriting. I'd made her swear not to send the same thing, since it was my idea. She'd promised and then had gone and gotten an almost identical box. "It's not fair," I'd cried like a kid. "She promised; it was my idea."

Another day I was dressing for a party, putting on my Fortuni long hand-pleated antique dress I'd bought from a contessa in Venice. It was a dress that clung to every curve. Marilyn came into the room and said, "Oh, no, Susie"—she made a gesture at the dress—"you can't wear a dress like that with underwear, your garter belt is showing. See . . ." She pointed. So I thought, What the hell, and took off my underwear, and she helped me make up. That night I got almost as much attention as she did.

My mother and father were invited to the White House for a dinner for the French minister of culture. I'd heard about Marilyn's affair with President Kennedy, but she was working and Mother was with her so they didn't think they could get away.

Ralph had talked to the president once. Marilyn had put him on the phone to give him some advice about his bad back, which was giving him a lot of pain. "I've heard a lot of good things about you from Marilyn. . . ." Those Bostonian tones rang clear. President Kennedy had even taken Max Jacobson with him on some trips. He was a New York doctor called "Miracle Max." He'd treated numerous celebrities for dozens of ailments with vitamin shots loaded with amphetamines.

As the time for the dinner drew closer, Mother called, "You go with Daddy. I can't leave Marilyn right now, she's in a bad way. I'll arrange everything."

I went to Loehmann's, a discount store for designer clothes, and fell in love with a Norman Norell dress. Norman Norell designed most of Marilyn's evening dresses. This one was more money, even at half price, than I'd ever spent on a dress.

"Buy it," Mother urged me. "How many times do you go to the White House?"

Geraldine Page, my father, and I took a limousine to Washington. She was talkative, charming, eccentric. My father adored her, and he was in good humor, telling stories. The time flew.

That evening, in my long ecru Empire *fille* dress, three-button white kid gloves, and my Chanel bob sprayed within an inch of its life, I clung to Pop's arm as Marilyn had years before at that first Actors Studio benefit. My dress purchase was justified; Jacqueline Kennedy's mother came over to me. "My daughter would like to know who made your dress."

President Kennedy fell asleep in midconcert. When his blue eyes were open, the president was charming, charismatic, and witty. I could see why MM was crazy about him.

Geraldine flew back to New York, and it was my father and me alone on the limo's backseat. The entire ride from Washington to New York, we never said a word. I couldn't think of anything to say that he'd be interested in. It was agony.

"It was wonderful," I told my mother later that night.

"I'm so happy you and your father are getting this chance to spend some time together before you go to work. Did you ask him about the part?"

"Not yet, but I will soon, I promise. There wasn't time." I didn't want to ask him, I wanted him to tell me. He was so brilliant, why couldn't he tell that I wanted him to talk to me?

Big secrets. Mom was coming home for a few days. Marilyn was flying in to sing "Happy Birthday" at President Kennedy's fortieth birthday celebration. She had ordered a special see-through dress, with strategically placed sequins, that had cost five thousand dollars. I couldn't believe it. Although MM hadn't been well, and had missed a lot of shooting on *Something's Got to Give*, she wouldn't miss this for anything. "Hell or high water."

When Mother arrived she seemed to be suffering from life. If she ate, she got fat; if she helped, she was ridiculed; if she loved, she was rejected; if she dreamed, she was disillusioned. I remembered her when she'd loved life, smelling of gardenias and jasmine, in wonderful silly hats with veils and flowers, wearing prints, pink-and-brown Mainbocher blouses, eating and cooking and touching, breathing deeply. When had her love affair with life ended? I'd been so involved with myself I hadn't noticed before.

Mother was a wreck when she got home from the rehearsal at Marilyn's apartment. "It keeps getting sexier and sexier. If she doesn't stop, it will be a parody. Richard Adler was crazed [Richard had written the special lyrics for the song], he made Peter Lawford call the president, who just laughed and said, 'Great.' "

"What did you say?" I asked. "Mom, why didn't you tell her the truth?"

She looked chastised. "She didn't want to hear it. She's determined to do it sexy," she told us. " 'How else can I top everybody else?' There's nothing anyone can tell her about this, except maybe your father, but he won't because it's not important enough to him. They'll probably blame me. . . . Maybe they'll love it."

Marilyn had worn out three pianists rehearsing for this song. She'd sung it in the bathtub, on the plane, night and day.

That evening I went to Madison Square Garden with my date. Mom and Delos were with Marilyn and Arthur Miller's father, whom she adored. I watched from a nearby seat.

She was high when she came onstage. All that held her up was the skintight dress she was sewn into, and her courage. The crowd roared when she made her entrance. She glittered in her sequins. The strange thing was that she glittered more when she was simply dressed, just being herself. She gave them what they wanted, she stole the show, and the attention was a shot in the arm, as intoxicating as a drug, but I hurt for her. From what she'd told me, each time she caricatured herself, she chipped a piece out of her own dream.

My father had refused to go.

At the private party afterward, when Marilyn and I hugged and kissed, her fingers bit into my bare arms, holding on. Her eyes looked a little opaque and lost, but she laughed and chatted away.

She was the belle of the birthday. Arthur Schlesinger, Adlai Stevenson, Robert Kennedy, the men all jostled for position to be near her, like teenage boys. These were the people who were running the country?

More disillusionment. Vice President Lyndon Johnson put his hand up my dress, then invited me, "Come sit on my lap, little girl."

I watched President Kennedy watching her. Those two glittering, charismatic Geminis were fascinating together, and apart.

The president and his Secret Service men departed. When Marilyn finally left, a few hours later, her exit was uncharacteristically reserved. She slipped out—no grand farewells. I gave her an Italian kiss on both cheeks and said, showing off, "*Ci vedremo presto, sogni d'oro.*" She liked the last part about dreams of gold. I wondered if she was going to rendezvous with the president as she had before.

I was torn between admiration and disillusionment. Nothing was what it seemed to be.

After Montand, she'd sworn, "No more MM's for MM— married men . . . honest. . . . Of course, he wasn't happily married." That differentiation seemed to make her feel better, and in Hollywood she'd warned me, "Be careful, Susie, it's full of men on the prowl, and half of them are married. Although face it, everybody is pimping their own trip. It's human nature."

Like most people, she'd advised, "Do as I say, not as I do." But I could understand her breaking her rule for the president.

Being in California again seemed to be eroding her confidence. Maybe that's what was meant by "You can't go home again." Of course, I was coming home, too. Home was where all the bodies were buried, all the old habits waited to pounce on you, all the old anchors and patterns. It was scary. When you went home, the past was alive in every familiar street or voice or look. It was harder to be a new self in an old habitat.

Mother wasn't working, so she was able to accompany Pop to Italy, where I was waiting for them. Pop was teaching a course in Spoleto. Marty was along, too.

Urgently, Mom was called back to the States. "Marilyn needs help." There were plots afoot, intrigues. MM was depressed. I hated to think it could be as bad as she made it out to be. The world couldn't be that mean-spirited. This wasn't war, this was life. Unless life was war. Once Mom had suggested that Marilyn might write the real story of her life. "It could be as dramatic as *War and Peace*." Marilyn was doubtful, " . . . It'll be mostly *War*." I wanted to see the glass as half full, not half empty. I wanted to be an optimist but perhaps my brother was right when he accused me of being naive and intimidated by reality. He didn't understand that in spite of everything I still believed in happy endings.

Filming resumed. My mother's calls became live coverage from the war zone in Hollywood.

In preparation for *Camille*, Pop, Marty, and I went to Franco's house in Livorno, on a cliff above the ocean. The clear Italian Renaissance light caressed everything.

There were men everywhere. I was courted, petted, fitted, flattered. All that male energy, all those expectations.

Pop was in his element. We weren't father and daughter, we were artists, equals, almost. Great knots of fear bunched and bumped about in my stomach. A hug from Pop would have been nice. It was hard to bend down from the pedestal I'd been put on to get one. Besides, I would have had to ask.

One evening we watched a sunset, fiery orange that faded to starry black.

"It's so beautiful." I was filled with emotion.

"If it's beautiful, why do you have to say it's beautiful,

darling? Can't you just watch?" Pop was matter-of-fact. I hid my tears.

I woke up from nightmares I couldn't remember, sweating, tears oozing out the corners of my eyes. As my fear increased, I'd awaken wetting my bed. Totally humiliated, I wondered what to do. Desperation brought inspiration and ensuing guilt. I blamed my dog. "Bad. Bad Camille." She gazed at me, uncomprehending. If I'd known I was going to play the part, I would have named her something else.

If this was even partially what Marilyn had lived with for years, my heart went out to her. If I took this any more seriously, I'd kill myself. The expectations were so high. What if I wasn't able to fulfill them?

Father had to go home. The calls from my mother and Marilyn had become more frantic. "George Cukor has turned against Marilyn and me. He used to be a friend, and Marilyn says I pay too much attention to Susie, but how can I be when I'm here with her. The script she accepted is being rewritten. Every night they give us white pages instead of yellow ones so she won't see they're new. We'd have to be idiots not to know what we've read. I feel terrible, this is killing me."

ARNOLD SCHULMAN

It was coming back to L.A., with the Lawfords, and the Kennedys, and what Fox was doing to her. Whatever they would say to her, all of them, they were treating her like a whore. And that's what had to come back to her. She was back to her roots; back to the way she'd been treated when she was giving blow jobs in the afternoon.

Here she'd come up the hard way, worked her ass off, gotten real respect as an actress and as a human being in New York. She'd started out with this stigma and worked

*her way out of the garbage pail. She'd married the most
respected sports hero and playwright. She got back to Hollywood, they put her back in the hookers' junkyard. All her
idealized fairy-tale protective hero-fathers had abandoned
her. She was a queen, but not to those people. They patron-
ized her—"You're not really one of us"—so she was in
limbo.*

*She had the psychology of a woman who's been treated
like a whore, loving/hating men. She was getting to that
age in Hollywood where they reject you. She was a sensitive,
intelligent human being with no different problems from
all of us. Everybody is addicted to something, except she
was fifty times bigger than life, so it was all magnified.*

Marilyn was worse off than she'd ever been. There were
more pills, more potential betrayers, more intrigue. The doctor
MM had adored wasn't able to stop her destructive behavior.
She now had moments of hostility toward him, too. Her drink-
ing escalated because she was around people who drank a lot.
Her discrimination was confused by people who were amoral.
Her ego got hungrier around people who fed it.

"It's different this time, Susie," Mom confided. "It's different. I've never seen her like this, pulled in so many directions.
She's running to psychics, afraid the Mafia is after her, that all
her friends are using her, and yet she has other times when
she's very clear and nothing seems to be wrong."

What was Marilyn doing? She was a lightning rod for tragedy; it followed her everywhere. My mother was finally in the
midst of a drama big enough to satisfy her wildest dreams, only
it was a nightmare now.

Marilyn made headlines doing a swimming scene for *Something's Got to Give* in the nude. Mom was concerned. "If she
wants to be taken seriously, she can't jump into a pool naked

anymore." But MM had pushed Elizabeth Taylor and *Cleopatra* out of the headlines, which she'd wanted to do, so she'd gotten what she wanted.

Elizabeth and Richard Burton were in Rome. They'd begun their highly publicized affair. I tried to avoid them.

Growing up wasn't turning out to be as easy as I'd thought it would be.

RALPH

She asked me if I'd heard the rumors about Bobby and her. She said, "It isn't true. Anyway, he's so puny. Bobby is trying to break up MCA and he asked me to help him." She loved helping to do something like that. About Greenson, I felt he had a big ego, like a lot of doctors he wanted to be God, and of all the analysts in L.A. she found him. Inger Stevens was his patient, too. She killed herself later. On that last July Fourth, Kennedy was visiting Pat Lawford and Peter, and Paula was giving a big party at the beach. You were still in Italy. Marilyn was very torn. She told me, "I don't know what to do." She went to the Lawfords'. And though she'd promised your mother she'd come there after, it was just down the beach, she never showed up. Paula had a wall-to-wall celebration, as only she could. Lots of other actors, studio heads, not MM. Lee didn't seem bothered, but your mother was furious. She took it very personally.

On that last film Marilyn felt very strongly that Greenson was involved, too involved with Fox. Additionally his twin sister was married to Micky Rudin, MM's lawyer in L.A. She told me he was still pushing her to get rid of Paula and Lee and me and trying to substitute himself for everything she'd built up those past years. She decided he was anti everything she wanted. She was radically turning on

Greenson and Mrs. Murray, the woman he'd put with her, she felt, to spy on her.

I'd cook steaks and bake potatoes on the barbecue in her backyard and make a salad. She wanted to bottle my salad dressing before Paul Newman did his. She knew it would be wrong for her to stay in California. She bought the house as a place she could close up when she wasn't doing a movie. She knew she had to work out there, she needed the money. Marilyn was planning to turn the garage into an apartment for Paula or me or friends to stay in—she said it was separated enough, we could all have privacy.

STEFFI

I was there on the set of Something's Got to Give *the day she did the nude scene, and there was your mother. It was one of the saddest moments I've ever seen. Pat Newcomb was in the star dressing room with Marilyn, and your mother was eating her lunch alone in that outside room off a tray. I adored your mother. She could do no wrong, she was always marvelous to me. I said, "Paula, what's wrong?" She said, "Nothing, I'm just tired."*

Marilyn looked terrific and beautiful and happy, but your mother looked miserable.

I think if it hadn't been for Lee, Paula would not have stayed so long. Someone always had to be there to hold it together for Marilyn. That was her pattern. Your mother was ambitious for your father, for you, and she wanted the best for Johnny. There was a deep love and concern for the whole family, and I felt at that time she was torn. I felt your father was saying, "You can't let Marilyn go alone, it will be a reflection on the work, on me. If you leave her, it makes me look bad." That was the way it was done in those days.

The wife worked for and through the husband, and Marilyn was the best opportunity for your father's work. But it came to the point where not only your mother suffered, but she felt her children were suffering. It must have torn her apart, because she must have already known she was dying and she felt she was losing control. She wanted to be with you and Johnny, and I'm sure your father said no. I didn't know she had cancer. No one talked about cancer if they had it in those days.

I think Marilyn felt your father wasn't paying enough attention to her. He always sent your mother, and remember all those long-distance phone calls. She wanted more, so any resentment she had about not getting attention from him she took out on your mother.

My father still had me listen in on their conversations, only now I listened with one ear. I mean, who needed all this neurosis? I think the pills and alcohol had made her paranoid, and she was paranoid enough before them.

Marilyn never said "Paula and Lee," she'd say "The Strasbergs are against me," or "Pat is sitting out there plotting against me," or "Greenson is using me." Everyone was plotting against her or using her.

Maybe what she was expressing on the phone was that she felt trapped by the expectations of all the people, Pat, her doctor, the Strasbergs.

My father by then had had breakdowns and shock therapy. He'd seen and recommended to Marilyn a neurologist who was doing experimental work, but I don't know if she ever went. Dad felt her therapist wasn't helping Marilyn alleviate the problem. He told MM the doctor was trying to control her. She agreed. They were so much alike. My father was so secretive, like Marilyn, to the end. After he died, I cleaned out his desk at Schwab's. In his locked drawers, he'd hidden all these little notes from Marilyn, all crumpled up so no one could see them.

She was rejecting everybody, and two months later she was dead.

As I was packing to move out of Rome, over six thousand miles away Marilyn was unpacking and moving in.

Mother called. "I can't wait till you get home." She reminded me of all the things I had to do, then she added, "Go buy *Life* magazine. Marilyn did a wonderful interview for them. Read it, you'll like it."

So I schlepped with a friend to the Via Veneto and had a *granita di caffé* and cannoli and watched Anita Ekberg unsuccessfully dodge the same paparazzi she'd fired on with a bow and arrow the week before when they'd tried to get pictures of her in her house. John Barrymore, Jr., fell out of a cab, drunk, in the gutter. I said hello and good-bye to the numerous American actors who came to the Veneto because you could usually find an old friend and read a paper in English if you felt homesick. I bought *Life* from one of the newsstands that specialized in foreign magazines and read the interview.

In it, Marilyn spoke with the voice of the person I'd known in our kitchen, in my bedroom, the bright, smart, funny, sad, thoughtful woman. She talked about fame, "but that's not where I live," and said she'd been married to two of the nicest men in the world, DiMaggio and Miller. What particularly astonished me was how much she had adopted my father's philosophy. Pop told us, "Never borrow anything. Steal it outright and make it your own." She had.

He had said fame was like chocolate—good, but not at every meal, or it could make you sick. She substituted caviar. "The sensitivity that helps me to act . . . also makes me react," she stated. I heard my father's ideas leap off the page the way I saw my mother's coaching in Marilyn's on-screen performances.

"The actor is his own instrument. Isaac Stern takes good care of his violin. What if everybody jumped on his violin?"

Pop again. His favorite Goethe quote about talent needing to develop in privacy was there. Despite everything I'd heard was happening in Los Angeles, she seemed to be able to articulate more coherently than before what was really important in her life; she seemed to have accepted herself in a new way. I would have been proud to give that interview. She was funny and witty, yet she hadn't made fun of herself. I thought I'd write her a note and tell her how good her interview was.

My phone was ringing as I entered my marble-floored Italian apartment. The hand-carved angels on the walls smiled down at me enigmatically. I'd been at the beach in Frigene all day with my girlfriends, actresses Tanya Lopert and Jo Pemice Fales, whose son, Enrico, was along with his male nanny. By the time I got home I was reeling from the sun, the taste of wine and salt water on my lips. Throwing my sandy beach robe on the floor, I ran to answer the phone. Like my father, I couldn't stand an unanswered phone call. He explained that as a young, poor boy, the only reason anyone called was to report an emergency or a death. In a piss-elegant English accent, a stranger inquired, "*Pronto*, is Miss Susan Strasberg there?"

TANYA

I'll never forget, you were standing at the side of that old brass bed you'd bought at the flea market and I didn't know who you were talking to, but it turned out to be some journalist. You turned very pale and you didn't talk much, you just kept saying, "Yes . . . yes . . . yes . . ." Then, "How did it happen?" You didn't ask any other questions. When you hung up, you didn't cry, you started pacing around the room like an animal. You started to leave the room, then turned around at the door and came over to me and said, "Marilyn's dead. Oh, God, I have to call my mother. What am I going to say to her? My poor mother . . . oh, God, what am I going to say?" So you called and you seemed pretty calm. You asked, "How's Pop doing?" You didn't ask to speak to him.

Afterward you broke down sobbing, and I held you. You were hysterical, weeping, sobbing uncontrollably, and you kept saying, "I'm so sorry, I'm so sorry," as if it were your fault, and you started to talk about how you had met her and about how there were so many things you could have done and should have done and would have done and that now it was too late. You said that in a way you'd turned away from her because you'd been so jealous of her, and you said, "I'm so sorry, now I'll never have a chance to tell her what I wanted to tell her." You didn't say what it was, except that she tried to share a lot more things with you and you hadn't been able to. You told me about how when you'd shared the room on Fire Island, she'd wanted to know what books you were reading, what makeup you wore, where you got your clothes, and you didn't want to tell her, and you'd tried to change the subject. . . .

It seemed impossible to me that she was gone, just like that, with no warning. She'd been so alive, maybe too much so. Everything had been so heightened for her as she'd struggled so fiercely for the new life she'd dreamed of. I prayed for her and talked to her the way I had to Anne Frank years before, feeling crazy, but not caring, telling her I was grateful she'd been like a big sister to me, that I'd miss her, that it didn't matter if she messed my room up . . . that I was sorry for being jealous, that I'd loved her . . . Finally, my heart pounding, my throat tight with held-in tears, I walked up the one hundred and twenty-two steep steps near my apartment to the Church of Santa Maria in Ara Coeli. I lit a candle for Marilyn at the thirteen-hundred-year-old Altar of Heaven. And then I lit dozens more, as if I could surround her with their pulsating, radiant light. I asked her forgiveness for not really looking at her, not always hearing her. Did anyone really live life, every minute, as if it really mattered? As if there were a purpose to it all? It was terrible, but along with the grief, her death made me feel so alive.

I'd thought Marilyn was an iron butterfly, but she'd turned out to be more gossamer. I'd forgotten that butterflies are very beautiful, give pleasure, and have a very short life span. She had beaten her wings against the cage of her own cocoon. Knocking from the inside, she'd finally succeeded in getting out. The butterfly is the symbol of eternal life.

My mother's guilt was a thousand times more intense than mine. My mother, who had seen so many of her "children" shot down in flames, self-immolating stars. My mother castigated herself, as I had: "If I had been understanding, if I had stayed in California instead of coming home, if . . . if . . . if . . ." All the what if's and might have been's and if only's were too late. The fact that all Marilyn's friends felt this same sense of responsibility didn't assuage her despair. Millions of strangers who had never met her felt they could have made a difference, too.

RODDY MCDOWALL

Years before she died, in 1956, I went to a midnight show at the Roxy, after my play had ended, of Bus Stop. Afterward I was hysterical with laughter. I knew, I realized, that I was the only person in the world who could help her; she brought that out in people, as did Monty and Judy [Garland], and Jimmy [Dean].

Society does things to these people. It needs something from them, not the talent, something else, something to be filled, and it lionizes and victimizes them at the same time.

I think Will Rogers said that these creatures get into a position of such power, surrounded by people who reflect them. I don't think they could reclaim themselves. Once they discover success is not a panacea, they have this need to extinguish these personalities that are so enormously beguiling. Oh, my God, if one is so full of self-loathing, they can't see the persona up there on the screen, all you see, blown up there, is your own despair.

Mira, Monty's coach, used to tell him, "You have to live like a monk. Only the work counts. . . ." Of course it becomes everything to someone who can't deal with human relationships. They don't think about living. "Catch me before I kill again"—the persona, not the talent.

My father was so distraught in the days that passed, he could not keep silent. Gray with his effort to control his grief, he said, "She promised me that if she was ever tempted, if she ever got into that sort of mood, she'd call me first. . . ."

Ralph despaired. "She told me that, too. . . ." There had been a message from a slurring, soft-voiced woman who'd called his service and hadn't left her name. Had it been Marilyn?

She'd made this same pact with all of her closest friends, my father, Ralph, May Reis, Norman Rosten. It hadn't helped. She'd died alone. I imagined her saying, "Hey, you're born alone, you die alone. . . ." Now that she was gone, she would always be the woman who might have been . . . the woman who almost was. . . .

Keats had died at twenty-six, ten years younger than Marilyn. He too had lived a life of ecstatic pain. "Darkling, I listen; / and for many a time I have been half in love with easeful death, / Called him soft names in many a mused rhyme, / To take into the air my quiet breath; now more than ever seems it rich to die, / To cease upon the midnight with no pain . . ."

Marilyn, half in love with death, half in love with life . . . another flip of the coin, heads or tails, life or death. All those overdoses, all those near misses; the odds had finally turned against her.

She was the one person I'd known who wasn't afraid of death. She'd talked about it as if it were her best friend, her ace in the hole. A poem she wrote cried, "Help Help Help, I feel life coming closer, When all I want is to die." She'd had faith in death even when it seduced her.

Death had embraced her like a final lover.

Marilyn's half sister, Bernice, was overwhelmed by the funeral arrangements. Joe DiMaggio, who'd met her in Florida, helped. He decided not to allow any of Marilyn's Hollywood crowd into the funeral because he felt they had been bad influences and partially responsible for her death. Frank Sinatra and Peter Lawford were turned away at the gates. Unfortunately, right or wrong, people she'd cared about and who'd cared about her were shut out. Joe hated crowds. MM had loved them. They'd validated her. I wondered whether even DiMaggio felt guilty. Before her death, a friend of Marilyn's and his had called and told him of the terrible time she was having. He'd said, "I'm sorry, I can't help the girl. I've tried."

Her funeral fell on a typical Los Angeles sunny day, the city shining bright in mourning for its native child. She was buried in her favorite green Pucci dress. Whitey had done her makeup for the last time. He'd promised her he would if ever . . . As a joke she'd given him a money clip engraved, "To Whitey, while I'm still warm. . . ."

We're born, someone smacks us, we cry, and everybody laughs. The way I wanted to die was to go laughing and let everybody else cry. Full circle.

I got an image of Marilyn looking down at all of us, saying, "It was great, so what the hell!" Wherever she was now I hoped she was laughing.

In the small chapel at the Westwood Memorial Park, between a parking lot and an office building, the minister read Psalm 23, the Book of John, chapter 14, excerpts from Psalms 46 and 139, and the Lord's Prayer, my mother's favorite.

Many friends were absent: Mrs. Chekhov, widow of her first acting teacher, who was in her will; the manufacturer from New York who'd lent her money when she so desperately needed it. There were no girlfriends except the women who had worked with her. I was in Rome packing to move back to New York. Hedda and Norman Rosten hadn't come; many preferred to mourn privately. Ralph was there, but Sidney Skolsky, who had just gotten out of the hospital, couldn't come, although Joe had asked for him.

My father, the man with whom she'd had the longest, most sustained relationship of any in her life, wrote Marilyn's eulogy.

A week later I received a note from my mother describing how my father had been too grief-stricken to speak at first. Weeping, he began by saying, "I know she would not have wanted us to mourn, but grief is human and words must be spoken." He had gone on, his voice shaking with his sorrow, and Mom had worried he might not be able to finish, but he had. She enclosed a copy of what my father had written. Mom spoke of Marilyn's optimistic plans for the future and how they had expected her to fly into New York the next weekend. "Unquestionably it was an accident. But that is how the wheel turns. We are all sad. We love you." Sitting on my brass bed from the Napoleonic campaigns, the carved Renaissance cherubs on the ceiling watching silently, I read my father's words.

Marilyn Monroe was a legend.

In her own lifetime she created a myth of what a poor girl from a deprived background could attain. For the entire world she became a symbol of the eternal feminine.

But I have no words to describe the myth and the legend. Nor would she want us to do so. I did not know this Marilyn Monroe, nor did she.

We, gathered here today, knew only Marilyn—a warm human being, impulsive and shy and lonely, sensitive and in fear of rejection, yet ever avid for life and reaching out for fulfillment. I will not insult the privacy of your memory of her—a privacy she sought and treasured—by trying to describe her whom you know, to you who knew her. In our memories of her, she remains alive, not only a shadow on a screen, or a glamorous personality.

For us Marilyn was a devoted and loyal friend, a colleague constantly reaching for perfection. We shared her pain and difficulties and some of her joys. She was a member of our family. It is difficult to accept the fact that her zest for life has been ended by this dreadful accident.

Despite the heights and brilliance she had attained on the screen, she was planning for the future; she was looking forward to participating in the many exciting things which she planned. In her eyes and in mine her career was just beginning. The dream of her talent, which she had nurtured as a child, was not a mirage. When she first came to me, I was amazed at the startling sensitivity which she possessed and which had remained fresh and undimmed, struggling to express itself despite the life to which she had been subjected. Others were as physically beautiful as she was, but there was obviously something more in her, something that people saw and recognized in her performances and with which they identified. She had a luminous quality—a combination of wistfulness, radiance, yearning—that set her apart and yet made everyone wish to be part of it, to share in the childish naïveté which was at once so shy and yet so vibrant.

This quality was even more evident when she was on the stage. I am truly sorry that you and the public who loved her did not have the opportunity to see her as we did, in *many of the roles that foreshadowed what she would have become. Without a doubt, she would have been one of the really great actresses of the stage.*

Now it is all at an end. I hope that her death will stir sympathy and understanding for a sensitive artist and woman who brought joy and pleasure to the world.

I cannot say good-bye. Marilyn never liked good-byes, but in that peculiar way she had of turning things around so that they faced reality—I will say au revoir. For the country to which she has gone, we must all someday visit.

Once I began to cry, my tears wouldn't stop. I didn't know if I was crying for Marilyn or myself or for all of us. Buddha and Mom were right, life was hard. But at least I could learn from Marilyn and not make the same mistakes. And then life would get easier, wouldn't it?

I thought about how fleeting fame was. Marilyn had said, "Fame may go by and so long I've had you fame, but that's not where I live." I thought about how fickle the world was. As much as it loved and mourned Marilyn now, in time it might forget her; but I knew I never would.

EPILOGUE

I'm used to not being taken seriously, but it's only the "light-hearted" Anne that's used to it and can bear it; the "deeper" Anne is too frail for it. . . . I'm always fighting against a more powerful enemy . . . finally I twist my heart round again so that the bad is on the outside and the good is on the inside and keep on trying to find a way of becoming what I would so like to be, and what I could be, if . . . there weren't any other people living in the world.

ANNE FRANK,
The Diary of Anne Frank

What we need most in life is to have something to live for.

Our problems are not what we think they are—the material problems. . . . The real problems are in our need for fulfillment, our desperate need to make sense of life and to have the strength to live. We know that life is worthwhile only if one is pursuing a purpose that is greater than one's own personal purpose.

Every soul is born with a purpose that is ignited as one goes along. God is the creator . . . the artist that keeps on improving His work of art—and you are both the Artist and the work of art.

HAZRAT INAYAT KHAN,
Mastery Through Accomplishment

The man who falls in the pit is giving you a wonderful message. He is teaching us something at his own cost.

PUNDIT RAVI SHANKAR,
Seeds of Wisdom

Hollywood, California, 1991

IT'S ALMOST THIRTY YEARS SINCE MARILYN'S DEATH—that sad summer day in 1962 that seems a lifetime ago. I was wrong to think that Marilyn might be forgotten. Not only is she remembered, but today she is more famous, more loved, more talked and written about than when she was alive. "I want to be a serious artist, don't make a joke out of me. I don't mind making them but I don't want to be one," she'd begged her last interviewer. Her wish was fulfilled. She achieved respect, recognition, and appreciation beyond her wildest expectations. It just seems so ironic to me that she had to die to do it.

And in the long run, her own life turned out to be the greatest drama she ever starred in.

Marilyn would have been sixty-six next year. I, who was always the youngest in the crowd, will be fifty-four—seventeen years older than Marilyn when she died at thirty-six, and two years younger than my mother was when she passed away

267

four years after Marilyn at the age of fifty-six. I guess I'm middle-aged, except that the older I get the further away middle age seems to get. These are the years when I'm realizing how much I messed up in my life and how little time I have left to correct it. Life goes so fast, too fast. I held it too tightly in my clenched fists and it ran out like sand. Many years ago my mother dreamed of writing a book. "I'll have to write the story of Marilyn," she'd told a friend, and here I am . . . the unfulfilled dreams and desires of our ancestors are imprinted in our genetic codes along with the color of our hair or eyes. I often wondered if my mother had been right, if our lives were "meant to be."

A number of years ago at a Hollywood party writer Henry Miller ran into me, literally. He tripped, hit me, knocking me to the floor, and fell on top of me. Ice broken but no bones, intimacy established, we discussed destiny versus fate, if there was a difference, if they existed. His opinion was unequivocal. "Of course they exist, and the difference is that destiny is what you're supposed to do with your life, and fate is what kicks you in the ass to make you do it." The aborigines in Australia believe we don't create stories, they already exist, and they go around looking for people to be in them, sort of central casting for God. So maybe this story was out there, looking for Marilyn and me and my family. Maybe Mother was right, it was all *bershert*.

I don't know. What happened to all the things I was so sure of at sixteen? Is this maturity, knowing that I don't know?

Something I do know is that Marilyn was not the victim she's been painted as. She would have hated the label. She fought too hard and took too much responsibility to have her life trivialized like that. Yes, she was wounded in her early years, and yes, she was treated badly in the later ones, but she was a complex woman who lived a complex life always aspiring to reach higher. Carl Jung believed that if we didn't recognize and confront our own shadows they would be forced to manifest in our lives as our fate. Marilyn of all people was aware of her shadows, even when she tried to evade them in pills or drink. In that paradoxical way she had, she was the biggest liar and the most honest person I knew.

It no longer amazes me that Marilyn died so young, but that she lived so long and accomplished so much. From the moment she entered the race, she was the dark horse, running as a long shot with a heavy weight of handicaps on her back. Many opinions have been expressed: she was schizophrenic, manic-depressive, paranoid, neurologically damaged, undergoing a spiritual crisis. Again, I don't know. She'd been an addict so long, her real symptoms, emotional and physical, were totally masked. She remains the mystery queen, and by her secrecy she allows us to project our dreams and fantasies onto her.

So many people now seem obsessed with her death: Who did it, who was she sleeping with, how many times? As if they could capture her essence or measure her spirit by who, where, when, how much, her measurements, her age, all those "facts" that too often have little to do with the truth. To me the real mystery is how she lived, not how she died. Maybe one reason we're all so fascinated by her, so determined to decipher her, is that she became this huge mirror in which we see ourselves reflected with all our vulnerability, longings, and desires. Anyway, life isn't a problem to be solved; it's a mystery to be lived. With all the speculation, expert opinions, innuendoes, the goddess remains veiled in mystery—as she should be.

Another thing I was mistaken about thirty years ago was that life would get easier. It doesn't, but I take it differently, so it is. What did MM say? . . . "Maybe I just took it all too hard." Now I take life a lot easier. I'm discovering that the greatest freedom I have is the freedom to choose my attitude, and that makes all the difference. These days I consider myself a reformed hysteric. It still tempts me but I've replaced panic with yoga breathing, and if all else fails, there's always choco-late. I collect aphorisms hoping to find one that will get me through the day. I pin them on the refrigerator—as my mother did—*Life is too sacred to be taken seriously.... Stay calm, nothing is under control.* Talking to God, I pray; listening to God, I meditate. Learning to be accepting even if I don't approve has helped; and as to changing other people, it's hard enough to change myself. And besides, maybe it's not about changing oneself, but about *being* oneself. And I'm beginning to take responsibility, the ability to respond. I love that. When I look back at the way I was, I feel like Sam, the old Jewish man from Brooklyn who went to synagogue for eighty years every day. At the age of ninety-eight he knew he was dying and prayed to God, "Just let me win the lottery before I die, not for myself, for all the people I could help and in case you forgot I'm the Sam who lives upstairs at 124." The next day he returned to shul and berated God, "You couldn't have answered my prayer yesterday? Some shmuck won but not me. All I ask is once to win the lottery." The next day Sam returned, more upset than before that he still hadn't won. Suddenly a luminous light filled the temple and a deep voice intoned, "Sam." He fell to his knees. "Yes, it's me, God." The voice continued, "Sam, meet me halfway, buy a ticket." So I remind myself to buy my ticket and life goes on.

Johnny lives in Paris. He is an internationally acclaimed director/teacher, and has been given his own theater in France. He continues to weave the visions of our father and mother's house. He and I are close, as we were when we and the world were young in the forties and fifties.

My brother lived in many cities, many countries, and drove many cars, but none took him so far so fast as that black Thunderbird Marilyn gave him.

Mother, whom everyone thought was a hypochondriac exaggerating her pain, had bone marrow cancer that began before *The Misfits.* Her pain had been real, and fatal. She was deeply mourned by all the "children" she'd sustained, encouraged, loved, and fed. Her spirit, her life force, was so strong I feel her with me always. Just before she passed away, she told a friend, "Even if Susan destroys herself, she'll still survive, because she's a survivor, and at least she'll have experienced a great passion."

Her last prediction came true.

Not long after Marilyn's death, I experienced a devastating professional failure and personal disillusionment, which I wrote about in my first book, *Bittersweet*. I fell into a dark night of the soul as Marilyn had. Abandoning career, fame, friends, family, and faith, I was swept into the whirlpool of the sixties. My life became punctuated by the drugs, violence, and sexuality of the *folie à deux* I became seduced and enmeshed in, my great passion. Like Marilyn and my father, I too was fascinated by the underworld, the darker aspects of consciousness. Four years later, with the birth of my daughter, I awoke from that dangerous nightmare game, confused but alive and grateful, feeling blessed. So I fulfilled Mother's prophecy and Pop's judgment: being "sensible" finally saved me.

In 1966 my beautiful child Jennifer was born, one month before my mother's death. Jenny inherited Mom's strawberry blond hair, luminous see-through white skin, and even her sign of Pisces the Fish. She was also born with a congenital birth defect that was corrected by open heart surgery when she was six years old. She is now a healthy twenty-five years old, and three inches taller than me to boot. Again I was filled with gratitude and counted my blessings that after my dark age came the renaissance.

My mother's next-to-last prophecy was, "I'm not worried about Lee because in six months he'll find another wife who'll take care of him and he'll be fine." It took him about nine months. How did my mother know us so much better than we knew ourselves?

He married for the third time (his first young wife had also died of cancer, like my mother). He had a second family—two beautiful boys almost the same age as Jennifer (who baby-sat for her uncles)—and became an Academy Award-nominated movie star at the age of seventy, proving you're never too old and it's never too late to do anything you have the courage to do.

Pop died unexpectedly nine years ago. He was eighty years old but still too young to die. Fifty years before, he'd danced in a chorus line in a George Abbott show. Three days before the stroke that took him, he danced in another chorus line with his students and coactors Al Pacino, Robert De Niro, and Dustin Hoffman at "The Night of a Hundred Stars" on television. Was it full circle? My father left a legacy of inspiration to generations of creative people. As Harold Clurman had predicted, even people who had never heard of the Actors Studio or my father were influenced by his work. Through his students, who became teachers, his method has been handed down to the newest generation of actors.

Recently Julie Newmar, a student of my dad's, remarked, "You know, Susan, your father loved three things: beautiful women, psychotics, and geniuses." I realized that I'd tried to be all three. What Lou Andreas Solome said about her friend, Sigmund Freud, reflects something I feel about my father. "When confronted by a human being who impresses us as being truly great, should we not be moved rather than chilled by the knowledge that he might have attained his greatness only through his frailties?" Maybe the baffling contradictions of our personalities are the measure of our humanity. And in the end love is all that matters.

Marilyn and Pop were kindred spirits, rebels and dreamers. He gave structure to her dreams. They were both outsiders. As MM used to say, "It's them against us." In the final analysis it was their work that mattered; it contained the best of them.

When Marilyn died she left the major part of her estate and personal possessions to my father because she knew that he would cherish her memory and never exploit it. Until the day he passed away twenty years after her, he never did. Her trust in his integrity was justified.

For years after my father died I'd wake up in the morning, my pillow wet with tears. In dealing with my grief, I realized that in some way his death was the cataclysmic event of my life. Over the past forty years I'd sought the love and approval of that remarkable, brilliant, and domineering man and now there was no one left I had to please but myself, only I didn't know who that self was or what my deepest desires were.

There were times in the years that followed where I felt like I was enrolled in one of those crash courses in accelerated learning. Life was a school and I was back in kindergarten, hoping I'd get to first grade before I died. I began to see that problems were also opportunities, challenges, or even gifts depending on how I used them. These days when things seem to go wrong I remind myself about the Chinese farmer who had one horse that ran away. The villagers said to him, "You're the poorest man in town now, what bad luck."

He replied, "Good luck, bad luck, who knows?"

When his horse returned a month later, leading a herd of wild horses, his neighbors exclaimed, "Now you're the richest man in town, what good luck."

He shook his head. "Good luck, bad luck, who knows?"

Taming the horses, his son fell and broke his back and was bedridden. "What bad luck," the people moaned.

"Good luck, bad luck, who knows?" he said.

The army came through the village and took the young men to war. They were all killed except his son, who was home in bed. Once more the village gathered. "You have such good luck," they said enviously.

He replied, "Good luck, bad luck, who knows? . . ."

Most people think of getting older as "bad luck" but I trust that, like wine, I'm getting better as I mature. Someone said maturity is when you do what you really want to do in your life, even though it makes your parents happy. Now Johnny has a theater, he and I teach acting, carrying on our father's work. I'm writing as Mom wanted to and I've fallen in love with acting again. My parents would approve. Actually the best reason I can think of to grow up is so I can become childlike again, without hurting myself anymore. That's child*like*, not child*ish*.

Near the end of his life, my father was still dreaming, planning a repertory theater. He sent Al Pacino to intercede on his behalf and speak to a famous actor about joining them in the company. When Pacino returned, Pop demanded, "So, what did he say?"

Reluctantly, Al answered, "Lee, he said it's impossible, that you're dreaming."

My father drew himself up to his full height. "Well, darling, I may be dreaming, but he's the one who's asleep!"

Last night I dreamed. I was sitting on a mountaintop in the Himalayas in the lotus position, and as I gazed at an infinity of blue sky, breathing the cool, clean air, lost in the silence, an Indian guru appeared, clad in a loincloth. As he began to adjust my spine like a chiropractor I protested, "Stop, you're giving me a lot of pain."

"No," he responded dispassionately. "I'm giving you change. It's your resistance that's giving you the pain."

There were other nights when I awoke from unremembered dreams, my heart and mind racing. Disturbed, I thought about all the what if's and might have been's and if only's that came before today. I must have what if 'ed a good part of my life away. Filled with remorse, I was unable to sleep. Then I reminded myself that even if I had turned down another corner of another street, I would still have arrived at here. Here is the best place I've been so far, and if I had to go through there to get here, what use are regrets or guilt? Johnny says that if you're going to feel guilty, at least make sure you're doing something sufficiently pleasurable to make the price you're paying worthwhile. Besides, whatever we imagine about the past, now is inevitable. Recently I read that scientists have a new theory that the part of the brain that carries memory also is the pathway for imagination.

And as Shakespeare asked, "Where does fancy start, in the head or in the heart?" In Marilyn's case, both. Her life was carpeted, end to end, with dreams. The Bard suggested that the purpose of acting was "to hold as 'twere the mirror up to nature." But in their waking dreams of passion, she and my father aspired to do more than mirror life. They hoped to illuminate it.

In her legend Marilyn has become the only blonde in the world, but to me, she is the little girl who dreamed herself, invented herself. "The dream is like a woman. It will have the last word, as it had the first," Carl Jung said.

She's special to me, not because of her neurosis or craziness or pain (we're all predictable and alike in that) but because of that spontaneous shining core of hers that I was fortunate enough to know. When I was growing up I identified with Marilyn's loneliness for some significant other to complete her. Now I'm beginning to suspect the significant other is *ourself*, that part of us we are separated from as children.

Marilyn and I suffered from "meaning" hunger. We were constantly searching for the reason for everything, for that thread of connection that would help us to make sense out of our lives. It's no longer the meaning that's so important to me, it's the experience of living fully. "Life is a banquet," Auntie Mame proclaimed, "and most poor suckers are starving to death." At least Marilyn *lived*, impulsively, compulsively, not always wisely, but fully.

It's strange, but I've always felt an intangible but real connection between Anne Frank and Marilyn, born within three years of each other, and sharing the same astrological birth configurations, as well as a longing to know themselves and to contribute something to the cosmic melting pot. Anne Frank wrote that she was grateful to God for her gift of writing because she wanted more than anything "to go on living even after my death." Marilyn, too, felt that way. Both these young women, who entered and transformed my life in that spring of 1954, have become archetypal symbols. Both were in jail—Anne literally imprisoned in hiding and then in a concentration camp, Marilyn imprisoned and at war behind the bars of her own psyche. They showed me the light and shadows of this incredible molecular dance we're all engaged in. Marilyn knew she was supposed to be an evangelist for something; she just wasn't sure what. Her life has become the message, the gift she had to give us.

She was a trailblazer not only for her public but for the actresses who came after her, who might have wound up as just sex symbols or hired help: Jane Fonda, Barbra Streisand, Sally Fields, Jessica Lange, Michelle Pfeiffer, Ann-Margret, Kathleen Turner, Julia Roberts . . . Kim Novak left Hollywood after MM died to live a more normal life elsewhere. When anyone teaches you something about yourself, they perform a service for you. Marilyn has done this for millions of young people who never knew her and were not even born until years after her death. A young taxi driver in California told me he had been transformed by reading about Marilyn. He learned about her favorite writers—Truman Capote, Carl Sandburg, Tennessee Williams, Arthur Miller, Rilke—names he might never have heard of otherwise. Because she had liked them and he had loved her, he read their books and plays to know her better. The new worlds that opened up for him changed his life. Marilyn would be pleased. Sometimes I imagine her as a beacon of light on the top of a lighthouse, flashing out a guiding light to steer us clear of the treacherous tides and rocks. "Pay attention. Wake up, smell the flowers and the coffee, ask for more, take responsibility, discriminate and above all, follow your dreams."

I'm not my father's daughter for nothing. I've struggled to be objective here, but it's been said that "we don't see life as *it* is, we see life as *we* are." During my last book tour, I was on a TV show describing the pain I'd suffered during my affair with Richard Burton. A woman in the audience raised her hand and commented: "Susan, I envy you your relationship with Richard Burton."

Taken aback, I blurted out, "Why? I've just told you, I suffered so much I was suicidal."

She was adamant. "Better to suffer over Richard Burton than over my husband."

We cut to a commercial before I had time to respond. I wanted to say that yes, it was all relative, but that no, it wasn't better or even necessary to suffer over anyone, ever. All those falling, self-immolating stars who blazed a brief golden trail testify to that: Richard Burton, Margaret Sullavan, Judy Garland, Robert Walker, Elvis Presley, William Holden, Billie Holiday, Vivien Leigh, Gail Russell, Janis Joplin, Freddie Prinze, Carole Landis, John Belushi, Dorothy Dandridge, Modigliani, Jim Morrison, Elizabeth Hartman, Romy Schneider, Pier Angeli, Gig Young, Monty Clift, George Sanders, Anne Sexton, Inger Stevens, Karen Carpenter, Capucine, Charlie "Bird" Parker, Jimmy Hendrix, Jean Seberg, Lenny Bruce, Sylvia Plath, Ernest Hemingway . . . Why are so many of these Americans?

When the late songwriter Arthur Schwartz was a young man, he had this long conversation with producer Max Gordon, a tough, pragmatic man who loved the theater more than anything. They discussed life, love, death, money. Arthur asked Max what he thought of "that nonsense about reincarnation."

Max got mad. "Hey, I absolutely believe in reincarnation."

"How could a man like you say that?" Arthur was shocked.

"Listen, kid, I can't believe I close here and don't open somewhere else!"

I too believe in reincarnation. I imagine that nearby, in some alternate reality, Marilyn, my father, Mom, and all the rest of those bright spirits are alive and well. It's true. I know it. Unless it's not. Then again, they may have reopened here. One of my favorite fantasies is that Vincent van Gogh, who died penniless, reincarnated to buy his own painting, *The Irises*, for forty-some-odd million dollars. Why not? Benjamin Franklin said he'd return in a hundred years, clothed in a new body. And I know that it's only the envelope of the body that dies. The letter of the soul still exists.

Recently a skeptical friend said to me, "What if you're making all this up?" After thinking about it I answered, "In that case, I like what I'm making up better than what you're making up." Who knows?

When Marilyn was a young girl, whenever she was going to do anything important she asked her friends, "Hold a good thought for me." She believed that energy followed thought. Toward the end of her life, when she was in trouble, at a turning point where life held both more promise and more pain, she asked again, "Please hold a good thought for me," an urgent letter delivered with a smile.

There's a poem of Sara Teasdale's that reminds me of Marilyn:

I saw a star slide down the sky,
blinding the North as it went by,
too burning and too quick to hold,
too lovely to be bought or sold,
good only to make wishes on
and then forever to be gone.

Only she isn't gone. She is still here.

My mother believed Marilyn was "a true star, a self-illuminating body." Now Marilyn is like one of those stars we look up at to make wishes on. It has died, but its light is still traveling toward us.

And we are holding a good thought for her.

ACKNOWLEDGMENTS

If this book were a baby, its godparents would be Shelley Winters, who encouraged me to write this story for years, and Norman Brokaw, the home run king, who made it possible. My thanks and appreciation to my editor Nanscy Neiman and the people at Warner Books, Harvey-Jane Kowal, Jackie Meyer, among others, who helped give birth to the "baby." I am grateful to those who contributed their voices and observations, and whose interviews gave another dimension to this story: Martin Fried, Delos Smith, Jr., Dorothy Monet, Roddy McDowall, Tanya Lopert, Ralph Roberts, Andreas Voutsinas, Steffi Sidney Splaver, Arnold Schulman, Geraldine Baron, and my brother, John Strasberg, who told the truth even when I didn't want to hear it.

I also want to thank the many people who shared their time, memories, photos, expertise, information and encouragement: Nancy Aylesworth; James Haspiel; Greg Schreiner of "Marilyn Remembered"; George Zeno; Linda and Keith at William Morris; Marcy Posner; Pam Bernstein; Sona Vogel; Jane Freeman; my cousin, Ruth Lippa; my extended family, Barry Parnell and Cynthia Adler; Rona Jaffe; astrologers Jeanne Avery, Jeffry Geist, the late Ruth Oliver, and the dean, Sidney Omarr; Mary Schwartz; Violet Arase; John Patrick; Pepi Oden; Lee Grant and Joe Feury; Justine Compton; Franco Zeffirelli; psychic and writer, Patricia McLaine; Richard Stolley; Phil Vance at Photovision; Paige Olson; Pam Tisdale; Cathy Leslie; Curtis Roberts; Deborah Tilton for above and beyond; Anna Garduno; Gladys Hart; Marshall Flann; Jess Stern; computer maven Richard Grosser; David Blasband; Joseph Hoenig; and John Springer.

Finally, my love and appreciation to Thomas Constantinides and my daughter Jennifer Strasberg for being there. And to the late Peggy Feury and William Traylor—in spirit—thank you, too.